TURNED ON

TUNING IN, IN A TUNED-OUT WORLD

TURNED ON

TUNING IN, IN A TUNED-OUT WORLD

DAVID NORRIE

Ainsley&Allen
PUBLISHING

ISBN: 978-1-946694-36-2

*I dedicate this book to fathers, to my earthly father
(thank you Dad), to my spiritual fathers for their direction,
and most of all, to my heavenly Father.*

*The fate of the world lies in hearts and minds of fathers everywhere,
may God equip you all to lead lovingly and courageously.*

TABLE OF CONTENTS

INTRODUCTION

THE PROMISE

I named this book *TURNED ON* because I want *TURNED ON* to be a metaphor in your life for all the things you desire to achieve but may seem far away. I will make you see that turning on your life is as easy as turning on a light switch when you walk into a room. It's a very simple yet still a cognitive decision you must make—to flip it on or not to flip it on. Choose the latter, and you are in the dark, you increase your risk of bumping into things, getting hurt, and going the wrong way. Make the simple choice to turn on that light and everything is illuminated, your eyes are open, and you can see where to go and how to get there.

In my entire career, as both journalist and coach, my main focus has been to bring a common-sense approach to life in order to make people happier and achieve more. I understand that as human beings, the majority of us like things that we can easily make sense of. In fact, life in the 21st century has become so easy that to do anything that requires even a little effort often seems too much. (i.e., You mean I have to get up off the couch to find the remote? You want me to get in the car and come all the way over there? Ugh, I have to make dinner? You sent me a six-minute video that would change my life. Do you have a 30-second version? I'm too busy with... you name it.)

In the pages to follow, you'll find that all the things you dream about, all the things you value, strive for, and hope to attain are so much closer than you think. They are so much easier to attain than you could ever imagine. There are two main reasons you don't have them yet; first is that you've been conditioned to believe just the opposite—that they are only for

2 · DAVID NORRIE

the chosen few, the geniuses or relentless workers who possess some superpower that you don't. Nonsense! In all my years of learning from some of the best mentors, I've come to realize this one truth, perhaps more than any other; we're all more alike than we are different and that none of the people we hold on pedestals wears a cape or has X-ray vision. The main thing that separates them from you is that they are doing the little things while those struggling debate over how to get started. And second is that you've been conditioned to take a path of least resistance that has lulled you to sleep, stripping you of the life force that God put inside of you in order to help you accomplish your mission and attain happiness.

In a journey of a thousand miles, the best way to get where you're going is to always recognize the need to make simple course corrections and smart, common-sense decisions. The amount of effort it takes to be happy in a relationship, successful at business, healthy in your body or calm in spirit is well within your means to achieve. It's no secret. As long as the sun comes up in the morning, you have the ability to create meaningful change in your life. Just like the airplane that takes off every day from Los Angeles destined for Hawaii, and we ask, "How can it possibly navigate 2,558 miles over open water and land on a tiny island in the middle of the Pacific Ocean?" The answer? Course correction.

Sometimes the light in your world can go dim, either from the intrusion of technology or simply because our society is so driven by instant gratification. We must turn on the light to see, to course correct in the areas of our life which bring the most happiness (Relationships, Health, Business, and Faith) and to realize that the opportunity we seek is just a flip of the switch away. Let's get *TURNED ON!*

CHAPTER ONE

WHO TURNED
THE LIGHTS OFF?

> *At the end of your life, you will never regret not having
> passed one more test, not winning one more verdict,
> or not closing one more deal. You will regret time not
> spent with a husband, a friend, a child, a parent.*
> — *Barbara Bush*

Did you wake up today and tell yourself what you had to be?

I have to be a father, a mother. I have to be a parent, a child. I have to be a boss, an employee, a role model, a teacher, a student, or an adult for that matter?

The bigger question is, did you wake up today and tell yourself that you had to be alive?

Philosopher and theologian Howard Washington Thurman said, "Don't ask yourself what the world needs; ask yourself what makes you come alive. And then go and do that. Because what the world needs is people who have come alive."

Cut, print, and send it to your memory bank. Did you receive that? The world needs people who have come alive. Amen! Every day I try to do something that makes me come alive. It's my jam, almost to a fault. I thrive on experience, movement, adventure, and connection. I cherish the day God has given me and plan to live it to the fullest. I enjoy making my own fun, creating connection, and searching out opportunity. I enjoy simply being alive.

But hold on, I have to be honest, I wasn't always like that. Well, I was, then I wasn't and now I am. Allow me to explain.

I've always been the type of guy to grab life by the horns as they say. I'm naturally an optimist, full of vigor and positive vibes. You could say I'm like a mash-up between Lionel Richie and the Beastie Boys, I'm easy like Sunday morning and I'm gonna fight for my right to party. But somewhere along the way, I got a chink in my amour, and I began to feel less and less alive. I found myself feeling disconnected and slightly depressed, but I didn't know why. That's not like me, I thought. You're David, the guy your friends say could make friends with a tree, the guy who always sought to soak up every ounce of life available.

Well, I wondered, maybe it's in my head, or maybe it's a phase I'm going through. So I waited it out. But then others began to notice as well. My wife said I seemed irritated more often and that I was getting frustrated during times of inaction or relaxation. I'd get angry seeing other people who were busier than me and start to beat myself up in comparison. I felt disheartened when I witnessed people who were achieving things, and I either began to punish myself mentally or scold them internally.

These feelings began to creep into other parts of my life. I was short-tempered with my kids when I was reading a news article or making a social media post. They'd ask me a question and my response was to snip at them as if they were causing some monumental disruption. This breaking news I was reading or the post I was crafting was important! Or so it seemed. The fact is, my life had suddenly become inundated with outside influences, most of which were beyond my control. They were greatly affecting my home and my happiness. At times, I became so discontented that I just wanted to bury my head in the sand and scream.

The tension mounted as my children weren't behaving the way I wanted them to and my relationship with my wife seemed more distant each day. I stopped going outside in nature and felt like time was always escaping me. Suddenly, the world was on fast forward, and I was struggling to run alongside and keep up.

Then one day, while on vacation at Disney World, I was at dinner with my family, and as I looked around the restaurant, my eyes caught the attention of a family like mine. Immediately I thought, "Ugh, how are the four of them going to sit there at dinner and all be on separate devices?" And that's when it hit me. I was living in a highly connected world yet feeling more disconnected than ever. I was operating in this parallel world that was my life, but yet so far from reality.

My obedience to my work, my phone and my *brand* was making me disobedient to my wife, my children, and my sanity. The guy who woke up every day as if it were Christmas was now waking up as if it was Tax Day. "Come over here and hug me" was more and more, "Leave me alone. I'm trying to finish something." "Let's go outside" was now "I just need more time. Give me five more minutes." and "What can we do?" became "What do I need to do?"

My perspective immediately changed when I saw that family at dinner. It was obvious they were majorly out of touch and distracted, and I realized that I wasn't too far off.

That's when I decided to write this book. I began researching and dialing in on the issues facing families. My wife and I felt the cause was so grand that we wanted to go all-in on it, and we purchased the TurnedOn.com domain and began recording a podcast. You'd think that was the beginning of a turnaround, but guess what, it got worse, not better. The more I read and the more I wrote about the topic, the more I was consumed. At first, I was in disbelief thinking, "I can't be writing a book about the distractions of the modern world and continue to be further and further seduced by them." But I was. As we approached the launch of our podcast, I became more and more consumed by followers and algorithms, taking on a huge degree of stress over having a successful launch. As we readied for our first live event, we became consumed by social media ads and email lists and how many likes and comments we were getting. An entirely new and unique set of stressors that hadn't been available or known to us just ten years ago were now dictating our bank account, our happiness, and our sanity. It dawned on us that the nature of how we live recreationally and how we work were both being heavily influenced by technology and the obsession with being busy.

GET BACK TO WHERE WE ONCE BELONGED

What do you do when you get frustrated? Scream? Exercise? Drink a glass of wine? For me, it's a no brainer. I go to my record player. Something about the needle crackling and the spinning of the turntable helps me to relax and focus. One day when the algorithm, alerts, and scrolling got the best of me, I took refuge in my mid-century room (aka man cave). It's my Eden, inspired by Elvis' famous Jungle Room at Graceland.

So there I sat, looking for the right album when I came across The Beatles *Let It Be* LP. And there it was, the perfect song at the perfect time, "Get back. Get back. Get back to where you once belonged." And that's when I knew what I had to do. I had to get back to where I had once belonged. I had to course correct and get back to the simple things that once brought me joy.

So much of what turned on means deals with course correction and getting back to the activities in our life which bare the most fruit and produce the most happiness. As we explore more of what that means to you, I'd ask you to start by examining your life and what's most important to you. What truly brings YOU happiness and what are some areas of YOUR life that seem to have gone a bit dark over the years. What will it take to get them back? To achieve a new perspective? To regain the power to live in the light again?

My ask of you is to see with new eyes and listen with new ears. By doing so it will be like a filter that you swipe on the lens of life which helps you to see the world clearer and with more vibrant color.

IS IT REALLY JUST THE WAY IT IS?

Seventeen years after Lennon and the boys hit No. 1 with *Get Back*, a much lesser-known act, Bruce Hornsby and The Range, would hit No. 1 with their song *The Way It Is*. The chorus goes, "That's just the way it is, some things will never change." It speaks of the economic and social dilemmas that plague our society and begs the question, is it really just the way it is or can we change. Change, in this case, when it pertains to the things in the song, like correcting racism and fighting poverty, is very good and much needed. But other types of change, that which is hasty and reckless, not well thought out, or simply just for the sake of change, must be met with a bit more discernment. When social constructs such as family, faith and community are threatened by change, we should question the source it's coming from and why. When staples of civility, manners, respect, and human interaction are subject to change, without good reason, then we embark on a path that could lead to disaster.

These days, people are more than happy to brush off our culture's lack of connection and courtesy by telling you that the world is simply evolving, but do you see it that way? How's that working out for you? I say, in a sense, we're *devolving*, as once typical, dare I say normal, face-to-face communication and civility has almost become awkward.

It seems to me we're avoiding one another on a grand scale and that most people would rather text than talk, look past you and not at you or go around you rather than toward you.

It also seems as if it doesn't benefit our social media, brand or business, we'll often choose not to interact at all.

Throughout this book, I will use pop culture as a means to communicate the message and lessons. It is my experience that if we can draw a visual reference or trigger, to paint the picture so to speak, then it's much more fun and easier to digest. That being said, let me ask you this, you remember Forrest Gump, sitting on the park bench saying, "Life is like a box of chocolates, you never know what you're gonna get." Right? We all put on a big grin when we hear it and think, "Awe yea, that's so true." But is it really? To an extent, sure, you bump into people, make a few moves due to circumstance and maybe have a few cosmic collisions or impromptu adventures. But one could make an argument for the flip side of Mr. Gump's assumption and say to the contrary, in life, you know exactly what you're going to get because you get out of it what you put into it. You possess the key that opens the door you choose.

Allow me to counteract one fictional character's quote with another which I think makes a lot more sense in today's rapidly changing world; Lemony Snicket said, "Fate is like a strange, unpopular restaurant filled with odd little waiters who bring you things you never asked for and don't always like." In other words, if you leave your destiny to fate, like opening a box of chocolates, chances are you're gonna be forced to settle for a lot of flavors you don't necessarily want nor like. As human beings, don't you think we prefer choices and options? We want control over what we order and that is what lies at the heart of a turned on life, taking action and responsibility for your happiness. Nobody wants to have their boss call them into the office and hear them say, "We have to let you go," or for their spouse to declare they just aren't happy and want out. Nobody wants the doctor to walk into the room and say, "We have a problem." When these situations occur, you don't want to say life is like a box of chocolates and, therefore, feel helpless. You want control of the ON switch to power up your business, your relationship and your health.

When we power-down by taking on the mindset of "that's just the way it is" it can be a devastating blow to our sense of free will and furthermore, when we take what is given to us because it's the easier path, it in effect lulls us into believing we don't have much control of where we should go. Basically, it's the world's way of deceiving us into relinquishing our dream of an ideal life. However, I know, and you should know that there is a greater authority, an author, a teacher, who has given us the capacity to shape our lives. In fact, to believe the illusion that we are just floating on this rock in outer space lying at the mercy of the wind takes a lot of work and it couldn't be any further from the truth.

To turn on means to shape your future by making small choices each day based on faith and knowledge that you were put here for a reason. You matter. Take that truth and combine it with the fact that now, more than ever, we live in a time when the gathering of information and the pursuit of happiness have never been more attainable. Now, more than ever, we find ourselves with opportunities to learn at a faster rate, to make connections quicker and to change our circumstances easier than ever. This is the true light. This is real freedom. And it's right there in front of you if you choose it.

But first, you must understand this; there is a huge difference between dreaming and doing. Dreaming you can do with your eyes closed lying in bed. It's a beautiful thing, but it's not doing. Doing is action steps, plain and simple. It's been my "a-ha" experience that what most people crave in the self-development world are two things: (1) action steps and (2) accountability. Think about this, 99 percent of you reading this right now are doing so because you want a better life and you believe reading this book will make some small (or large) difference in achieving that. And I'd be willing to bet that the same 99 percent of you really just want those two things in life—how do I get there and who or what can hold me accountable. You notice I said, "or what" because many of you are self-starters; you don't need a mother or father or boss telling you, "Get to it," but you do need something to hold you to your word. Maybe that's your inner voice. Maybe it's the responsibility of a family. Maybe it's just keeping the heat on and a roof over your head. But you do crave accountability—some means of reward or motivation.

Here's where we go to sleep at the wheel, when the outside voices (our peers, our culture, our world) are louder than our internal voice (our spirit, intuition), that's when we get depressed and feel helpless. There is a power struggle, make no means about it. Each day you open your eyes and put a foot on the ground, there's a power struggle between you and what lies out there. How will you equip yourself to win?

I say the solution is easy. It's the action steps. There is a great divide between dreaming and doing, and Winston Churchill said it best, "We've become note rich and application poor." Lots of info. Lots of scribbling down and learning. Not so much doing. It's a big problem I've noticed over the years in my line of work. Many of us have become so obsessed with obtaining knowledge but not so great at implementing it. We've become privileged to see, on a tiny screen in the palm of our hand, all the things that life has to offer, but we also seem content to do just that, view it rather than live it. We have the resources to know everything about history, yet often it seems we aren't learning from it, and we're destined to repeat the mistakes of our past.

My greatest question to you, as you dig in here, is this; How do we get back to experiencing life in all of its richness, the human kind rather than the virtual type? Have we let go or tuned out the parts of our existence that make us feel most alive, content to watch through a screen and dream about *what ifs*? If so, how do we flip the switch back on again and reclaim control?

Answer me this, when you walk into a room that's dimly lit, what's the first thing you do? You look for the light switch. Is there an easier task on the planet than flipping that switch? No, it's so easy a toddler can do it. It's that one small thing which is the catalyst for all other actions. You must illuminate your space and make everything visible in order to complete the next task.

So, we start by asking what area (or areas) of your life would you like to shine light on first? What can we turn on so that everything else is easier to see and do? Not the giant leap just yet, but one small step?

Overweight and can't fathom how to get in shape? Turn on your faucet and begin your day with eight ounces of water. Drinking water is the easiest thing you can do to start making a difference in your health. Hate your job and want to start a new career but can't see over the fence? Take one set of notes that you took from a seminar or book and put it into action instead of letting it sit and collect dust. Want to save your marriage but think it's beyond salvage? Gather five seconds of courage and humility to take the lead, showing your spouse real, accountable action and lay out exactly what is wrong with it but also what is right. Spiritually bankrupt and searching for a higher purpose? Open the Bible to any random page, put your finger down, and start reading. I can't tell you how many millions of people have completely changed their lives doing that one small act.

Churchill's words about being *application rich* make a lot of sense when you pair them his other words, "Success is not final; failure is not fatal: It is the courage to continue that counts." A Super Bowl winning coach still has to field and team and get it ready the next season the same way a coach whose team only won a few games does. What separates the long term winners from lonesome losers is the courage to keep working, improving and trying.

To put it simply, attending a seminar doesn't change you any more than reading this book does, but they both provide instruction, or ammunition or fuel, for you to take action. And when you take a collective series of small actions that's what creates the big leap, the massive shift toward happiness. You may not have the courage to change your life in the blink of an eye, and, as I said, it's not even realistic, however, I know you can muster up a tiny bit of courage to continue with one step and then another and another. Sometimes our life feels like it's in neutral or even going in reverse. That's when you pump the brakes, put some gas in the tank and agree to turn on one thing at a time. Once you possess the fortitude to turn on one piece of the puzzle, it leads to the confidence and conviction that you can do the next and the next and the next.

WHEN THE HAND GRABS THE DOORKNOB

You pull into the parking spot, put the car in park, gather your keys, your wallet, cell phone and you exit the vehicle.

Perhaps you're tired, maybe distracted by the moving parts of your life. Perhaps you're going into work, or a coffee shop, the gym, or church. Regardless of which one, this is probably a walk you've made many times before. So much so, you can almost do it with your eyes closed. You're on cruise control.

Now, for a moment, imagine that you're walking in slow motion, everything slows down like in a movie. You can see one foot slowly going in front of the other, your arms swing slower now, and you can feel your chest inflate, and your eyelids close and, even slower, begin to open. You're caught in the middle of rest and awareness, as you get ready to start your day.

It's decision time.

Do you flip the switch that says TURN ON—my spirit is open for business, or do you stay on autopilot and recluse? Turn on, and a world of possibilities awaits, a world in which all of your hopes, your dreams, and your ideal life are within your control. A world in which you're alive, alert, and everywhere you go and everybody you encounter has massive potential to bless your life. Or even better, you have a massive potential to bless theirs. Your ability to grow is limitless, and your creative tank is always one step away from being filled. It's like you possess the keys to a car that can take you to the places you've always wanted to go.

But then there's the other option—the cruise control button. After a tough week, sometimes you just want to check out and go on autopilot. This button is definitely the easier option because it's comfy and takes less effort. Still in slow motion, you've entered a subconscious conversation in your head that every-body has. The choice plays with you, one side says, "Chill, you are exhausted, and nothing is going to change if you just go through the motions and stay in your tiny cocoon." It's routine living. You're still alive, only less interested and engaged. And hey, you're not hurting anybody, you're simply going to go inside and take up some space for a bit, nestle yourself into that neat little puzzle like so many of the people around you.

The colossal irony of this second choice is that you quite possibly went to bed the night before praying for a blessing, an answer in your life to that which ails you. You dreamt of bigger things for yourself, maybe even promised God to do something on your end in order to achieve gifts from him on the other.

"God, if you could just open a door for me."

Guess what? He already has. The door is open. It's always open. But there's only so much He can do for you. The next part is up to you—you must take the step and Turn On. There is a strange space that exists between the dreams of your future and the prayers you made the night before. It's called conviction. It's like when you were a kid and told yourself all day, "There's no way I'm going into mom and dad's room tonight. I'm not afraid of the dark." But when nighttime came, what happened? Your mindset shifted, and you lost your conviction as your best intentions went out the window, and you were right there between Mom and Pop.

Here's the problem, you're not a child anymore, and Mom and Dad aren't there. It's time to step into conviction and put the fears of the past behind you.

We all look at our bellies in front of the mirror at night and say, "Tomorrow is the day. I'm getting to the gym and turning this ship around," only to find ourselves tired the next day, maybe looking at that doughnut plate in the break room, feeling a little sorry for ourselves, and looking for some immediate gratification. We say to ourselves, "Awe, what's one more doughnut gonna hurt?" So, we delay the start of our new body in lieu of temporary happiness.

Life today has no shortage of easy options and comfortable distractions as we're all reaping the spoils of a world that has made going on *cruise control* the new norm. Not sure about that? Consider that for most of you reading this, a roof over your head, clothes on your back, and three squares a day are all a given. No matter how tough you think things are right now, I'm guessing most of you aren't worried about those three. Yet we still have the ability to feel as if life isn't working in our favor. We've become so comfortable with life's necessities that we have time to contemplate being bored with life, so we check out.

Be it our smartphone, social media, or any number of the endless entertainment options we have at our fingertips; we're giving them dominion over our lives. We allow them to foster or replace real human-to-human interactions, the kind which let us know what it's like to feel real emotion and what it means to make real connection. It's almost like we've become afraid to smell, touch or get close to anybody.

So, in a way, we've become sort of emotionless. And who is to blame? After all, we've freely chosen to turn on all of the distractions, yes? Meaning nobody is forcing us to. Exactly, nobody is forcing us to turn off, but that's not to say we haven't been led to by something or somebody.

C.S. Lewis wrote, "The safest road to hell is the gradual one, the gentle slope, soft underfoot, without sudden turnings, without milestones, without signposts." I know what Lewis was speaking of, but I'll let you ask yourself, who or what is leading or encouraging you to become emotionless, to turn the lights out and go on cruise control.

And there is a bigger question that follows—what have we turned off in our lives as a result? Relationships? Adventure? Creativity? Friendship? Community? Charity? Purpose? There's a scripture in the bible that reads, *No temptation has overtaken you except what is common to mankind. And God is faithful; he will not let you be tempted beyond what you can bear. But when you are tempted, he will also provide a way out so that you can endure it.* (1 Corinthians 10:13).

What you are feeling is what we're all feeling in some way. Don't think you're alone. It's common to mankind. But like the Word says, God provides a way out. He's not the one tempting you, that's not his game. He's the redeemer. The door opener. The giver of light, the giver of life. He is allowing you to choose and choosing to get turned on is your way out. And again, the way out begins with you seeing with new eyes, hearing with new ears, and making better decisions in the moment. Ninety-nine percent of the time we know right from wrong instantaneously. It's what's called out inner voice or intuition, and it's one of the ways God speaks to us.

Our conscious is very good at knowing what to do. But we can be equally adept at blocking it out as well. We know the difference between what will produce fruit and that which is fruitless yet still we allow that tennis match to occur in our head, which eventually leads you to… yep, you guessed it, the path of least resistance. Do I take the $20 I found on the ground and turn it in or put it in my pocket? Do I order the sugary drink or say no and ask for water? Do I wake up when my alarm is going off or hit snooze? We know, we know, we know. But we don't always follow through.

THE BIG WHAT IF?

Let's go back to the moment when you turn off your car, grab your cell phone, and reach for the door. You're walking into the same coffee shop that you've walked into dozens, maybe hundreds of times before, again thinking about that first sip of latte. Time slows down; your tired eyes slowly close and then open again. You take those long strides, and you're in slow motion again as you reach for the door handle.

NOW, PAUSE. You're frozen, like in a movie, only this time in an instant, you're able to step outside your body and assume a third person's point of view. For a moment, you're allowed to become an observer of your life, so while you're there, frozen in time, ask yourself what it is that you want from your days here on Earth? Is it more money? A new career? Perhaps you want to meet more interesting people. A new love interest or a spouse? Prospects for your business? Or just somebody that gets you and your oddball sense of humor? Again, it's decision time. You're a grown man or woman with free will and the dignity of choice. You have every right to stay on cruise control, comfortable in your routine, blaming outside forces for whatever it is you lack. This comfort zone yields a fairly predictable outcome.

Let's go one step further while we imagine this scenario at the coffee shop where time has slowed down, and you're just an observer. Let's say there's a woman behind the counter making the coffee. We will call her Sarah. Sarah hates pouring coffee. In fact, she loathes pouring coffee, but you'd never know that by looking at her because she has an award-winning smile that she wears like a mask. Nine out of ten customers don't see her smile or notice she spells her name with an H at the end because they are looking at their phones, half asleep at the wheel of life. Sarah with an H could be many things: an amazing friend, an awesome wife, or a genius in the making with Shark Tank-like ideas in her head. Or maybe Sarah has such a strong connection with God and an immense knowledge of life that she's the spiritual guide you've been hoping to find. Regardless, if you open that door and stand in line with your head down, saturated in the superficial, you'll never know what Sarah with an H, or anybody else for that matter, can do for your life because you've lost connection, abandoned your life-force. And it doesn't have to be a coffee shop; it can be anywhere you go at any time. You have to ask yourself, am I a person who is open for business, open for community, open for relationship, for friendship, for love, adventure, excitement, philanthropy, prosperity?

Allow me one last allegory that helps explain what many people are facing today. Imagine you're a painting hanging on a wall, and the highlight of each day for you is wondering who will come by and look at you. You're eager to be noticed, eager for attention and praise, but you sit there helpless, at the mercy of the passers-by, because you're a painting. Passers-by may point and gaze at you, even talk about you for a bit, only to walk off. Your anticipation with each new person is ultimately met with the same disappointment as the one before as they walk off, one after another after another. After a while, sitting there on the wall, everything and everyone begins to look the same. You have no control. You're just staring at the same scene with no ability to move or even engage the passers-by. You're simply looking out at a world that is moving, that's full of color and conversation. One that is alive. But you're not. That's not how life was meant to be lived.

This is life happening to you, not for you.

If you really thought about that scenario, right now, you're like, "Well, that's awful. I certainly don't like how it felt." That is what happens when we surrender all of your identity to Instagram or Facebook. People walked by and look at it, but it lacks the human connection that we really crave, and we end up getting our hopes up that we'll find some type of relationship, but it fails to crack the surface and doesn't really add to your life or your happiness?

That's what happens when you abandon your humanity, by tuning out to the people right there, in your home, your neighborhood, your office. Facebook, Instagram, YouTube and Netflix don't care if you park yourself on their sites all day. They practically put out a warm blanket, footstool, and a cup of coffee for you. Get comfy, no need for anything besides us. That's a huge lie. These distractions are all more than happy to wake you up in the morning and tuck you in at night, almost literally. But one thing they can't do is feed your soul and deliver on your need for true face-to-face connection and fellowship.

THE FOUR HALLWAYS

I just spent several pages laying out choices and taking the power back in your life. Wouldn't it be easy to wash our hands of responsibility and blame this on machines, smartphones, or technology rather than ourselves? We must ask, are we to blame? And if so, what we can do to fix it because the stakes are high, extremely high, and if we don't fix it, we will continue to relinquish a little bit more of our humanity each day.

SO WHERE DO WE BEGIN?

Awareness: having knowledge, being cognizant, informed or alert. That's where we start. We begin with being more aware. Human beings know when they are eating too much, drinking too often, and yes, spending too much time in frivolous mind-numbing activities. Just by reading this, a seed has been planted in your head, a reminder of what could be if you just make a few simple decisions here and there. But turning on is about much more than figuring out how to communicate in an advancing culture. It's about an inward desire to work and live to your highest capacity by drawing more attention and light to that which serves your life rather than that which subtracts from it.

In my years of coaching, I've become painfully aware of that people will kick and scream about having a better life, then find the craziest excuses not to. In other words, we can subconsciously be afraid, avoid or sabotage our ability to live in accordance with our highest potential or self-actualize, as psychologist Abraham Maslow coined it. And when we lack congruence between what we're doing and what we're capable of doing, regret, frustration and depression can enter the picture.

To pursue being turned on offers a solution to push back against the daily blockers and distractions that create walls between the life we wish we had and the one we are living.

My job is to help you get past the pain or sticking points in what I call "The Big Four Hallways" of life: Relationships, Body, Business, and Faith. I choose to refer to them as hallways for a reason. Let me explain.

HALLWAY ANALOGY

When you choose to turn on, you decide to be diligent in search of your gifts. Gifts that have been entrusted to us in a written agreement that we will use them. Gifts which each one of us surely have because we have been chosen to be here. Yes, that's correct, we are indeed chosen and not by mistake. You may not know, but you are one of the very few who made it here, and it was not easy. Do you want to know what your chances were? Experts say about 1 in 10 x 2,685,000 power. That's a 10 followed by 2,685,000 zeroes.

The Buddhist described it this way: "Imagine there was one life preserver thrown somewhere in the ocean and there is exactly one turtle in all of the oceans swimming underwater somewhere. The probability that you came about and exist on earth today is the same as that turtle sticking its head out of the water in the middle of that life preserver—on one try."

Does that kind of blow your mind or what? Makes you realize you're not here by accident, doesn't it?

Let us be aware that not only is our body a vessel which carries us from one table to another, eating or talking, but it houses a soul that has an ability to know, love and share gratitude or sadness. Now, if something went wrong along the way and you thought it might be easier to turn off and give up rather than to stay in the fight, I assure you, read on, your situation is correctable. In fact, everybody loves a great comeback story. My friend, author and speaker Tim Storey, is known as the "Master of the Comeback," having worked with names like Quincy Jones, Lee Iacocca, Smokey Robinson and Robert Downey Jr. He said something to me one day that I think you should always remember, "God gives you the sight, the right and the might to do great things, but you have to develop the fight!"

One of the main obstacles to achievement is that our problems (or setbacks) are something our minds always tend to make bigger than they really are and, therefore, the *fight* which Tim speaks of can often feel insurmountable. But fight, or grit as I like to call it, is what we must obtain at some point in our lives, perhaps even over and over again as we age because our world can indeed be a rough place at times. In my days of covering the NFL, players used to say a guy was good or tough because he had *some dog in him*—meaning grit. I believe we all have some dog in us that allows us to muster the courage to dig in and turn our lives around.

I'll be the first to admit, I've had some introspective ping pong go on in my head over the years being a Christian. Can I have dog in me? You won't find the word dog or even grit in the Bible but make no mistake, the feeling is there 2 Timothy 4:17-18 *But the Lord stood at my side and gave me strength... And I was delivered from the lion's mouth.* Luke 21:19 *Stand firm, and you will win life.* Isaiah 54:17 *No weapon formed against you shall prosper.*

We find strength when we find light, as you've heard people say, "There will be light at the end of the tunnel." The word light is mentioned 272 times in the Bible, and since light is the only thing that can pierce darkness, we need to find the switch to turn it on. That's just a start though, just because you turn it on once, doesn't mean it stays on or that you won't have to find it again. The sun comes up and goes down, fires burn hot, then fizzle out, you turn the lights on, but somebody or something turns them off. One of my spiritual fathers, Dr. Keith Rogan, put it like this, "Keeping your mind renewed is like keeping your hair combed, ya gotta do it every day."

This is where the four hallways come in. Imagine each one of the Big Four Hallways I mentioned as hallways of your life; they represent your marriage and family, your health and well-being, your vocation or career, and your spiritual walk or faith. I presume it's safe to assume that you should want them all to be very long hallways, right? You want to live long, have a lasting marriage, earn a living that keeps you comfortable over the years and have a personal relationship with your creator.

Let's go down each one of these hallways and explain.

RELATIONSHIP

Our lives are made up of relationships, relationships between spouse, family, friends, co-workers and neighbors. I use the term "Home Team" to refer to the family in your house, and if the Home Team is solid, then those other relationships have a lot better chance at being solid too. At the heart of the Home Team is marriage, and if we hope to see a better future for our children, this is where we start.

In the beginning, every marriage is extremely bright. We say, "I Do," and the butterflies are zooming around in our belly 24/7. This hallway is so bright on our honeymoon we think that it would be impossible for it to go dim. But any happily married couple will tell you, it's going take a lot more than butterflies to power that light over the long run. Keeping the lights on past the honeymoon takes work and commitment. Unfortunately, we've been exposed to an enormous amount of negativity about marriage over the last three or four decades, conditioned by so many Hollywood romances and supermarket tabloids to believe at the first sign of strife it's OK to bail on it in lieu of something better. You know the old cliché, *The grass is always greener on the other side*. Yea, the light isn't always brighter in another hallway. Even if you think you chose the wrong hallway all together, it's probably not the case.

What happens in many marriages is that the path of least resistance (A.K.A the cruise control button) gets turned on. This is where the husband or wife just decides, ya know what, my marriage is safe, so I'm just gonna reach over here and flip it on automatic pilot, because it knows where to go. We say *wake me up if anything drastic happens*. Well, guess what, it will happen. Even the best marriages between the most kindred of souls will attest to that. The bonds will be tested, so we must be consistently looking for ways to keep the lights on. Be proactive and know what to expect ahead of time to avoid becoming a statistic. If you decide to take control and search for a light when your marriage is already in a nosedive, chances are you're too late.

Relationships between children and parents are equally at risk these days because the lure of distraction combined with a lack of communication has put parenting on autopilot. Combine that with the fact that the pop culture role models being shown to a younger generation these days aren't exactly stellar, and it's easy to see we've arrived at a crisis. The light shines brightest when we, the parents, reclaim our responsibility, schedule quality time with our children and become massively aware of who or what is influencing their lives.

BUSINESS

As we continue to reiterate the importance of balance in our homes and family, we must realize that what we choose as a vocation has a great deal to do with those relationships. Being in a high-stress position or worrying over finances takes a huge toll on our Home Team. Time spent away from our spouse or children is valuable time that we must make the most out of, that is why this hallway is so important in relationship to the others, because regardless if you're single or married, we all must earn a living and prosper. Like my father always said, "Somebody has to pay to keep the lights on and the food on the table."

In keeping with one of the storylines of this book, this hallway of your life is more and more likely to be subject to change because of the speed of technology and how that affects today's business environment. If there were one light that we can bet will require being turned on over and over, it could very well be this one.

The average person will switch jobs seven to ten times over their lifetime, and you may be turned on and cranking in your job right now, but where will your industry be in a decade? Or better yet, how will your interests and abilities change over that same period of time? It's not *if* that switch will need to be found but *when* and *how often*.

Don't you think we can all agree that it's important to strive to be content with our work as it takes up a significant portion of our time and plays a pivotal part in our day to day happiness? Like Steve Jobs notably said, "Your work is going to fill a large part of your life, and the only way to be truly satisfied is to do what you believe is great work. And the only way to do great work is to love what you do." As you will read, God gave each of us gifts and a mission to which we can use those gifts. That is where the bridge between the business and the faith hallway is made.

FAITH

It is perhaps the most pondered question of all time, "Why am I here?" It's the quest of all quests, the search for the meaning of life. Be you an atheist, agnostic, casual practitioner or full-fledged believer, this hallway of (let's call it) *something greater than me* exists in all of us. Nobody skips this question, but many avoid it. In my opinion, life is not really worth living unless we're actively seeking the answer to the question, "How can we contribute to something greater than ourselves?" In fact, I'd venture to say the true definition of being turned off may be the disposition to solely be concerned with oneself.

If I may use a sports analogy to describe this hallway, I say it can be easily described in terms of a baseball game. Each of the bases represents a stage of your life. When you're young, let's say in your twenties, you've reached first base. You're just happy to be on the bag. Let's be honest, life can be quite superficial at this stage, maybe you're fixing your uniform, peering into the stands to see who's watching you and you're full of excitement just to be playing the game.

Now anybody who knows even the tiniest bit about baseball can answer this question; what's the first thing you do as a runner on first base? You look for the third-base coach.

Why? Well, for three reasons. (1) the third base coach has experience and a wealth of knowledge about the game and the strategy. Typically way more than you, the base runner. (2) The third base coach is strategically positioned to see the entire field. He can see things which you, at first base, cannot see. (3) And lastly, the third base coach has a top priority. Perhaps you can guess what that is? Yes, it is to get you home.

By this point, I'm also guessing you know who the third base coach is. It's the Holy Spirit, or God's earthly presence. Wouldn't it be great if we all had a clear vision of the third base coach in our twenties while on first base? Life would be a lot easier. But let's be honest, some people don't search him out until they are at second, in their thirties or forties, and halfway home. Not only do they have things in front of them at this point, but they have some things behind them as well, such as children, mortgages, employees and responsibilities.

And then still, there are those who won't discover that coach until (or if) they reach third. At this point, He (God) is right in your ear as you are a lot closer to home. Better late than never, you'll want Him there for this stretch. To try and go through life separating the spiritual body from the physical one is a choice I feel is the hardest to make.

THE BODY

Let's look at our physical body. Without it, we can't do much in terms of turning on the lights in our home, work and places of worship. It gets us where we need to go, and it's the source for physical connection and communication. In its prime, let's say about age 19 years of age, this hallway is beaming with light and really turned on (in more ways than one). Our hormones are raging, and the body's abilities appear endless. We feel alive and invincible and, therefore, more likely to take our health for granted. It's like "Darn, I only can see four abs, not six? Well, maybe I'll just have one Big Mac next time." If you're young and reading this, thank God for your fast metabolism, and don't take it for granted, it doesn't last forever.

As we blow out the candles on each birthday cake, our bodies will begin to change, and we will recognize there will need to be a greater effort to keep them lit. When major lifestyle changes occur in the form of a new house, new job or new baby you could find yourself suddenly in a darker hallway with your health. Maybe being turned on at this point means paying closer attention to your diet, stretching more, watching what you drink (alcohol) and being more concerned about stress management.

When the light you had at 17 or 27 is not as bright anymore it's easy to panic and begin flipping every switch you read about in a magazine or hear on the news looking for a quick fix, but again, from a one small step approach, it's about real solutions not tomorrow's newest fad. In this particular hallway, the key word is longevity. We take an inside out approach that speaks to both mental and physical health and asks the question, what's the simplest way we can get our physical body and spiritual body in synch with one another.

THE BIG PICTURE

Now that we've gone over the Four Hallways, can you clearly envision them in your life? Can you see where some may have gone dark? In which ones would you like to produce more light? Are you anticipating brighter days ahead?

It's been said that the one inevitable in life is that it will constantly change. No matter who you are, where you are reading this or how long it's been since it was published, these concepts won't change. They are too simple and too obvious. And in full transparency, the biggest thing I realized in writing this book is this: even when you're in it, researching it, and writing about it, if you don't stay turned on and intentional every day, the distractions will creep back in.

I found myself writing these chapters and feeling the pull to answer frivolous emails rather than play with my kids, to eat more for pleasure than for sustenance, to walk away from difficult conversations rather than embrace them and to avoid prayer when I needed to be grounded in it.

When we choose to turn on, we must realize that the tendency and opportunity for distraction and disconnection are often greater than our desire to do that which makes life richest. Now, more than ever, we have a slew of distractions from which to choose. And why is it so hard to fight distraction? I think we can begin by defining the word attrition—the wearing down or weakening of resistance, especially as a result of continuous pressure.

Ask yourself right now, in what areas of your life do you feel you've been weakened? Where are you meeting resistance and feeling continuous pressure? Has comparison on social media made you devalue your body or career? Does your relationship not look like a Hallmark Christmas movie? Has the continuous pressure of your job worn on you to the point where you've contemplated throwing your hands up and saying, "I'm done. I'm don't know what my alternative options are, but I'm done." Or maybe your faith has been church hurt or worn down by sickness or disease within your family.

In a culture up world, attrition can wear us down with every turn we make. We now possess unprecedented access into other people's lives, seeing things that we really have no business seeing or need to know and things which may have no true basis in reality, meaning a combination of photoshop and fake news. Day after day, we stack these imagines atop one another wearing them like a new layer of clothes until we reach the point where it's just become completely uncomfortable, and we feel weighed down and constricted by the trivial rather than the truth.

There's a story about a young girl who was driving down the highway on a road trip when out of the corner of her eye, she noticed a chocolate bar on the dashboard. Eager to get it, she took off her seatbelt and reached over as far as she could. Unfortunately, she took her eyes off the road and ended up driving into a ditch, severely damaging her car and hitting her head.

The lesson in this parable is this: how many times do we wreck something in our lives because we were simply distracted or reaching for something else that was not as important?

The chocolate bar is a metaphor for everything in life that is instantly gratifying and pulls at us or distracts us from that on which we truly need to focus. You will see in the chapters that follow, the things holding you back, distracting you, lulling you to sleep, or offering a quick fix are the same things affecting your family, co-workers and community. So often we hide these dark spots and insecurities because we fail to realize we're all falling victim to the same circumstances.

Reaching in this story can show up in many forms. We can reach for shallow intimacy instead of love, the bottle for comfort and distraction, or social media for relationship and companionship. The bigger question is: What's at stake that we could potentially wreck? The answer is the big four or most important things in life: our hearts, health, careers, and salvation.

Unless we step back and do the work, the simple work, we will continue to spiral into the shadows, wondering where or how we let life escape. We must wake up and become alert to a higher quality of relationship and reject the preoccupation with the superficial. Author Robin Sharma says, "Your billion-dollar ideas don't show up in the middle of dramatic distraction. They show up when you have the business and personal discipline to make space for your creative mind to flourish."

I know this to be true because every time I exercise self-discipline and turn on the areas of my family, faith, career and health, I get an enormous feeling of gratification, an endorphin rush from achievement and sticking to my priorities. However, when I allow for distractions and procrastinate on those same things, I beat myself up, wallowing in self-pity and frustration.

REACH FOR THE LIGHT

So, are you ready for some light? Are you prepared for good news? Isaiah 52:7 says, *How beautiful upon the mountains are the feet of him who brings good news.* The good news is that course correction is there for you, a few simple switches away. But be warned, just because something is easy doesn't necessarily mean it's comfortable. Hebrews 12:11 says, *No discipline seems pleasant at the time, but painful. Later on, however, it produces a harvest of righteousness and peace for those who have been trained by it.*

Tiny moments of discipline create a string of small victories and ultimate change. I think the easiest example to demonstrate this is with our bodies. We see a doughnut in the break room. We know doughnuts aren't good for our diet. Duh, that's easy! The right decision is what? Painfully obvious. Yet the discipline is unpleasant.

We must practice restraint and delayed gratification. Where does that come from, you ask? Is there some kind of Jedi mind trick we can practice? Is it in our head? Yes, it's in your head, but not entirely. It lies in the ten inches between your head and your heart. C.S. Lewis called it "Leaders with chests," which John C. Maxwell expounded on saying, "The head (reason) must rule the belly (sensual desires) through the chest (character and spirit)." He said that without a strong chest, we succumb to the excuses. And we know that these days if we are looking for an excuse to hide from our spouse, an excuse to eat out of control, an excuse not to talk to our neighbors or not go to church that they are available in abundance. We must therefore trust our gut, think with our heads and lead with our chests.

CHAPTER TWO

TURN ON YOUR DAY

"You can't be that kid standing at the top of the waterslide, overthinking it. You have to go down the chute."
— Tina Fey

Do you know what more than 45,000,000 people search for on GOOGLE *monthly*? Four words: **How to be happy.** Wow, that means 45,000,000 people are searching for light.

The pursuit of happiness rather than mere survival may seem like a first-world problem, but I believe man and woman have been in search for peace of mind since leaving Eden. Strangely though, we've arrived at a rather ironic point in history, one in which progress has afforded us all of life's external necessities in a quest to make us comfortable while giving us the time to contemplate the one thing it can't deliver—true happiness. There is no plug-in, no app, for that. And when you stop to think about it, can't we say that man is trying to counterfeit that which cannot be manufactured? And by manufacture, I mean both in the literal sense (by inventing and using machinery) and in the spiritual sense (fabricating a false reality and emotional experience).

Our grandparents and great grandparents worked hard each day for necessities such as food and shelter. The continuation of the species was still the main struggle. Happiness was a luxury set aside for the very little time when they weren't simply trying to survive.

Should we feel guilty? Haven't we've earned the right to bathe in the spoils of our riches? It would be silly and very old fashioned for me to revert to the exhausted "When I was your age" cliché, so I won't. Well, not exactly. You see there is a good point to be made here, one that John Lennon and Paul McCartney made back in 1964—money (or things) can't buy you love. If it did, 45 million souls (most of which have money in their pockets) wouldn't be searching for it on the internet each month.

You've probably heard the term "Motivational Monday" which I've always found quite comical. We have a system in our home that cools or heats air to the exact temperature we desire at the push of a button. We can prepare a hot meal in a micro- wave in 60 seconds. We can watch shows we like on television or listen to music on the radio on demand anytime we like. If we have a toothache or headache, we can have pain reliever delivered to our doorstep that day, and it immediately relieves what ails us. We can fly from California to New York in just under five and a half hours. Cross the Atlantic in six.

I say this to draw a clear point—we have all the luxuries a person could imagine, and yet we have to find inspiration to get up and get out of bed on a Monday?

Think about what your great-great-grandpa would say if you could ask him what he did for Motivational Monday. I'm guess- ing he said something like, "I woke up at the crack of dawn to milk a cow, gather eggs or churn butter before school. Then, I came home, did some type of manual labor around the house, ate dinner, studied by candlelight, and went to bed to get ready to get up and do the same thing the next day."

I'm not trying to be acrimonious or petulant; I'm just saying we've become trapped in a values inversion by allowing ourselves to be depressed and unmotivated at a time when we possess every imaginable convenience to make life easy.

Therefore, the first thing you need to do to turn on your day is to stop taking it for granted. Be grateful your eyelids opened to see a new light, and you woke to the perfect temperature, flushed the indoor plumbing, washed in a hot shower, and only had to open a refrigerator to satisfy your hunger. If that still sounds like old fashioned rhetoric then simply be grateful that you most likely live in a country that operates by democratic principles and, therefore, you get to decide your fate on this day. That very important fact still isn't a luxury in some parts of the world, yet in free societies, we take it for granted.

YOU CAN'T ALWAYS GET WHAT YOU WANT, BUT YOU GET WHAT YOU NEED

Let's think about intention vs. necessity. In other words, the way you *want to* versus the way you *have to*. We don't have to get off to a good start each morning, but we should want to as it is a crucial element to success. The attitude we step out of bed with is our responsibility, so regardless of the tasks ahead, to blame anybody but ourselves is a copout. So step one in a turned on life is to reclaim one critical area of your life—personal responsibility.

Wouldn't you agree that when you feel like you're in control of your life, you also feel empowered to do more and be more? And the only way to truly take control is to strip all others of having authority over your situation. Be it good or bad, you are where you are right now because of the decisions you've made in the past and it makes sense that when you lay your head down on your pillow tonight, you will be where you are because of the decisions you made today. So why not start to get turned on by claiming dominion over your day by making one small decision in your favor. It could be as small as taking a 20-minute walk or learning a new word (like acrimonious) or setting your alarm to go off thirty minutes early. I call it rising with an attitude of intention rather than one of necessity. For four years, my wife Angelike and I led a 6:30 am devotional group called *Rise with Intention* because we knew the importance of beginning one's day with action and accountability.

REST OVER RUSH

What's your relationship with the snooze button? Do you hit it once, twice, or are you a perpetual snoozer always gambling with the clock, bartering your productive time for a couple more minutes of sleep?

Can you recall ever hitting the snooze button on Christmas morning? Probably not because you knew that day would be special, and you were aware of the possibilities of joy that it brought. I won't tell you to treat each day like Christmas because, while it sounds nice, we know that it's much easier said than done. But you do need to wake up with the idea that today offers momentum and that each morning brings an element of hope.

If you are looking for a simple way to create some momentum quickly in your life, then let it be this: the second before you open your eyes, flip a mental switch, before that first light hits your iris, make a choice to awaken your spirit. Know that you are in charge, nobody else, not your boss, your aching back, or your ex-husband. The most important decision you make is how to start your day without the snooze button and with personal responsibility. Then, you will have time (peace) and authority (dominion) over the rest of your day. Perfect. What's next?

When I wake up and put foot to the floor, my mind goes to coffee. For many, many years, that cup was my morning partner, and its best friend was called social media. Coffee and social media absolutely loved one another; they were like Ross and Joey, Scooby and Shaggy, Bert and Ernie. The only problem is, Ross and Joey sat in man chairs most of the time, Bert and Ernie rarely left the bedroom, and Scooby and Shaggy, well... we know what they were doing. So, let's just say coffee and social media weren't the most productive combination to begin my day.

I really needed them to be more like Han and Chewie, you know, saving the universe and all. But, one of them had to go, and guess who wasn't leaving? That's right, coffee. Be it now, a month from now, or 20 years, coffee knows he and I are lifelong friends and that he ain't going anywhere. So, we kicked out social media in the morning.

Do you know who was most happy with that decision? My kids. They hated sharing Dad in the morning. But since social media was, and is, critical to our business, I needed to be on it. So, I began crafting my brand or business posts the day before and just hit send in the morning, clearing the way for healthier habits and quality time with my family. Coffee was cool with the decision, too, as we welcomed relaxing music, self-development books, and scripture to the party.

Here was my problem though, and I know many of you share it, I have a short attention span. Friends describe me as a squirrel, and even the best of intentions can succumb to distraction by the slightest of temptations. So, for me to say I can wake up each morning and read a chapter of a book is far-fetched. And honestly, it is something I used to beat myself up for. I'd wonder, "David, how can other people read so many books while you struggle to stay focused on one? You're an adult who teaches connection and self-development, and you can't concentrate for 30 minutes, who are you kidding?" But then I eased up, allowed myself some grace, and told myself to do what I could for as long as I could and try to create a stronger habit. So what if I only read five or six pages? That's five or six pages more than I did before.

The turned-on philosophy is not to do a 180-degree flip in one day, but to take tiny steps that are comfortable and doable and then continue to do and build on those. So that's what I did, five or six pages at a time. I also got into the healthy habit of drinking 8 ounces of water first thing in the morning before my coffee. It wasn't easy at first but after a while, the habit stuck.

HOPE LOVES A GREAT MORNING

No matter your age, the key to the fountain of youth lies in three things: INSPIRATION, MOTIVATION, and REVELATION. Inspiration to see with new eyes and marvel at new experiences. Motivation to pursue your goals and keep yourself healthy enough to live out your purpose with vigor. And Revelation: seeking God's disclosure of himself and his will in your life. This may be the most important thing you will nurture and cultivate as you grow older, and they are really easy to focus in on once you can start to cancel out the outside noise. But because we live in a culture of sensory overload, where something is always pinging, beeping or popping up, it's no wonder why so many of us have a hard time dialing into our inner voice of hope and instead turn to despair.

Hope is a word I adore, but also feel is completely overused. Why? Because it's probably the most profitable word in self-development. Hope sells, and it sells in big-time dollar amounts. But remember, hope wasn't coined in a three-day conference or manufactured in an online course. Hope is divine and comes from above. It's mentioned 129 times in the bible and is one of the foundations of faith. Hope in a better future and hope to pick us up when we are down. But what exactly does it mean? My favorite definition of hope is the joyful anticipation of good. Yet, I think the reason a majority of people have difficulty finding it is because we currently live in a culture of fear. Fear is the expectation of bad; it's the antithesis of hope, and it's prevalent in just about every newspaper and late-night newscast in our culture. We've created a culture of fear that has crept into our houses and our minds. Let me remind you, though, void of these cultural fear tactics, hope and fear represent a 50/50 proposition, like up or down, left or right. There are only two ways to look at it. We know fear exists and is real, but we must also remember that it is not of God. We must also acknowledge that faith in God will deliver us from fear as the phrase "Fear Not" is mentioned 365 times in the Bible.

Keeping this simple, our first job is to decide which side of the coin do we wish to focus. Do you want to rise to a world full of conflict, what-ifs, name-calling and blame, or would you rather awaken to introspection, a higher purpose, collaboration, and more possibilities to connect with others?

Whether it's your vocation, marriage, health or faith, being turned on means having more reasons to be hopeful than reasons to be fearful. Many of you are stuck in a pattern of fear and subsequent stagnation, however, I'd be willing to bet that if you made a list, you'd surprise yourself that there is more in your life to be hopeful about than to fear.

So what's preventing that hope from overcoming the fear and becoming a reality in your day? The answer is in the form of a question; what are you tuned into and who are you spending the most time with? The information we consume and people we surround ourselves with contribute the most messages to the space inside our head. If it is constantly being fed into your mind that the world is unfair, you'll never experience financial freedom and that you should be scared every time you leave your house, then guess what? Yea. Fear will be your mindset.

Our current culture and the technological advances that have arisen from it are naturally, or perhaps not-so-naturally, forcing our brains to work overtime, stretching them, so to speak, to work at a greater capacity than ever before in the history of man. Stop to think about that for a second. For millennium, man would wake up and make basic life and death decisions like what to eat, who to congregate with and where to lay his head at night.

Even at the end of the 19th century, that was mostly the case. Now contrast that with your life and take a moment to count how many minutes or seconds go by in your day between messages. How many decisions is your mind trying to juggle at once? Where should you send your kids to school? What are you going to post on social media at lunchtime? Should you be scared that somebody got robbed two counties away? Which Presidential candidate will lead you to financial ruin or a nuclear holocaust? Are you too fat? How many wrinkles on your face is acceptable? Is there somebody you could sue in order to get money? What products are in your house that may be killing you?

Have you had enough information overload? Do you realize that we are living in a culture of constant input and little rest, continuous fear-mongering, and little faith? It's overwhelming, and we can blow off steam complaining about it from time to time, but then go right back to the accepting that's just the way it is. No! Fear loves company and makes a lot of people a lot of money, but it can't exist without agreement. It cannot spread without willing parties. So in unison and with hope, we must get turned on and become eager to sweep fear aside and usher in a culture of hope.

If you agree that you'd like to invite more hope, or light, into your life, you must first assess the places in your life where darkness has crept in. After that, you must place absolute faith in the notion that light has to power to overcome darkness as scripture says, *For nothing is hidden that will not become evident, nor anything secret that will not be known and come to light.* (Mark 4:22).

Physically, spiritually, and metaphorically this battle between the two forces is playing out in our homes, offices and communities every day. Physically, we're being bombarded by blue light —in our house, from our TV, from our computers and smartphones. Over time, it causes retina damage and vision problems. From a spiritual standpoint, it's become harder to distinguish God-given light from an artificial spiritual light, i.e., that from the universe, metaphysical mediums or enchantresses, and fictional superheroes. The traditional church has done a rather poor job educating believers on the supernatural power of God, and subsequently, many people are enticed to those counterfeit sources of hope I just mentioned.

Allow me to use the words of a woman who lived her entire life in the dark to illustrate that hope doesn't come from artificial or counterfeit sources of light but rather the one true light.

> *"Optimism is the faith that leads to achievement; nothing can be done without hope and confidence." – Helen Keller*

Not only was Keller not privy to our modern sources of consumption (television, internet, smartphone), she lived her life absent of sound and sight. She would write about her life as a girl who for so long had no concept of death or days, light or dark. She was a person who would simply eat, drink and sleep without hope or anticipation of joy. Then along came Anne Sullivan who opened Keller's mind by teaching her to spell and read with her fingers. This part of the story most of us know, Sullivan was the Miracle Worker immortalized by the film of the same name. The part of the Keller story most people don't know is the name John Hitz. Hitz was another one of Keller's teachers, and he introduced her to the book Heaven and Hell by Emanuel Swedenborg, a Swedish theologian and philosopher. His work gave her a new faith which helped her to understand the separateness between the soul and body which she would later write *brought her to God's city of light and that by walking there, she has known joy that has conquered darkness to such an extent that it has given her the strongest reasons to overcome her limitations.*

How eloquent she put it, *God's city of light*. Reading that for the first time I thought how could I not feel tiny and shallow for being depressed or upset with life when here was a girl who never heard a guitar or saw a sunrise. Yet, Keller felt the light, and it gave her the strongest reasons to overcome her limitations, which were great. Wouldn't you agree that the world is ready for light, that you are ready for light? Couldn't you use some strong reason to overcome your much smaller limitations? I feel like we're ready to be grateful for the things that God has made rather than man, I feel like so many of us are poised to reclaim the bits and pieces of humanity that an advancing culture and technology may have taken from us. I feel like the world is ready for a revival of grand proportions.

MIND AND BODY REVIVAL

One winter morning, while sipping coffee, Angelike looked at me and said, "Wow, you need moisturizer. Your face looks really dry." Nothing like a subtle nudge from the wifey to tell you something isn't right about yourself.

So, I went into the bathroom and found some moisturizer. I closed my eyes and began to rub it on my face, and in doing so, I had an epiphany. I relaxed and began to feel the contour of my cheeks, my eyes and my forehead. Something I imagine Keller did early in her life that I had obviously taken for granted for too long.

With one sense shut down and another heightened, I had the thought that God gave me these eyes to see with, this nose to smell with, and these cheekbones to smile with. It was a very honest and simple shift in thinking. I went from feeling sorry for myself that perhaps I was getting older to thinking, "Hey now, this is an easy enough task to make part of my routine, and it's something to better yourself with David. You're nourishing your skin, feeding it life-giving nutrients and, at the same time, getting in touch with a newfound appreciation for what I do have, rather than that which I lack or I'm losing." I couldn't see my hair turning gray or the wrinkles around my eyes, but I was grateful I could open my eyes to see that I had wrinkles and that I had hair still.

It felt good to wake up and take control over that part of my day, to shift from non-productive to proactive, to go from feeding the brain with despair to massaging it with appreciation. Not only was I taking a simple moment to get back in touch with my physical self, but I was nourishing my skin with something that would make a tiny improvement that day. When I repeated that, I felt and saw a difference. I was turning on my body.

The big lesson? Investing in yourself each morning is always a good way to start your day. And just like that, I decided to be a morning person, and that may be the best decision anybody can make.

This is a man's man talking here. I'm not a self-love guru or love child of the 70s. My hope is to encourage even the manliest men not to just think of themselves as a sack of random cells waiting to expire. We are fearfully and wonderfully made in the image of God, and in that, we should appreciate ourselves for the miracle we are. Isn't it amazing that our bodies never stop working, even while we sleep? That at night, it goes to work repairing and replenishing itself? The morning isn't for being a sloth; it's not for waking up and thinking what do we have to do; it's for waking up your body, rewarding it, and then asking ourselves what can we do?

With hands that can dial, grab, caress, and wave and with ears that can hear birds and guitars and eyes that can see amazing color and depth to communicate that beauty to a receptive brain, we have to acknowledge the miracle of being human. We're not machines. We're not programmed to do the same thing every day and perform emotionless activities. We were given the power to create, but how has that power taken some of our life away?

Perhaps the best way to understand this is to look at it through the lens of pop culture. Surely many of you are familiar with the character Neo and *The Matrix* movie. He woke up to a world which dictated life to him rather than being in a world which he could control himself. Maybe you are familiar with Bill Murray's character in *Groundhog Day*, waking up at the same time, repeating the same day and going through the same mundane motions in the same setting over and over again at the mercy of a world where nothing changes. The common message in both stories is that we're all faced with one question; is life happening to us or for us? If it's happening to you, like Murray, then you risk the huge regret one day of seeing it from a different perspective and asking, "WHY DIDN'T I TURN ON?" If it's happening for you, like Neo chose, then you agreed to take personal responsibility to create a world which you truly desire to live in.

The next step in turning on your day comes down to your intention over the next 12 hours or so. If we're honest, the majority of people would gladly trade just about anything for an extra 30 minutes of sleep in the morning. I know those who can't imagine what life would be like without a snooze button. However, getting outside within the first hour of waking up could drastically change your perspective. Remember, hope loves a new day because it brings new possibilities. The sunlight, the smell of fresh air and the sounds of nature (even if you're in a big city) will outweigh anything you'll find on your television or computer.

Remember the psalm of David says, "He makes me lie down in green pastures, He leads me beside quiet waters." It doesn't say, "He took me to Starbucks and leads me to the Wi-Fi." The morning is the perfect time to get in touch with your spirit. My favorite thing to do is to walk barefoot outside, even for only 10 minutes, in order to ground myself with the earth.

Nobody will ever accuse me of being a Tree Hugger, but the facts are there and studies show that when the body is grounded (meaning your bare feet touch Earth), its electrical potential becomes equalized with the Earth's electrical potential through a transfer of electrons from the Earth to the body. It has also been revealed that this habit neutralizes free radicals, increases immunity, and reduces pain, inflammation and stress. And best of all, it takes almost no effort.

Another great benefit to going outside shortly after you wake up is to get a big dose of Vitamin D, or the Sunshine Vitamin. Do you know why it's called that? Similar to how plants absorb light and convert it into energy, our skin absorbs UV-B rays and converts it into vitamin D. While most people are aware of the dangers of too much sun and skin cancer, most aren't told about the reverse—not enough sunshine. Studies suggest that by going outdoors and getting nature's Vitamin D, you can help protect against osteoporosis, cancer, depression, heart attack and stroke. And the consensus is that Americans, especially those who live in the northernmost states, don't get enough. That's another reason why it's important to spend at least 10-15 minutes outside on sunny days or take a supplement during the winter months. In addition, the oxygen-rich environment helps your immune system and digestive system function better.

It's hard to see God these days because we've extracted ourselves from nature, living in concrete jungles and even suburban ones. In our Turned On Method course, Angelike and I give our clients this simple assignment in week one: go outside and find three things in nature that prove God's existence in your world; a caterpillar, a flower, a bee. Then the next step is to find three things that prove God's existence in you, look upon your child, embrace and caress your spouse or smell that same flower. He's there, we've just stopped looking for him at times when we are distracted.

So the biggest no-brainer in the history of happiness is to get outside before work just for a little bit each day and watch what happens in your life.

Remember, when you say "no more" to snoozing and "yes" to putting your bare feet on the ground, you'll quickly realize that everything you did prior to that was just an effort to delay getting your day (your life) started.

DESTROYING THE YOKE OF DELAY

And this brings us to one of the most critical concepts of the book and a Turned On life. What is the snooze bar except something that only delays the inevitable? Eventually, we have to wake up and have to get into action, which is why I want to urge you to think of Turned On as a kind of wakeup call. It's an alarm for your spirit which goes off internally and urges you to stop putting off the important things in life and to begin building the small habits which lead to true optimism.

While I will reference many famous writers and teachers in these pages, perhaps it will be the least known or most obscure who delivers this most important message.

Dr. Sola Adetunji is a Bishop and teacher from Lagos, Nigeria. I stumbled upon a sermon of his years ago, and it immediately grabbed my attention and opened my eyes to something very powerful. He said, "Destiny is a function of time. And it is the devil's target. Satan does not attack you because of your past, he troubles you because of your future—that is his primary target! For most of the time, when Satan sees that he cannot derail you in destiny, he delays you; for when you are delayed long enough, you are destroyed."

Yes indeed! The devil is in the delay. In simple terms, each of us is born with a divine purpose or destiny to be fulfilled. Sadly, a large majority never reach it and go to their grave with what I'll call unfinished business. The reasons and excuses are endless:

I was born with bad genes; I had a really tough break along the way; My business partner sold me out; my wife left me; I got sick; I got injured; I had to take care of somebody. The money ran out; My addiction prevented me from doing it. All strong, very valid excuses, but still none are as common as the one spoken by Dr. Adetunji, the one we least want to admit—I got distracted. I got sidetracked.

As humans, we're susceptible to distractions, and today we have them in abundance. There's always something dinging, beeping, or asking for our attention. And while it's obvious these things take our focus away, it's easier to blame what? Others, right? It's always easier to blame others for our shortcomings than to take personal responsibility and correct them ourselves. By giving people, situations, vices, and devices authority over our lives, we hit the metaphorical snooze button allowing our dreams to be delayed.

As it was written, your destiny is only a function of time. Some have longer than others, but we know about how long we have on earth. Now, the devil, or the Enemy, can't take what God put on your heart, he can't steal your dreams. They belong to you. The Enemy is powerful but doesn't have that kind of power. His power is external of your spirit and feeds on manipulation, lies and, most of all, distraction.

The enemy is not concerned with what you've done in your past. It's been done, and that's irrelevant now. No, the Devil has his sights set on your future, your potential. That is very much his target because if you have a dream in your heart, a kingdom serving game plan, then he is going to set his sights on disrupting it. He wants to bring chaos to order, deceit to belief, and replace hope with fear. Think about some of the obstacles he may have already placed in your path to divert your attention from your calling.

Understand that distraction takes on many forms from frivolous romances to mindless video games, to the more serious
speed bumps that cause major stress like illness and financial
strife. Or maybe it's not monumental. Can you recall a time when
you were working on something important only to be interrupted by a text message or email? What happened? You broke
your concentration, became frustrated, and said, "I'll have to get
back to this later." Did you? How many times do you just put it
off indefinitely?

When it comes to the Four Hallways, when he delays you
long enough, you'll either forget or just give up because it seems
too big of a hill to climb. That's when the enemy can claim
victory. He couldn't stop what was in your heart, but he delayed
you long enough to put off that reconciliation, to put off starting
that charity, to put off that diet or that business. Remember, the
safest road to hell is a gradual one, so start your day right. Don't
get distracted.

TELL YOURSELF THE TRUTH

Over the course of writing this book, I experienced massive
distraction and resistance on many levels. The amount of stress
in my home seemed to skyrocket as I felt the pressure to get this
message out to individuals and families alike. Because of the
power distraction holds over us and the need to escape, there
were times when I wrote with incongruence or when I found
myself looking at my phone more and retreating into diversion-
ary activities when the moment seemed overwhelming.

Remember, our day and our inability to stay focused on its
tasks often fights against the very things that provide distraction. If food companies do research on what color to put on a bag
of potato chips or exactly how many cookies to put in a bag, you
must realize it's not big business that has your best interest in
mind? If cable television networks and social media outlets

benefit by having you spend more time on their channel or site, what lengths will they go to ensure that you do?

The struggle is real, and the allure to escape the responsibilities and nuances of the day have never been more appealing. Questions like, "Do I deal with the dirty dishes, go to the gym, play with my son, finish that sales presentation, or take 15 minutes to pray?" Go head to head with distractions like, "Should I play another game of Madden, scroll through my Instagram feed, shop on eBay, or order a pizza?"

Just because we know something is right, doesn't mean it'll be an easy decision. It's like a funnel cake at a fair. I can watch the dough being dropped in the deep fryer and see the powdered sugar being sprinkled on the dough and have every instinct in my body tell me, "Wow, that's not good for you," but still there I am handing my money to the cashier. For what? Ten minutes of pleasure and a couple of hours of regret? That's the kind of pull our generation is dealing with in terms of distraction. We are pulled so hard by advertising and the quick escapes that we ignore our instincts and ignore our family.

We can't ignore what's happening as a result.

CHAPTER THREE

TO BE HUMAN AGAIN

> *"I would risk anything to kiss you again."*
> *– Lumiere*

A turned-on life is such a simple concept that even kids get it. As I drove down the street one day, I saw a neighbor walking her dog and I waved. She didn't wave back because she had her head down in her phone oblivious to both my voice and my action. My seven-year-old said, "Daddy, she's not turned on."

I've found that children are a lot more perceptive and intuitive than we give them credit for sometimes. But, at the same time, they will only do what we teach them, so it's imperative we grasp what it means to be present and steward the message intentionally.

Unfortunately, as we start to adult as they say, life begins to get heavy with responsibility, and we typically do two things: first we forget the importance of connection and interactive play and two, begin to look for an escape from life stressors in the form of subversions that relieve us from the heaviness.

Like many of you, there are days when I just want to come home, sit on the couch with a glass of wine and watch a movie. There's nothing wrong with that. But I realized that it can make for an easy escape which, if not put in check, can become a habit that shifts the balance of life, slowly stealing the time we could be investing in other things.

Now if you're a mom or dad of young children, the movies you watch typically come in the form of a children's story or cartoon. Such is the life of a parent. You know you've had one too many cartoons when you find yourself singing to communicate with your spouse even after the kids are asleep; *Do you wanna go to bed now, or let's stay up and pray, I never sleep good anymore since you've begun to snore, our life is so cliché.* If you're laughing you've done it. If you're not laughing, you don't have kids yet.

Anyway, every once in a while, one of those children's stories ends up waking up something inside of you. In one particular case, it woke me up to the fact I might be taking life for granted. The movie is *Beauty and the Beast* and it's my daughters' favorite. We've seen it at least a dozen times. We know all the songs by heart, and I'd say, without a doubt, my favorite is "To Be Human Again." It comes during a time in the movie when the cookware, the candelabra, and the clock find themselves longing for a life they once knew, one in which they were not just objects becoming less and less human but rather one when they can finally break the awful spell they're under and become full of life again. It's an important reminder of all the things we take for granted — cooking, singing, playing, dancing, twirling and love. Things that, one day we'll look back on and ask why I didn't do more of that? To the contrary, when you're old and in the later stages of life can you really imagine yourself saying, 'Why didn't I shop online more', 'Why didn't I play John Madden more' or 'watch Vin Diesel do another 360 spin in his Dodge Charger?' Probably not.

I know in our house there is often a longing to hear one of Papou's old war stories or to be able to kiss YiaYia one more time.

Maybe it's a walk with your dog, a story with your kids or a slow dance with your spouse? Whatever it may be. When you are human again, and only human again, that's when the world, once more, will make sense.

It seems like we, as a culture, haven't been receiving this message our children's movies have been teaching for some time now. Another favorite of ours is Pixar's *Wall-E*. It's a sweet film with very little dialogue that takes place in the future when the earth has been rendered uninhabitable due to accelerated industrial growth and pollution. *Wall-E* is a garbage-collecting robot left to clean up the mess the humans, who have all abandoned earth, have left behind.

While at heart, it's a love story between Wall-E and Eva, another robot sent to earth to see if any real life still exists, there is a much more prophetic and troubling byline to the picture — what the future could look like if we choose this path of least resistance and go on cruise control. In this future, human beings are relegated to hovering chairs that are equipped with interactive computer screens where everything from ordering food to virtual entertainment is at their disposal with a simple voice command. (Sorry, Alexa, you may want to cover your intake speaker here).

Their food is brought to them and their communication is limited to what show or activity they will occupy their time with next. In one scene, two men complain of boredom as they ride side by side on their hovering chairs. But they aren't looking at each other. Even though they are next to one another, they are speaking to each other via their screens. Sound familiar?

In the end, as you might imagine, Wall-E awakens the passengers to what they are missing back on earth. What it's like to be, as you might guess, human again. And of course, as all feel-good stories go, they see the error of their ways, revolt and restore life to how it should be.

Lesson learned right? Apparently not. *Beauty and The Beast* was released in 1991. *Wall-E* was released in 2008. According to BoxOfficeMojo.com, they ranked No. 15 and No. 14 among the all-time highest grossing children's movies.

So plenty of children and parents have laid eyes on them and the lessons they teach. But have things progressed or regressed since then? It seems like we, the consumer, get it. We love the storyline, nod (or clap) in agreement and watch them over and over, but do we heed the message? Not really.

I was curious to learn more about *Wall-E* and its creator, so I Googled it. It was co-written and directed by Andrew Stanton, and, no surprise, he turns out to be a pretty insightful guy. And it just so happens that his Ted Talk titled "Clues to A Great Story" made one of the most significant impacts on my life and career. I even made his key point of the Ted Talk into a central part of my course instruction over the years, and that is: MAKE ME CARE. He explains it so simply, adding, "Because we all know what it's like TO NOT CARE."

YES! Make me care. Make us care that these movies are sending a message we can't afford to ignore. Make us care more about connection and spending time with our family than flipping stations or getting distracted by trivial endeavors. Make us care that we have a limited time with our children while they are small and still want to hang out with us. Make us care, in general, because life is too short to not care.

Now I want you to think back to the Big Four Hallways of your life. Where does else does "Make Me Care" fit into each one? Something has to make you choose a career, a love interest, a reason to exercise, and of course a reason to know that there is hope beyond this life. What inspires you to get out of bed each morning, put your feet firmly on the ground and get after it? Where are you deriving your energy from as you seek inspiration and adventure?

AN INTERVIEW WITH A VAMPIRE

I've spent the better part of my adult life as a journalist, interviewing thousands of people and telling stories. It was my job to observe, be curious and ask questions, and I was very good at it because I'm an observer with a curious spirit by nature, so people watching is something I have always enjoyed. I'm also a massive extrovert and anywhere I go, I'll strike up a conversation with anyone and find a common thread.

After newspapers died (lost their relevance), I thought my career was dead as well. From a very early age, I remember having conversations with my family, friends and college counselors about what I wanted to do with my life. I always said, "I like to tell stories," something nobody really believed at the time could ever translate into making a living.

Ironically, it has. For the better part of the last twenty-five years, I've been telling stories, my own as well as others. In fact, I began to call myself a student of human interaction, taking what I loved, watching people interact with one another, and marrying it with what I was good at, being an extrovert and telling stories. I got so good at it that I began teaching it, helping young entrepreneurs feel more comfortable coming out of their shells to tell their stories.

And that leads us back to this story, perhaps the most important one of our era, one that is becoming more and more overtly obvious; and that is humanity, human beings, are becoming less and less engaged with one another? In my time as a reporter, telling stories, some people I interviewed just sucked the life out of me. You may know them as Energy Vampires and one doesn't have to be a reporter to engage with them. Surely, you've been at a party and got stuck talking to somebody who you felt just drained you. It happens. Some people seem born to drain us of our life force by no fault of their own. But what about the modern vampire? The one that was created because technology sucked the life out of them? It's the person who can't look you in the eye, can't hold a conversation and forgot how to be human because they've relinquished their days to distraction. Traded their personality, their charisma, their identity for distraction.

These modern vampires seem completely bereft of the ability to interact with other human beings unless it's absolutely necessary. And it's reaching epic proportions. The second we get bored we go right for the phone. We, as a culture, don't seem to know how to rest or handle downtime anymore. We must constantly be occupied with some form of visual or electronic stimuli.

The bigger consequences which are forming are that we're becoming afraid of silence, afraid of being alone with our own minds, and, at the same time, it appears as if we're becoming more afraid to be in the proximity of another human without a buffer like a TV, computer or phone.

We've almost become afraid to look another person in the eye. Perhaps it's most obvious when one is forced to work with or interact with someone in public. You know the cashier who appears to be counting the seconds before your receipt comes up because the awkwardness of having to look at, or speak to you, seems utterly overwhelming. Or the clerk who you go up to in a store to ask a question and they appear to panic with fear as if that is not a normal part of the job requirement.

If your curious about the validity of this, ask yourself how you'd answer these questions:

Today, do we have…

- A better grasp of language or more primitive communication?
- More close friends or more online acquaintances?
- A deeper understanding of who we are or more confused?

- A stronger desire to interact with people or more avoidance?
- A more intimate relationship with our spouses or more distant?
- A bond with a majority of the people we work with or simply on a need-to-know basis?
- A knowledge of who our closest neighbors are or more skeptical about who they really are?
- A detailed understanding of what makes our children tick or a parent/child understanding of what the rules are?
- A relationship with our creator or a religion which we practice?

If we're not connecting on a personal (human) level, what are we doing instead? We're making excuses not to answer our phones or our doors, hiding behind a cloak of busyness that allows an alibi to avoid conversation and intimacy. It seems like even texting has become too much of a burden on our brains, so we've just gone backward to caveman days of using pictures (emojis) to communicate. That's evolution you say? It would be kind of hilarious if it wasn't so sad.

It's not only draining us of our emotional wellbeing; it's physically hurting us too. There is a condition called text neck which occurs when a person is continuously emailing, texting, or watching a screen in a hunched over position. The toll on our bodies, researchers say, can lead to things like bad posture, spinal degeneration and ultimately surgery. And I'm not hypothesizing or generalizing. Being a journalist and avid user of social media, I have seen my posture deteriorate, experienced neck and back pain, weight gain and neurological pain in my thumb (ulnar collateral ligament to be exact) from texting. Over the course of writing this book, I even developed severe pain in my right eye that kept me up at night. I spent the better part of two months going to eye specialists who told me my issue stemmed from being in front of a device so often.

The more we detach, the more we continuously consume electronic stimuli, the more it will permeate into the most important relationships in our lives. Perhaps you've already been witness to it; husbands and wives sacrificing intimacy as technology crowds the bedroom, devices babysitting our children or constantly occupying our teenagers. Young people in their early twenties are reporting higher levels of depression and feeling more stress than ever and in the workspace, as in our neighborhoods, we don't know who is around us; we just see bodies coming and going with no real attempt at connection.

Author and speaker TD Jakes said it best, "We wonder why we are so lonely. You're lonely even when you're around people. We are living in a cocoon, because our senses and everything alive about us is covered. It's phony."

Think about that, we're lonely even when we're around people. Is this news to you or all too familiar? Are you or somebody you know suffering from some degree of depression even though they have friends and loved ones surrounding them? It's crazy. You're not crazy. It's crazy that in an era where it's easier to connect and meet people than ever before in our history that people are feeling this way.

Want to know what's even crazier? When we think of the type of person who may be most susceptible to or damaged by this loneliness or depressions that our society is experiencing as a result of this disconnect, we always try to fit them into a box or stereotype. We try to place them into a category or pigeonhole them into something that explains their plight. Ah, they must be a neglected child. Maybe an outcast, a teenager who is a social misfit? Oh, she's lonely and depressed? Probably a widow or a recluse? He's a hermit and that's why he feels like he has no real friends. The type of person going through this might have financial troubles which left them with feelings of failure and ultimately isolation.

We could postulate that the uptick in reported loneliness and depression is due to a lack of validation, notoriety or hope. Yes, that would be a good answer or easy explanation, I'm sure. But it's not so, because of one telling example and that is this, when the commissioner of the National Basketball Association, Adam Silver, comes out and makes a public statement saying he believes the young men in his league (all famous millionaires) are suffering from depression because of social media, well then, that blows up any notion that this affects only a particular segment of people. We're all in jeopardy.

"We're living in a time of anxiety," Silver said in a 2018 interview with ESPN. "I think it's a direct result of social media."

That's a bold statement to make and it would still be easy to dismiss as the opinion of just one man, on the outside looking in, however former NBA All-Star Dirk Nowitzki chimed in on the issue as well saying "(In my day,) guys would sit around the locker room waiting for the coach to talk, and during that wait there would be conversations taking place. Now it's 15 guys on their phones, win or lose. There's not much time being spent together."

Add to the argument the fact that Philadelphia 76ers guard JJ Redick went public with his decision to delete his social media accounts saying it was interfering with his time with his kids among other things.

"It's not even conscious," Redick said in a 2018 interview with BleacherReport.com's Tom Haberstroh. "I hate to admit it, but anytime you're at a stoplight and your phone is within reach? You pick it up. It's become instinctual. Even if you put the phone down and walk out of the room, you're always aware of where it is. It's become an extension of you. That's f---ing scary."

That is a very bold testimony to say the least, but before we go any further, let me remind you that this book is not an assault on television, social media or technology, but rather a rallying call for humanity to place more emphasis on the balance we need to seek moving forward. Yes, we must point out the dangers which we've all seen with our own eyes but there is also good which can come from our technological advances as well.

DON'T THROW AWAY YOUR SMARTPHONE, JUST BE SMART

I'm grateful for my smartphone in that it allows my children to see and speak, in real time, with their grandparents who live 700 miles away every morning on our drive to school. Technology allows me to run my business from anywhere in the world and to connect with people all over the globe. It's allowing me to write this book in my backyard in the presence of chirping birds and the smell of the forest. Would I wish it to go away? Absolutely not. Plus, we couldn't go backward if we wanted to. We can't unknow what we already know or undo what we've already created.

That said, nearly every single person I've spoken to while writing this book has acknowledged the existence of a pull they feel from technology and they also admit feeling (or seeing) resistance, either in them or the people around them, to engage with another person in social settings.

This brings up perhaps the most frightening aspect of this, and that is some of you are OK with disengaging and don't see the dangers in it. To that I must say, alright then, it's your choice, but at the same time it's not just about you, it's about the impact your decision to disengage is having on other people like your spouse, your children, your friends and co-workers.

To get an expert opinion on this, I interviewed Dr. Kostadin Kushlev, an Associate Professor at Georgetown University who specializes in the Psychology of Health and Well-Being. He said, "If you think of something like the Apple Watch, the marketing is that it's easier and quicker, but what it's ignoring is that humans are very acute to when something averts their eye gaze. There becomes this very basic feeling of being excluded when we look away, and we're sensitive to that. Meaning, if somebody talks to me and I look at my watch, even if it's very quick, I'm sending a social signal to this other human being that I'm not engaged or what they're saying is unimportant."

When Dr. Kushlev said these words, I knew he was right on target because these things rang true for me in my own house. My children are very conscious to the allure of smartphones. They don't just want me to put it down, they ask me if I can put it in another room. They are quite cognizant of its threat to their attention and my time.

Here is a simple question I ask you; Has the presence of a phone or device in your house ever led to an argument or misunderstanding? I recall in our own house, Angelike and I having a spat concerning who was paying more attention to the children. I became angry with her saying, "All last night you were sitting there on your phone on Instagram or Facebook," to which she became defensive and replied, "I was not on social media. I was researching things going on with my health right now and it was very important stuff."

In the end, neither of us were justified. She felt what she was doing was important and I felt rejected and neglected. So, do you see, despite our best intentions, be it a quick gaze at your Apple Watch or researching health issues, how we make the people around us feel when we don't afford them our full attention?

Angelike and I were able to talk it out in a very adult and mature manner because our marriage is based on communication, but what happens when this distraction occurs between spouses or families with less than ideal communication or better yet between salesman and customer, neighbor to neighbor or strangers just making friends? One side ends up feeling extremely marginalized or rejected but rarely voices their feelings, leaving us to wonder why we didn't get the sale, get invited back to the next party, or get a second coffee date.

THE ALTERNATIVE

Sometimes the best way to explain one thing is to equally dive into its antithesis, in this case it is to turn off. Turning off is typically something we associate with electricity or energy. "Hey, turn off the lights. Turn the car off."

It's the same thing with humans. Being turned off is shutting down our life-force. It means to succumb to the addictions at our disposal, to give into our phones, our televisions, our video games and our desire to be social. For example, if your marriage is on the rocks, is the short answer to shut down, recluse to your Man Cave and drown it out with sports, alcohol or pornography? When your job sucks, is the answer to just go through the emotions and give the minimum effort while complaining in unison with a coworker who is equally unhappy? Is your body turned off? Would the escape be to look for articles or people who tell you that it's not your fault or not to worry because they are making a pill for that? And lastly, has the light in your personal house of worship been dimmed and thus your world seems to be falling apart at the seams? It's easy to blame God for all of your problems, not only in your life, but in the entire world. Why would God do this? How could He let this happen?

Remember this, to light there is dark, or the absence of light, just the same as to every hero there has to be a villain, and the same way we can't blame God for all that is wrong in the world, we can't make objects (phones, computers, TVs) the villain in this picture. No, we can't even make villains out of the people who create, sell or advertise them? But it's our human nature to want to place blame. We need to point the finger at a villain.

Is it us? You might be asking do we point the finger at ourselves? Sure, we have to take some responsibility for checking out. Nobody makes us neglect our kids or pass by our neighbors house. But perhaps there is a greater villain to seek out. What force or forces could be at work which would like nothing more than to see husbands and wives not talk, parents brush off spending time with their children or neighbors not congregate? Like many Christians, I call this force, or villain, the Enemy. Devil is a harsh word or concept for agnostics or casual believers, but the fallen angel exists and he has practically rolled out a red carpet and roped off a table with bottle service for anybody who is willing to give and relinquish their spirit. Without a doubt he wants you turned off. There is no question he prefers to see you frustrated with your life because that is when his bright red neon sign flashes brightest. It's like a complaint factory where you take your gripes and dissatisfactions and trade them in for temporary comfort. The Enemy puts your feet up on a lazy boy and massages your shoulders agreeing with you on how nobody gets you. He lulls you into a false sense of security which appears to ease your mind but ultimately leads to a trap door where the lights are always out and the future doesn't exist.

Hear me correctly, devices can be a device to lull you to sleep, to sway you to a false sense of reality. I am NOT saying your smartphone or computer is evil, that's ridiculous. I'm saying worshiping it and being a slave to it are the work of the Enemy and the Enemy is sly as a fox. He uses bright colors and melodic sounds to provide an easy and seemingly harmless escape from the world. A temporary shade from stress, which makes you feel connected but is keeping you from real connection. Subtle is his M.O. so make no mistake, your retreat from true connection will happen little by little. It will feel so natural and so harmless that you'll think of it as no big deal, lulling you to sleep and destroying your relationships. Again as Lewis said, "It's a gentle slope, a soft underfoot." I'm going to keep reminding you of that.

Here are some examples; You haven't called your parents in weeks, but your show is on tonight. Let it wait. Your kids want you to go play with them, but you're busy writing a post right now. Let it wait. Your neighbor said to stop by for coffee, but you don't really know them, and it takes too much time to get over that awkward part. Let it wait. Your client is important and deserves a phone call, but it's much easier to send a text and reschedule. Let it wait.

It's all very easy to put off, to delay until tomorrow. But one day you might wake up asking is this all life has to offer? I liken it to a great vacation: sometimes it's really hard to appreciate where you were until it's over. There's a sinking feeling at work on Monday, and we ask ourselves, "Why can't we just go back?" We say, "Awe, I'd like just one more day on the beach." Jim Rohn, a man whom I highly respect and who has an uncanny insight into human nature, once said, "We must all suffer from one of two pains: the pain of discipline or the pain of regret. The difference is discipline weighs ounces while regret weighs a ton."

Who or what will we regret passing up? What discipline will we regret not paying more attention too? I've heard that no pit is deeper than that of wishing you'd spoken to your parents more when they were alive, or that you'd spent more time with your children while they still lived at home.

So often it's hard to see ourselves as being turned off because it's become our new normal. If everybody is doing it, we're just fitting in. If something is hidden in the dark, you can't really see it or want it until it's illuminated by light. So that generation growing up in a virtual world might not miss what the generations prior cherished, human connection. I pledge I WON'T let the people closest to me miss out on it because I know it's not how God intended us to live.

BLINDED BY THE LIGHT

Where do we find the light? How do we un-train what has been ingrained in us? Better yet, why would we want to reverse something that we think has made our life easier, not harder?

Let's take a closer look at it and I'll use myself as an example. When I hit the 40 milestone, I felt like I was naturally slowing down a bit. I said, "Oh well, this is what happens when you hit 40," and I settled into the idea of wearing 36-inch jeans, settled into the idea of getting a bit more gray and putting a dent in my favorite couch every evening. I resisted changing my diet like a cat resists taking a bubble bath.

Angelike and I continually brushed off the importance of date night because we had a lot going on and it seemed easiest to push back. Like many people, we were searching for a path of least resistance and were more than happy to put some important parts of our life on cruise control.

Then one day I said, "How'd I get here?" I'm tired, lethargic, and I can feel the jiggle of my belly going over speed bumps. We haven't had a date night in months and the biggest passion projects I'd dreamed about (like this book) always seemed to be on the "Don't forget to" Post-It note.

I knew I wanted more and that I valued my life enough to look for that light switch, so I set aside my pride and asked for help. I needed clarity. I needed action steps. And a simple decision to seek out mentors and ask for help became a critical step in the right direction, a simple decision that caused a ripple effect in so many areas of my life.

I started by asking the most important question to the most important person; I asked God to put a Spiritual Father in my path. Then I asked Angelike for more accountability as both a husband and an entrepreneur. I asked some friends who were very successful if I could pick their brains, and finally, I spent some dough and invested in high quality-coaching.

The order of those requests is very important, I don't think it would've worked in any other way. And the fruits of those requests you'll soon read about and discover how to incorporate into your own success, finding your own light.

This now becomes about sharing simple steps that anybody can make with just a little commitment and consistency. So I beg you, don't throw in the towel, it's not too hard to be healthy. You are meant to find and keep true love. There is a path to wealth and certainly a path to spiritual enlightenment.

Anybody can give up, that's the easy part. But when you do that, you throw away the only life God gave you. And while it may be the path of least resistance now, at the end of your life, you may look back at your bucket list and say, "Well, I didn't do all the things I wanted to." And you might justify your lack of achievement in the BIG FOUR by saying to yourself "Well, I didn't hurt anybody either. I didn't cause any harm, didn't steal anything or do any damage to the earth or society." I say hey, that's awesome. Good for you. Go ahead and give yourself a huge pat on the back when that happens, cause heck, that's what you're supposed to do.

But don't expect to get a trophy for showing up and watching life when you should be in the game, participating, and competing to win. That's turned on. And I say this with love because we're not supposed to take this earthly body we've been blessed with and chaperone it safely to the grave. It's not only a waste to turn off to the world, sedate yourself with the pleasantries of life, and go on cruise control; it's a sure-fire recipe for heavy, heavy regret.

BACK TO THE FUTURE

> *We now face the danger, which in the past has*
> *been the most destructive to the humans:*
> *success, plenty, comfort and ever-increasing leisure.*
> *No dynamic people has ever survived these dangers.*
> *— John Steinbeck*

I'm sure at some point in your life you've been a little fed up with the prices at the gas pump or with your heating or air conditioning bill. *Geez, that's a ridiculous price to pay,* (you might say) *I need to find a better, more efficient way to* (heat, cool, power my car) *because this is draining my bank account.*

This makes sense, yes?

Well if that's so easy to see, why can't we see the price rising on our sanity and happiness that is happening in our culture? We are losing our own energy independence, trading life-giving for life-taking in a cultural reclusion of disturbing proportions. We're taking from that which is real and tangible and trading it for that which is counterfeit.

Nonsense, you may say. But is it? Let me ask you this, the last time the internet connection in your home went down, did everybody remain calm and just go about their business or did it look more like Leo and Kate racing around the deck of the Titanic looking for a lifeboat? Yea, I thought so. The panic without virtual connection, "Everybody STOP what you are doing and find the number of the cable provider and call IMMEDIATELY. Until then, life as we know it will be on hold."

Have you experienced that energy shift?

What about a social media energy exchange? Have you ever experienced a mood shift based on a post or the number of likes you were or were not getting? Or have you ever admitted, "Wow, I just spent a significant amount of time on Facebook looking at the same cliché quote, the same selfie poses or the same political rant." Then this little voice creeps up in the back of your mind and whispers "Pssst, nothing is really changing. Your life is being reduced to that of an observer of others."

It's like a volcano bubbling under the surface and then that inner dialogue says, "There's gotta be more, please tell me there's more."

This new normal is real. I know it when I walk through the food court at the mall and table after table after table is filled with teenagers sitting together in groups, all looking at their phones. When I say this is a manufactured and shallow existence, I mean it. That's why NBA millionaires can be depressed. That's why young people with their youthful looks, excellent health and the world in front of them can feel lost. A Center for Disease Control study in 2018 polled 15,000 high school students. It saw declines in sexual contact and the use of drugs like marijuana and cocaine but saw an increase in feelings of sadness and hopelessness, going from 28.5% (2007) to 31.5 (2017). (source CDC.gov)

Pew Research says 95% of teens have access to a smartphone, and 45% say they are online 'almost constantly.' The sad part is, our kids don't see it as bad. A large number of teens describe their addiction to social media as mostly positive (31%) or that it is neither positive nor negative (45%). So, dilemma number one is how do you convince an entire generation they're missing out on something if they've never experienced that which you're telling them they are missing out on?

The other situation, which I will continually reference is that we're becoming less comfortable being unoccupied. We must be engaged and have something to do almost constantly. I know this for two reasons, (1) I'm victim to it and (2) in a recent survey, 77% of people aged 18 to 24 responded "Yes" when asked, "When nothing is occupying my attention, the first thing I do is reach for my phone."

But do we really need studies and numbers to tell us something is missing? That something has gone awry? Of course not, we see it. All we have to do is step outside and look. It's like spiritual quicksand, slowly consuming us day by day, the search for what's going on in other people's lives and around the world. There is a preoccupation with what's happening over there rather than what's happen right here, in front of us. If we ask ourselves why we didn't experience this as much before, the simple answer is we neither had the technology to see into everybody else's lives nor the time to conjure up such feelings of comparison or emptiness.

Until recently, raising families and the tasks associated with survival were still numerous. The comforts of our culture have, by default, distracted us from what got us to this point in the first place—community and cooperation. We (the human race) have become so smart that we've almost written ourselves out of the picture entirely.

Do we need to go back to the old days? No, I'm not saying that. What I'm going to urge you to do, with your 21st century life, is to take the blindfold off, make a list of things that truly make you feel alive and most importantly, avoid putting the things that truly matter (family, health, business and faith) on autopilot. I'm going to ask you to make a conscious effort to create more time, more experience, and more relationship for those things which give back to us our energy, not drain it. Because if we have time to be bored, time to be voyeurs, time to examine, compare and criticize so freely, then we certainly have time to do the opposite, which is to create, nourish, fortify, explore, express, cultivate and to give life, not waste it.

It's time to ask ourselves, "Is there something I'm missing?"

SCIENCE FICTION VS REALITY

Two of the most popular forms of pop culture genre today are science fiction movies and reality TV. Just as easily as we can see our future laid out in children's tales, we can see the prophetic via our favorite adult movies.

Consider this: almost every science fiction movie of the 80s or 90s which was considered to be just that, science fiction, has pretty much landed on our doorstep. Allow me to give you some examples. Movies like *Looker* (1981 - Albert Finney) about the surgical quest for a perfect body and flawless facial features. *Runaway* (1984 - Tom Selleck) about tiny (spider-sized) robots monitoring our homes and lives via cameras and listening devices. *Natural Born Killers* (1994 - Woody Harrelson, Robert Downey Jr.) about serial killers who reached quasi-celebrity status thanks to an out of control 24-hour news media. *Outbreak* (1995 - Dustin Hoffman) about a dangerous airborne virus that threatens the entire world. *Gattaca* (1997 - Ethan Hawke, Jude Law) about science interceding in the creation of life and predisposing natural selection. *Minority Report* (2002 - Tom Cruise) which featured retina scanning and facial recognition as a main theme. At the time, these movies were all farfetched, that'll never happen, futuristic sci-fi thrillers.

Knock knock, we're there.

If the goal of being turned on is to maintain perspective, relationship and connection, how can we do that if our future world is more science fiction than real? What kind of life will our children inherit? Or better yet, in the quest to get ahead, what are we leaving behind?

We are bringing new science into our homes before we know the repercussions. *Let's wait and see* or *just trust the process* doesn't bring families back together or help cure the current crisis of depression.

People will argue that to become highly productive on a competitive level in today's world you have to be plugged in. Yes, to some extent, but not to the point where it interferes with your happiness.

In the coming years, I truly believe the answer we be less technology, not more, more outside than inside, more face to face than virtual. I believe in that so much I'm leveraging my career on it, betting that as more of what is real about life is taken away, the higher the premium on having human experiences will be. I liken it to HBO's hit drama Westworld where wealthy people in the future paid big dollars to regress to the raw and real old west. The only difference is, in Westworld the raw and real was the furthest thing from real. It was artificial intelligence made to mimic real life. Not the answer we will be looking for.

Angelike and I are committed to balance in our family and teaching it in our business. Yes, in order to reach the masses, we use smartphones, computers and video conferencing because they are the tools of the trade. But we have also made a concerted effort to do more live, in person teaching and coaching within our community.

This is where our home business merges with big business.

Big corporations and brands are softening up the public for a world that is anything but real. I'm betting on the fact that some people, I think a lot of people, will need a way to keep it real. If you watched the 2019 Super Bowl, you will probably recall a Michelob Ultra beer ad in which robots were running, golfing, boxing and biking alongside humans. The feel of the spot seemed to be satiric but everybody in the room I was in just sat there in silence for a second afterward, with frightened looks on their face. And then we all kinda looked at one another at the same time and said, "What the heck was that? Creepy!"

Tech companies and merchandisers are working in unison, producing whimsical or funny commercials, but what's whimsical or funny about losing our humanity? Are the *Terminator* movies funny?

I know that in setting up the thesis for this book I've really been hammering home this point of a technological war of intrusion and diversion. I get it. Should we be worried? Yes. Panic button worried, not yet. I would say at this point more highly concerned and aware of what is at stake and what lies on the horizon. There is a very eerie and pretty specific warning about such things in Romans chapter 1, verse 22 which reads, *Although they claimed to be wise, they became fools and exchanged the glory of the immortal God for images made to look like a mortal human being… They exchanged the truth about God for a lie and worshiped and served created things rather than the Creator.*

Regardless if you're a believer or not, how can you read a 2000-year-old passage like that and not draw a parallel? You don't have to hit me on the head with a frying pan (or drone) to get my attention. While the threat of robots taking over is still a little bit laughable, the infiltration of robotics and high-tech artificial intelligence into our homes is real. Because it always comes so beautifully wrapped and disguised as advancement and convenience, we don't see it as a threat. But when your family is at dinner and nobody is talking, or you can't stand in line for five minutes without having to look to your cell phone to entertain you, there is a problem.

HANGING IN THE BALANCE

Answer this simple question. How long could you survive without leaving your house? Sounds odd at first but really think about it. How long could you physically and somewhat comfortably survive without leaving your house? A couple days? A week? Months? Maybe even a year?

Should we congratulate ourselves that we've made it to the point where could survive in our house for months, if not years, without leaving? Don't get me wrong, we all love the convenience of Amazon Prime and I think we'd agree that progress is a wonderful thing when managed correctly.

But the essential question I'm going to ask you repeatedly throughout this book is, do we as humans possess the ability to manage ourselves when it comes to progress? Can we police ourselves to find balance in our homes, businesses, places of learning and worship?

Again, I refer to my conversation with Dr. Kushlev. In his opinion, based on his research, he's not so sure we do possess the ability on our own.

When speaking of our love affair with smartphones, I really don't think completely relying on oneself to resist will work. Humans are not good at fighting temptations. They (phones) are designed to be rewarding and capture our attention. They affect the circuits of the brain the same way that drugs do. As long as you have the phone on the table in your field of awareness, it will be difficult. Most of us don't even realize when we pick them up.

I'm guessing his answer struck a chord. Are you able to disconnect from your phone without stress or do you feel like you can't leave home without it?

We're an amazing species. Since the beginning of time we've used our imaginations and capacity to think critically to solve problem after problem. Look at just how far we've come in the last fifty years in our efforts to make life more comfortable. But at the same time, sometimes success in one area has resulted in negative consequences in another. In fact, we may be able to point to one thing, above all others, that has done just that and changed the course of our future.

So, let's, for a second, go Back to The Future, meaning let me use that pop culture classic to make the point. When Marty McFly (Michael J Fox) uses a time-traveling DeLorean to go from 1985 back to 1955 he has a front row view of human's fascination with our ability to improve life. Marty's skateboard, Calvin Klein underwear, Sony Walkman cassette, and Chuck Berry guitar wow his 1955 mother, father and community.

Now I want you to think about all the things you could take back in time now to impress your say 1979 parents: smartphones, MP3 players, and Alexa to name a few. You could make a Facetime call, stream music or order Alexa to bring up a YouTube video showing a commercial for a Sony Walkman, which was introduced to the world on July 1, 1979 ($150).

But what do you notice? Those are all contingent upon one thing... the internet. While the genesis of what we know today as the internet began in the late 1960's and early 1970's as a government project, the world wide web took off in the 90's and today 81 percent of the developed world has internet access. In fact the US News And World Report stated that in 2014, more people globally had access to cell phones than working toilets. So it's easier to take a phone call than take a... well, you get where I'm coming from.

American Author John Steinbeck who, in addition to his love of the country, appeared to have an almost clairvoyant nature to his writing, understood the impulses of man better than most. He seemed to have a grasp on the dangers of man's unquenchable thirst to advance yet wrote with amazing optimism about man being able to navigate and overcome when he reached too far.

He wrote, "Americas best impulses will serve us in the future as they have in the past, to clarify and to strengthen our process. We have failed sometimes, taken wrong paths, paused for renewal, filled our bellies and licked our wounds, but we have never slipped back—never."

America's best impulses. Hmm, what does that mean, you might ask? When Philo Taylor Farnsworth successfully demonstrated the first television signal transmission on September 7, 1927 do you think he intended it to broadcast good or bad? Perhaps he envisioned a nation watching the inauguration of a President, the latest weather updates or even a baseball game taking place on the opposite coast. But do you think he said in 90 years from now I can foresee shows about murder, adultery, and 24 hours of politically-biased bantering? Do you think he hoped that children might learn things about nature from TV or completely shut themselves off to the outdoors by consuming it?

The same thing can be said about the internet, we can use it to connect families and learn, we can use it to share stories and conduct business or we can use it to recluse from society, a medium to exchange sexually explicit materials, as a means to spy and gather information or as a vehicle for political slander. Can we, as humans, tame this beast we've unleashed and move forward with a healthy relationship with technology?

You've heard it before; lead, follow, or get out of the way. And when it comes to leadership there are bold leaders, false leaders, thought leaders, and cheerleaders. Which will you be?

How will you lead your family? Will you boldly set an example of what it means to be present or will you be the family with all four members in different parts of the house on different devices? How will you lead your business? Will you encourage a culture of face-to-face fellowship or run strictly on text messages and inter-office memos? And your body? Will you leave it to your grocery store, doctor or government to tell you what made up food or pill to put into it and trust what they give you or will you be proactive and take responsibility for your health and what goes into your body?

There is a revival coming. Know that. The pendulum will correct itself and not because of our need to be nostalgic or the desire to be a minimalist, it will correct because we're hard wired for human connection and we crave all that which makes us alive.

COMING OUT OF THE DARK

If you've ever walked into your bathroom in the middle of the night, you instinctively know where to find the light switch. The same thing goes for turning on life's hallways.

We instinctively have a good sense of where the light is, we just have to reach for it. To turn on means to ignite a leadership revival in your home and every place that needs light, our kitchens, dinner tables, living rooms, backyards, bedrooms and boardrooms. It may mean getting the family up a little bit early so that everybody's day gets off to a better start. It may mean everybody agreeing to show up to the dinner table without devices. It may mean taking the television out of your bedroom and leaving the phones behind when we go outside to play.

The movement for a turned-on family, neighborhood, city, or society begins with one person at a time. It means to become a champion of human connection who is willing to go against the grain a little in order to show others that life is full of opportunity when your eyes are open and your head up. It can start today. Right now. With you. You're capable of leading the charge, divinely appointed to lead by example

CHAPTER FOUR

TURN ON YOUR MARRIAGE

If the sun refused to shine
I would still be loving you
When mountains crumble to the sea
There will still be you and me

— Robert Plant

As somebody who wrote about football for a living most of my adult life, I'd say I fumbled enough in relationships to know that it takes two being turned on to put together a successful drive. I use a football analogy here because I was covering the NFL when I met my wife, and there's an old saying, "Everybody loves the long ball," but marriage isn't 80-yard touchdowns; it's short passes and one-yard runs. It's coming back from negative plays or interceptions, huddling up when down and distance aren't in your favor to push the pile and get that first down.

Sure, we enter the game for the excitement and the glory of the big play, but the great teams, the legacy teams, know it's sweaty and frustrating at times, but, like marriage, it's always a team game.

The statistics are out there—many marriages end in divorce. No big revelation there. Would it be safe to say that everybody goes into a marriage with the highest hopes? Nobody really goes into it saying, "Hey, this should be awesome for a couple of years, then let's let it fizzle out and go our separate ways." Of course not, we all think we're going to be the exception to the rule and make it last forever, till death do us part. I think that's absolutely the correct mindset to go in with, but we have to ask ourselves why or how we will be different.

I think Author and speaker Dave Willis put it best when he said, "Couples who make it aren't the ones who never had a reason to get divorced; they are simply the ones who decided early on that their commitment to each other was always going to be bigger than their differences and flaws." In my own presentations on marriage, I like to tell people, "It's not *if* you will argue; it's *how* you will argue." In both of the proceeding thoughts, it comes down to mindset, or the will to win at marriage even during the most difficult times. If you have a cut-n-run attitude, like the ones we are witnessed to in Hollywood, then, of course, it's going to end poorly.

MARRIAGE, A BAD RAP?

If we look at marriage in the 21st century from a culture perspective, we have to be honest; it appears to be on the ropes. But if we look at it from a Kingdom perspective, it's ready for a revival. A revival is an improvement in the condition or strength of something or an instance of something becoming popular, active, or important again.

What does that mean? Well, maybe it's easier to look at my affinity for marriage and compare it to something else close to my heart, hip hop. I was inspired to make the correlation when I saw a t-shirt that said, "MAKE HIP-HOP DOPE AGAIN," and thought, "Wow, ain't that the truth?"

While it may seem like a stretch comparison, here is where they're similar. When Hip Hop began, it was pure. Birthed very raw and uninhibited (without self-conscious), it was a natural form of self-expression that flowed and existed in rhythm and harmony with its surroundings or environment. On the streets, there was a need for companionship, to feel understood and yes, loved. It was intended as a force for good that allowed abandoned (lonely) voices to be heard. It was conceived to communicate hope to places where there was none.

I know. I know. You're thinking, "David, are you trying to make an analogy between Hip Hop and Adam and Eve?"

Indeed. But let me be clear, old school Hip Hop isn't Dr. Dre and Biggie. I'm talking the origins of rap (rhythm and poetry) like Grandmaster Flash and the Furious Five, who in their song "The Message," said:

A child is born with no state of mind
Blind to the ways of mankind
God is smilin' on you but he's frownin' too
Because only God knows what you'll go through

Somewhere along the way hip hop, as it was created, lost its soul. It was tempted, deceived and corrupted by those who lost sight of its roots and just wanted to exploit its goodness. It became tainted with the evils of sins like lust, gluttony and pride. Those who created it were marginalized, called old fashioned or out of touch. They were accused of not evolving with modern times. Their voices were drowned out by those who took over ownership of a new kind of hip hop, artists who thought their (newer) concept of how it should be made more sense.

Can you see it now? Can you see marriage in the same light? It was given as a gift from God. He created woman as he saw man was lonely and felt he needed hope, touch, and community. But somewhere along the way, marriage lost its soul too and was hijacked as well. People who believed in it were marginalized, called old fashioned, and told it just didn't make sense in our modern culture.

But as it often goes, evolution brings with it a revolution and ultimately a restitution. Restitution is defined as "the restoration of something lost or stolen to its proper owner." I see taking hip hop and marriage full circle, showing an entire new generation how it all began. In my heart of hearts, I believe Hip Hop will find its proper owner, its roots will be restored, and people looking for hope will grow tired of another rap about who has more money, women, or weed. And in my heart of hearts, I believe marriage is on a similar path. It will be shown to a new generation, tired of the reality shows, hook-up apps, and empty feelings of loneliness. The dissers of the Old School will eventually see that there is a good reason as to why it was created in the first place. It'll be cool again to a new generation, and the masses will come to realize that longevity only exists when something is pure and given from above.

ROMANCE, SHEER DELIGHT, HOW SWEET

In the lyrics from LL Cool J's 1987 hit "I Need Love," Cool James raps about wanting to find a girl to make his life complete. And while I'm guessing it did take more than a Fendi bag and a bad attitude to land him, LL literally met an around the way girl named Simone. The two had a chance encounter in 1987 when LL stopped by to say hello to a friend in the neighborhood. They were teenagers and would date for eight years before saying "I do" in 1995. They've have been going strong in marriage ever since.

Not only is this story a great bridge to this paragraph, but it represents what culture and dating was like in the pre-internet/cell phone era—a clandestine meeting of two people. Like everything else technology has touched over the years, relationships and marriage are no different. It's presented single people looking for "the one" with a path of least resistance in the form of websites and apps such as eHarmony, Bumble and Tinder.

Match.com was first on the scene in 1995, and since then, the format has seen steady growth prompting more than 1,500 dating apps and becoming a $2.5 billion dollar industry. And while it's somewhat early to know the long term impact technology will have on marriage, there is no question these types of apps have made it a lot easier to search, find and hook up at the touch of a button. Unfortunately, it seems the hooking up is really what the industry is becoming known for.

For instance, if you go to Bumble.com you can read a list of interesting terms like *Monkeying, Benching* and, my favorite, *the Bad Pancake.* In their own words, *monkeying* is described as "the same way that monkeys swing from branch to branch without touching the ground, someone who goes from relationship to relationship with no downtime in between." *Benching* is "putting somebody on the back burner, just in case you want to pick up and start dating them seriously again. It's said to be the human equivalent of the Maybe Pile when you're cleaning out your closet." And a *Bad Pancake* is a term used to describe "the first person you date after a breakup. The bad pancake is someone you don't see a future with who you use to test the waters of dating again."

Maybe these things existed before the world of tap-to-date apps, but the fact that these definitions are so casually dispatched and dictionaried should sound some alarms.

We, as a culture, seem to be marginalizing relationship, making derogatory satire of what is supposed to be the connection of two people. I mean, you can't bench your wife because she makes sub-par pancakes just like you can't monkey around on your husband because his waist no longer matches the size of his biceps.

So then I ask this; would you say it's fairly normal, when you meet a couple who are either dating or married, to pose the question, "So, how did you meet?" Sure it is. It's been my experience when I've asked this question to couples who met by way of site or app, I often get a "We met online, but..." Almost every time it's followed by the word *but*.

Why is that? Is it because we still have reservations about this modern way of dating and feel the need to defend a relationship of this nature? Not according to Pew Research which states the stigma associated with internet/app dating is getting better. There was a six percent shift (29% to 23%) among those polled saying people who use online dating sites are desperate. But that same report insists a vast majority of relationships still begin offline, despite the fact that one in ten Americans are now using online dating platforms. Even among Americans who have been with their spouse or partner for five years or less, fully 88% say that they met their partner offline—without the help of a dating site.

In all fairness, I know very happily married couples who met online or via social media. But here is the greater question; is there is a certain amount of romance lost when the meeting is not-so-clandestine? In other words, if asked, would those who met online say they'd have preferred to have met in a more serendipitous story?

Then, as with all other points-of-entry for technology into our human existence, we must ask what does it look like in the future? Will dating and marriage evolve into an online ordering process? Will fate be removed as we allow computer-knows-best to determine our best chances for success? If this becomes the preferred or customary way of finding a mate, do you think we have a greater or worse chance of decreasing the divorce rate? If nothing else, it's an extremely interesting topic, to say the least.

I found evidence of one study published in the *Proceedings of the National Academy of Sciences*. It stated people who met their spouse online said their marriage was more satisfying than those who met their spouse offline and that marriages that began from online relationships were less likely to end in divorce or separation. I was surprised at first but continued to read and learned that the study was funded by eHarmony.com. That's like asking New Englanders who the greatest quarterback of all time is. So again, in this age of information and misinformation, it's very easy to find or cite something that backs our view of how it should be.

Technology always creeps in. But it has no emotion, so it has no conscience when it comes to overreach or intrusion either. It wasn't intended for the internet to take pornography into our homes and destroy marriages, yet here it is.

I'll end this thought process here. In 1997 when the IBM supercomputer Deep Blue beat world chess champion Garry Kasparov, it was seen as a sign that artificial intelligence was now on par with human intelligence. Love, though, is not a computation. It may feel like a chess game, but it is not. Anybody who knows my wife and I knows we are polar opposites. No computer would have ever matched us up. Would I have favored or liked her on a profile? No doubt. But our love story is one I cherish, and it is one of a clandestine nature which you will read.

GETTING TO THE HEART OF THE MATTER

If you've ever seen the movie *My Big Fat Greek Wedding*, you remember how the father of the bride insisted the Greeks invented everything. Being married to a Greek woman, this is one of many parts of the movie I can attest to as being true to life. They are a storied and proud people, even if their famed King Leonidas in the movie 300 was played by the actor Gerard Butler, who just happens to be Scottish like me.

But I'll leave that alone for now and bow to the Greeks for their profound dissection of love. In fact, they have six different words or types of love; Eros, Philia, Ludus, Agape, Pragma and Philautia. For the sake of this segment, let's dismiss Philia (a deep friendship or camaraderie), Agape (a love for all people or family) and Philautia (a love for oneself) and concentrate on Eros, Ludus and Pragma.

Many people get together and sometimes engaged when they are somewhere between the first stage of love, EROS, or a physical kind of attraction, and the second, LUDUS, which is like a playful affection. Combined, the two amount to something like *I saw you dancing, I think you're pretty, you think I'm handsome, we both like the sushi and Sandra Bullock movies and your corny jokes make me laugh.*

Got it?

That's dating, not love, and traditionally it's how couples have come together, and it's very normal. They are turned on in the very literal sense of the word, hormonally. Is this a good time to get married? Probably not. Ask actor Nicholas Cage. He's been married four times and is 0 for 4 with one marriage lasting four months, and one just four days. This is nothing new or unusual by Hollywood's standards but certainly not what God intended marriage to look like.

To go from being turned on by hormones to being turned on and fully grown, we must look to what the Greeks call PRAGMA, which was the term for mature love. It is identified as a deep understanding between longtime couples, one in which making compromises for the good of the relationship and showing patience and tolerance over time is of highest importance. Compromise, hmm, not sure I remember that word being used in our vows. Pretty important though. Whereas the first two types of love are more associated with falling in love, PRAGMA is more in tune with staying in love and the effort that it takes, i.e., "Good morning Sweetheart could you make me a strong cup of coffee, I was up with the baby from 2 to 5 a.m. because he had a fever." Or, "We have to spend 32 days in a hotel to care for my mother who is dying of cancer."

Most people who have a successful marriage will say it takes work. You've heard this before. Well, let's compare it to starting a new job where the first couple of days or weeks are very exciting, everything is new, and the possibilities are endless. Sounds a lot like an Eros or Ludus stage. But then you realize that in order to be successful at this job and to get the highest return on your investment, there's going to be a long road of work ahead. Not every day is a payday, promotion or perk. Sure, you enjoy it but make no mistake—it's work. There's an old saying, "Stop saying marriage is just a piece of paper, so is money but you still have to get up every day and work for it."

Perhaps that is where so many are failing in and out love these days? Because, like our technology, we expect it to be easy. "Alexa, play Uptown Funk and order me take out." Whereas the microwave generation was forced to wait 60 seconds, now it seems like we're impatient if anything takes longer than six seconds. Has this restlessness infected our love lives as well? It must be quick and easy to obtain, and if it gets broken or even scratched a little just toss it and find another one.

THE SELF-DEVELOPED MARRIAGE

In the self-development world, people talk about "Burning the Ships," meaning once you land at a destination, you're there, and there's no looking back. You've burned the ship you came ashore on, and you either win the battle or die trying. This is mostly used by entrepreneurs and startups, but let's apply the same concept to marriage. How much harder would you work if you knew this was your only shot and there was no other person who would ever love you? Do you think the divorce rate would go down? Sure, it would. Options, regardless of how they turn out, are generally looked upon as favorable. But options also tempt us to look for things more quickly when we encounter the tiniest bit of resistance. Not so good. Being turned on in this case means turning off to outside temptations, aka the grass is always greener on the other side scenario.

Angelike really opened my eyes to this when she said that many people leave a relationship or marriage because their spouse wasn't giving or providing them with 20 percent of what they thought they wanted. Eighty percent was good, though. So they end up finding somebody that provides only that 20 percent they thought would make them complete only to discover the 80 percent was better.

DO BETTER

Our very first Turned On Live event featured Chengi Toubin, a love and relationship expert with her own YouTube channel and coaching business.

I was initially inspired to reach out to Toubin after seeing a particular video she did that caught my eye. It was titled "Do Better," and in it, she speaks of how mobile devices and social media have impacted our dating lives. She points out that because we essentially have the world in the palm of our hand, there is always the potential to find and do better. When our parents and grandparents were looking for love, she explains, they were often relegated by geography. Who was on your block, in your neighborhood or went to your high school? That's who you dated. Those geographic constraints of love are no longer there. Your perfect person or soul mate may be out there—in China, Australia or half a world away. With all of those options, how can we possibly settle? There must be somebody just perfect, absolutely made for us.

She then confirmed Angelike's point about what's missing isn't always worth leaving in search of. In other words, while we're trying to do better, maybe the person who we left because they didn't check off every single one of our boxes was actually more compatible. Maybe that 20 percent they fell short on is something that was just meant to be worked on over time.

This not only made sense in dating but resonated with other aspects of life. Angelike and I work from home, so the constraints of geography as to where we can live are endless. There's always a city we think might help us do better which ultimately leads to an endless array of what ifs and maybes that continually pop into our heads. Maybe Texas is better than Tennessee because they have bigger houses? Maui has better weather. The traffic, taxes and food are better there than here. Do you get where I'm coming from? Maybe we should be happy with the home we have that checks off 80 percent of our boxes and be willing to travel or work on the things that aren't perfect.

Sometimes our desire to do better doesn't get us better; it only confuses us and leads to more stress and second-guessing.

GETTING YOUR HOUSE IN ORDER

United States census data shows that from 2000 to 2015, the rate of home ownership declined in 90 percent of all American metropolitan cities which represents a major shift in thinking. Over that same period of time, the census bureau shows the average age of couples getting married has increased by almost three years for both men (27.1-29.8) and women (25.3-27.8).

This probably doesn't come as a surprise on either issue, particularly on marriage. If people are waiting a little bit longer to tie the knot, that isn't such a bad thing. It's actually better, in my opinion because it's my mission to put a dent in the divorce statistics, and I believe it begins internally with the individual.

In order to communicate effectively and really know another person well enough to live with them in marriage, one must first know oneself. This is called intrapersonal communication or our inner language of thought. I feel very confident speaking to this because I waited and waited and waited before I finally tied the knot, and during that wait I did a ton of talking to myself. Unfortunately it wasn't always good talk as I got really good at blaming everybody else for my singleness but me. Does this sound familiar? *There's nobody that gets me. They aren't good enough. They don't meet my standard of this or that.*

It wasn't until I slowed down and began communicating with myself, turning myself on (no pun intended) that I would truly find myself ready for a relationship. In other words, I had to get my internal house in order before I was ready to share a literal house with another person.

Now, for a second, let's use the home as a metaphor for the head. Just like you mow your yard, put the dishes away, and make your bed before you have company over, you must do the maintenance inside your head prior to inviting somebody into it. I had to ask myself, "David, what is it that you really desire?" and "What is it that you really have to offer?" These questions seem elementary at first, but they are not. To be available or open to a loving relationship, one must first stop kidding oneself about what is actually important and then stop hiding behind the facades we see on social media. The turned-on person wants real connection, something social media profiles don't really offer.

The turned-on suitor places an emphasis on real, time-tested personality traits like trust, honesty, compassion and tenderness. They don't run to blame, and don't look for a scapegoat when trouble arises. Real communication, real stability, and real faith are equally important. Everything starts internally with a quest to see oneself with new eyes, and once that happens, the world of possibilities opens up as others begin to see you with new eyes.

I'm not going to lie. It took a huge slap in the face to wake me up. I had to make some tough decisions. I stopped going out on weekends. I stopped talking to every pretty girl I saw. I stopped looking for somebody to take care of me and asked what I needed to do to take care of myself. I had to ask what I would think of myself from an outsider's point of view beyond my physical appearance and was I really ready to be loyal in ways there was no turning back from.

But I didn't stop there. I got comfortable being alone with myself and shed the feeling that to be happy, I needed to be with somebody. That was huge. And I know we all loved when Jerry Maguire said, "You complete me," but that's cutting oneself short. We don't need anybody to complete us—that's between our creator and us. We need to complete ourselves. Once that occurs, then we can look for somebody who complements us. This is an important shift in thinking for many people. Remember, if we go back to Eden, Adam was a complete being. He was an incorruptible genetic creation of God.

To complete somebody means there are holes somewhere to be filled. Another person shouldn't fill your holes. Adam wasn't missing a piece. He was simply lonely. When Eve was created, God didn't ask Adam for input and say, "What do you think you lack?" How shall I make your partner? No, he put Adam to sleep, and when Adam awoke, he saw Eve and knew her. He said, "Bone of my bone and flesh of my flesh." It was a complement to him, each whole and complete but better together.

I have weaknesses. Angelike has weaknesses. But we're not incomplete. When we meet our partner and follow in our favor, there is more fruit to be made. More abundance to have. But make no mistake, if you're looking for another person to complete you, you are not working in the favor of God; you're doubting that he made you perfect with everything you needed to have.

SURRENDER AND GIVE YOURSELF AWAY

Have you ever met a couple who described their meeting as serendipitous or completely natural? That was how it happened for me but not because it was my time, but because it was God's time. I'd try to push the button; I attempted to force it on my own for the better part of two decades, only to fail. During that time, there was plenty of exhaustion and banging my head against the wall. I wasn't being true to myself and subsequently ending up hurting others. Only when that got really old, and I was at my breaking point, did I throw my hands up and surrender myself to God. That is when it became natural.

Because when the time is right, you don't resist His will. When friends call to hang out at the club or to set you up with the next Mr. or Ms. Right, you don't have a problem saying *No thank you, I've been down that road*. In my case, I was content to cook, spend time on myself, and kick back with the occasional glass of wine. All on the solo.

I did a lot of reading and a lot of praying, and when it got too quiet and felt uncomfortable, I didn't panic and run back to my old ways. I allowed myself to sit in that silence, be still and observe how I felt. I leaned into God. I turned on to a feeling of self-fulfillment and self-reliance that I never thought I could obtain when I was actively looking for the woman to complete me.

Again, this is probably the most difficult part for some because being alone with ourselves and our thoughts is not easy but is enormously gratifying when you accept it. Granted, this was before Facebook and Instagram had exploded. MySpace was around, and I had the ability to see what was going on outside of my bubble, but singles today have to overcome that hurdle of seeing life through the crystal ball of social media, which makes it very hard.

SPECIAL DELIVERY

If you remember the 80s comedy classic *Weird Science*, you recall Gary and Wyatt, two teenage boys trying to make the perfect girl during an experiment. And boy did they, in the form of Lisa, their voluptuous Frankenstein played by Kelly LeBrock.

As you may recall, the boys had their shenanigans with Lisa, but all along continue to pursue two girls their own age from their high school. There's a scene toward the end of the movie in which Anthony Michael Hall's character Gary is asked by Deb, his teenage love interest, why he would ever want her over Lisa, the perfect girl they boys created in their experiment. Gary then says, "Lisa is all I ever wanted in a girl before I knew what I really wanted."

Granted, *Weird Science* is an 80s teen classic, that's more tongue-in-cheek tomfoolery than anything, but writer-director John Hughes always had a very special ability to tap into the very real, very mature, narrative of love. And in the case of Gary and Wyatt, sometimes what you think you desire in the perfect mate isn't what you wanted at all. They were essentially counterfeiting a woman. And while we can brush it off as just comedy, remember, life has a way of imitating art. If we go back to the Bumble.com glossary of terms, you'll find **Catfishing.** You may already be familiar with it. It means to present a false version of yourself online, either with fake or doctored photos or false profile information, in order to lure someone into dating you.

We're counterfeiting ourselves like Gary and Wyatt were counterfeiting a woman. People are falsifying who they are in order to appeal, attract or entice a person to like them. And we are wondering why relationships and marriages are failing. In *A Midsummer Night's Dream,* William Shakespeare wrote, "Love looks not with the eyes, but with the mind, and therefore is winged Cupid painted blind."

As a writer, I'd never be fit to even sharpen Shakespeare's pencil, however, I did write my own love story in the most literal sense you can imagine.

TAKE ME TO THE GREEK

Most people are familiar with 1 Corinthians 13:4 and the first six words of the scripture, "Love is patient. Love is kind." As I've alluded to, in my 37 years prior to one special encounter, love had not been kind to me, and I had begun to grow very impatient.

I scribbled my thoughts down each evening in a journal. Some entries I look back on now and laugh, and some I look back and say, "Ah-ha," and still there are others I look back on and ask myself, "What the heck were you thinking?" But it was cathartic. Even if you're not one who is into writing, journaling just has a way of helping you get stuff out, a way of coping that is very healing.

There is one very specific journal entry I always look back on with great fondness. As usual, I was feverishly chasing down my thoughts on paper, writing down all that I had experienced with my love life, a kind of "for the record" type entry that was equal parts to myself and equal parts a final plea to God. I quickly became vulnerable and, at the same time, frustrated while my pen tried to keep up with my thoughts. As I pressed heavier and heavier onto the pages, in a fury, I wrote these words: "GOD, PLEASE SEND ME AN ANGEL," and then signed my name in cursive with a big happy face next to it as if to say, "There ya go Big Guy. It's official. You know my request."

I put the journal away and continued on in my new surrender. A couple of months later, things came to a head, and one day I'd just had enough.

I'd just gotten back from Los Angeles, having been through five rounds of casting with the reality show Big Brother. I thought it was the big break I needed in my career (if you could call it that) and possibly my love life. However, as I thought we were set to begin filming, the producers knocked on my hotel room door and said they were recasting the show, sending us all home.

Devastated. That's how I felt. Humiliated for wasting my time and for the fact I allowed myself to think a reality show was the answer to my problems. How naïve I was.

I vividly remember going up to the bartender at LAX and saying, "Three red wines, please" and him looking curious as to whom the others were for, considering I was alone.

It's even embarrassing now to admit how depressed I was and how I sulked in hopelessness because I had no woman, no career, and no hope. Sad to say, at that point, my faith in God's will was severely being challenged.

That Monday, my best friend and publisher of the magazine I worked for, called me and I picked up the phone in a bad mood.

"What?" I asked.

"You need to go interview this girl for a story we're running," he said.

"About what?" I replied.

"She won a fitness competition."

"Isn't there somebody else that can do it?" I asked (as the new me I was surrendering to did not want to be tempted by another pretty face).

"No, you meet her tomorrow at noon."

OK, I subsided to do my job but convinced myself not to entertain her with fluffy questions, not engage her with cute conversation. "As a matter of fact, I'm not even going to make eye contact with her," I said to myself. I was turned off to the entire idea of having to interview a fitness competitor because in my head, I knew what I'd get. She worked at a tanning salon and was dating a guy twice her age who promised her a career in acting or something. She was going to talk about herself and her body the entire interview, and I would leave even more depressed than I was. But it's funny how sometimes when we don't feel like turning on, God has mercy on us and flips the switch for us. That's what a full surrender looks like.

So, there I was, looking down at my notepad asking boring questions one after another, asking myself how long this would take. She answered each one, and the door began to open. She spoke of her "real" career in medical sales, her love for her parents, and her love for Jesus.

It was as if God had tapped on my shoulder with a big smile asking me if I still wanted to stay in OFF MODE. As I became begrudgingly smitten during that interview, I wrapped it up as all good reporters do, by verifying the correct spelling of the subject's name. I said, "A-N-G-E-L-I-Q-U-E yes?"

"No," she said. "I'm Greek, and in the Greek alphabet, there is no letter Q. You spell my name Angelike (*Angel*-LIKE)." To this day, when people call our house and ask for Angel-Like, I have to look up to the heavens and wink at God. He couldn't have been any clearer in answering my prayers.

RESET BUTTON

In my case, the message was clear. I asked for an angel, and God sent me Angelike. But remember, I'd struggled my entire life until then. I had to shut it all down in order to open it back up. Everybody knows where that tiny button is on the back of their computer when the colorful pinwheel of death is spinning and spinning and you can't get anything done. As a last resort, you have to shut it down, because sometimes the only way to move forward, to make progress, is to completely turn it off and then turn it back on.

But there is always that question, "If I do that, will I lose everything I've worked so hard for to this point? " That is where faith comes in. Hit that button and hold it down. Turn off what isn't working and keeping you stagnant and waiting for the spinning wheel to end. That which you keep waiting to fix itself will not. In John C. Maxwell's words, "No man is an island. If we are to accomplish a divine mission, we must call upon a divine power." Finding a partner and a lasting marriage is a mission. That's why romance movies are an entire genre; it's our human nature to find love. The question is, are you getting the downloads from God when it comes to love? Are you really trying to make that connection with him before you make that connection with your partner?

NEXT GENERATION COMPATIBILITY

Webopedia.com defines compatibility as *the ability of one device or program to work with another device or program*. The term *compatible* implies different degrees of partnership. For example, a printer and a computer are said to be compatible if they can be connected to each other.

You don't have to be Steve Jobs to see the parallel between what technology considers compatible and that which humans do. Look at the key phrases in that definition: *work with, partnership* and *connected*. Now, put all three together and you see marriage is about working with a partner to stay connected.

Angelike and I could have easily gone down the slippery slope we'd each traveled prior to meeting one another if she and I didn't speak out on who we were and, more importantly, who God was calling us to be. During the first years of our marriage, we each made a lucid decision to personally grow ourselves and stretch ourselves because when one grows and the other one doesn't, it drives a deep wedge of jealousy and resentment in the marriage (or in any relationship). Trust me, it wasn't all roses and romance in that first year. The lights flickered. Remember the journal I mentioned earlier. On Tuesday, August 9th, 2011, just six months after we wed, there is an entry that reads, *What the heck am I doing? Are we doing? This is our first year of marriage and we're fighting like cats and dogs. I'm sorry that I feel this way because I want to be a good husband in a successful marriage, but I'm not sure what I'm doing wrong. God needs to be in the center of our relationship.*

Remember, I said it's not if you will fight, but how and with what weapons? Fights include weapons, yes? In a relationship or marriage, the weapons typically come in the form of words, meaning accusations and threats. But the Word found in the Bible is a weapon for good that combats those accusations and threats with reminders and promises. We went to the Word early and often in our first couple of years. We purposely turned on (more credit to Angelike here) and incorporated God's instruction as part of our communication.

Even when we're talking about people and friendships, they tend to grow apart because one person is pursuing how to communicate and update their compatibility while the other may be choosing to turn on the cruise control and stay in the same comfort zone. You don't leave those people behind, but you're moving forward, and they're standing still. That really happens in marriages. When I think of the couple that's reading this, it's people that are willing and open to grow and get vivid clarity on their personal role.

If we go back to the Eros stage of love, it's easy because we're working with our eyes, hands and lips to partner and stay connected. But if we are to get to Pragma, or mature longstanding love, it's a completely different set of tools, primarily the brain, the gut and the heart. Comedian Will Ferrell joked, "Before you marry a person, you should make them use a computer with slow internet service to see who they really are." Now that's funny because we don't often show our true self until we are put under some degree of stress. How do you handle sickness in the family, financial downturns or even how you react when your husband doesn't restock the toilet paper roll or throw pillows just how you like them? (Not that I'd know that) If it's the same way that you cope with slow internet service, it's probably not good?

For just one moment, let me speak to the men. I know it's in our nature to think we can solve all problems with our lips and hands, but we know that's not the case. Compatibility in marriage is as much about the physical connection as what color your Mac Book shell is to the number of gigs inside of it.

When it comes to intimacy in a marriage, I can't begin to stress its importance. At the same time, one quickly realizes sex in marriage is not exactly the same as when you were single. This is a tough subject for me to tackle because I did not live by biblical principles as a single man. I wasn't saved until I was married, therefore, for me to speak on this, I know, can sound a bit hypocritical. But I'm going to do it regardless.

Single men typically think when they get married, their wife will give them sex whenever they want as if it's part of a binding contract and because that's most likely how it worked with their partner when they were single. Oddly enough, there is a rather plain to read biblical contract that pertains to sex, something I was at the same time shocked and happy to know. These revelations were brought to me by the Greek priest who presided over our wedding and who performed months of premarital counseling leading up to it.

For anybody like me who was raised Catholic, sex was rarely spoken of, and it typically carried an enormous amount of guilt. But Greek priests are permitted to marry and, therefore, I felt blessed to have a frank discussion of sex within the marriage with our priest. He eased my mind telling us that God did not put these urges in us to test us and that sexual intercourse was a gift from God meant to be shared as a bond between a committed husband and wife.

Proverbs 5: 18-19 reads *may your fountains be blessed, and may you rejoice in the wife of your youth… may her breasts always satisfy you and may you ever be intoxicated with her love.* Corinthians also speaks of both the married man feeling anxious over how to please his wife as it does the married woman being anxious over how to please her husband. It also says to not refuse one another (sexually) unless it is of mutual consent for a period of time, such as prayer or fasting.

Now that you have some biblical insight to sex and marriage, let's look at the worldly side. For the most part, there's typically been an unspoken give-and-take struggle concerning sex because men crave physical contact, and women tend to want to be loved on and have an emotional tie in. It's kind of like a quid pro quo in marriage (i.e., if you get the kids to bed, we can have some adult time). Although sometimes I do the quid only to find the quo fell asleep on me. I joke because be you male or female, if you're married and reading this, then you know that all those ideals of what your sex life would be like once you got married went out the window about year two. Not because you didn't like sex anymore but because life just happens and sex can slip down the list of priorities if you are not focused on nurturing it. Kids are certainly a factor in the equation, as we had to go to Europe on a second honeymoon in order to have a second child. Other contributing factors can be work, stress and just complete lack of effort or attention. The one cure-all is communication, both spoken and unspoken. It's the cornerstone of a healthy marriage and a healthy sex life.

We must be willing to have blunt and sometimes odd conversations with our spouse. Men often need to be vulnerable, and women often need to transparent and honest. If we aren't clear on who we are and what we require, then all we're doing is delaying a more serious or difficult conversation down the road. My advice to couples is to learn how to articulate your needs and desires early and effectively. If we can't talk to our spouse about sex, then frustration enters the picture, and it's easy to develop a hidden resentment. Then both sides rationalize, blame, complain, and justify the reasons why things don't seem to be working out in the bedroom or in the marriage. That's why a turned-on marriage eliminates technology (TVs and iPhones) from the sanctity of the bedroom. The turned-on bedroom is for three things only: sleeping, talking (or praying) or making love. Anything else has to go.

Don't forget, words matter, and conversation is the glue that holds a marriage together. I'm not going to speak for all couples, but I think I can speak for the majority when I state that the woman goes into a commitment saying to herself, "I know this is going to work, and this is going to be my husband for the rest of my life; it's going to be my fairy tale." The man, on the other hand, can sometimes be guilty of thinking, "I hope this lasts. I hope I can do this." Even though he is in love, his thoughts and feelings are often not articulated as easily.

If you look at the more pragmatic couples, they tackle communication and the differences in the sexes knowing the pitfalls and not acting like they are bulletproof. And it's quite normal for a man or woman in the early stages of marriage to think, "Oh my God, I'm not sure I know what to do, I'm flying by the seat of my pants," as long as you follow that up with the idea that "Perhaps we need some guidelines, mentors or a plan of action in terms of how we talk to one another about our feelings." The big "D-Word" problems occur when you ignore the conversation and think communication is not supposed to feel like work.

Times have changed. Technology has changed. Everything around us has changed. When you look back at a man and a woman, when it comes down to laying side by side in a bed, that's where a real marriage and real communication takes place. It's in those moments of silence when you're completely alone without distraction that you can turn one another on, and I'm not speaking of sex.

The bedroom is a sanctuary; it's where the deepest passion and the most heated conflicts typically take place. The conversations between a man and a woman will always remain constant whether you were living in a tent 2,000 years ago or you're living in a condo in present-day New York City.

Turning on your marriage is about respect and a mutual adoration. It's about sacrifice. Just because technology has changed, just because the things around us have changed does not mean that we have to fall victim to them.

Couples who consciously choose to engage in conversation about their career, children, and sex are happier. If we retract and shrink, going back into a place where it's easy to experience fear and suffering, then we will end up a statistic.

In this hustle and grind world, with the busyness of today's world, it's easy for husband and wife to get their priorities distorted, and that is why these words by Chip Gaines echoed so loudly for me when I read them. He said, "Obviously, Jo and I, as a couple, we just don't want to redline. You know, we don't want to run so hard after some dream or some goal only to find out that we've neglected the thing that means the very most to us, which is our marriage and our relationship."

Redline means no heartbeat, and ironically, Angelike has always said, "When we are asked to do something, I always ask, does it fit into our arteries (metaphorically speaking) because everything has a pulse or rhythm that runs through the main arteries, God, family, health and business."

So, when you are making decisions that impact your marriage and family, make sure they fit your pulse. Ensure that the people, purpose, and passions you pursue outside of the home feed into the HOME TEAM concept and contribute to drawing you closer together, not farther apart.

To wrap up this chapter that is so near and dear to my heart, let me finish by saying this. I've traveled to so many different cities around the world, and I've witnessed so many different communities and cultures and ultimately there is a single truth:

we're all looking for happiness and harmony, balance, and success. I've seen broke couples who were happy and rich couples
who weren't. I've seen city people move to the country to try
and find happiness, and I've seen country people move to the
city. It seems as if there's a dividing line. People either have a
lack of desire to create a home, or a lack of ambition to create a
career. In our house, we know we can do both at a high level if
we communicate and work as a team.

And that's what it comes down to. When you care about
something, you put intention into it, and when you put intention
into something, good things happen.

CHAPTER FIVE

TURN ON YOUR CONNECTION

> *"We use words to either connect with someone or control someone.*
> *If you use your words to connect with people,*
> *you'll have a relationship.*
> *If it's to control people, you won't have a relationship"*
> *— Mark Driscoll*

Looking back, I remember how beautiful my wife looked. It was a Saturday night, the first time in what seemed like forever that we were able to relax as we had our most trusted babysitter in town, my mother-in-law. She was the best because we knew she wouldn't allow the children to sit in front of the television and watch cartoons. Instead, Mom preferred to bring out games, crayons, and coloring books.

The occasion? Our fourth wedding anniversary. In four short years, we'd grown a million-dollar business, moved three times, and had two children. We had been anticipating this particular Saturday night for a long time. Not only were we going to celebrate our love, but we were also celebrating our business and hitting a new milestone as entrepreneurs.

Angelike was wearing a stunning black dress, one she wore proudly as she was once again able to fit into her pre-pregnancy style again. We pulled up to a new restaurant we'd heard amazing things about. The maître'd sat us at a beautiful table overlooking the sun-kissed Arizona valley as the evening's cool air was approaching in late February. As I placed the napkin on my lap and scooted my chair in, Angelike did the same. I took in a deep breath of gratitude for all that we'd been through and all that this night had to offer. And then, I did what no beautiful wife would ever want her husband to do on their anniversary night. I pulled out my cell phone and began to respond to a text message that I had received.

"Are you for real, David?" Angelike said. And my response was probably typical to one you have perhaps given or heard before, "Yea, babe, I'm sorry, it's just that…"

"No!" she said, sternly interrupting me. "Uh uh, not tonight. Nothing is that important that you have to answer it right now."

As I foolishly tried to reconcile my motive, she would have nothing of it. I responded by doubling down on my stance, saying that this text deserved my attention. And then I even got defensive and pushed back harder against her plea for me to be in the moment. Let's just say the first 15 minutes at the table was uncomfortable. The server steered clear of us. Definitely not how either of us had envisioned this highly-anticipated night going.

And then there was silence. I can only imagine what was going on in her head. Eventually our sever gathered the courage to break the tension and greeted us politely. In a frustrated voice, Angelike gingerly responded to him saying, "We're going to need a moment, please." That's when I knew this was serious.

It didn't take long for my defensiveness toward her to turn into a disappointment in myself. Alone with my thoughts, I couldn't help but think how right she was. "Geeze, what a stupid and selfish act David. Look what you've done. All that planning and excitement, and now you're behind the eight ball. What were you thinking? Idiot! You disappointed your wife for what? A stupid text message?"

So, I mustered all the courage I could find and pushed my foolish pride aside, offering the sincerest apology that my heart would allow me to give. Thankfully Angelike accepted. But never one to let a good teaching moment go to waste, she kindly forced (OK encouraged) me to talk about what had just happened. Guys, if you're like me, you know that we can bury an uncomfortable spat quicker than Steph Curry can bury a 3-pointer, or at least long enough until it eventually goes away. Women, on the other hand, often have a different philosophy. They like to talk. For some reason, they like to bring out this word they love—clarity—and tell how much they need it. In my entire time as a single dude amongst my guy friends, I can say with 1000 percent accuracy that I never used the word clarity. So, this was new to me.

For the next thirty or forty-five minutes, we did just that. We got clear. She spoke about the priorities in our lives and in our marriage, and we both agreed that if we were to have another four years of marriage, that our phones were going to have to take a back seat most of the time. Then we agreed to turn mine off and put hers on vibrate in her purse, just in case Mom needed to get ahold of us.

And who would've guessed it, we talked the rest of the night, uninterrupted, not only salvaging what could've been a disastrous anniversary, but we also made some pretty solid progress and set some very important standards for what was to come.

IT'S A CHOICE

One of the first steps to getting turned on is to realize that it is a choice. It begins in your head. From that night on, I got in the habit of handing my wife my phone to put in her purse when we arrived at a dinner together. I can't say I do it willingly every time or even all the time, because I'm what's called a squirrel and not good at policing it, but I am very conscious of the fact now and do it often.

As I mentioned in the story at the beginning, Angelike and I were living in Arizona at the time, the state motto of which is *Ditat Deus* or "God Enriches." And wow, did he ever. I remember praying for strong spiritual leadership, and he led me to The Trinity Church and Pastor Mark Driscoll. Driscoll is a man's man, exactly what I needed. I respected him for his knowledge of the Bible, his example of a loving husband/father, and because he is an expert communicator.

If the conversation which took place on our anniversary concerning the cell phone had happened six months earlier, it most likely would've ended in disaster and Angelike and me not speaking for a few days. I was hard-headed, full of self-righteous pride, and hated to be corrected. But we'd been in the pews when Driscoll spoke of communication. He said something that really knocked me upside the head and stuck with me, and that was, "If you love people, you're willing to have conflict with them so you can have relationship with them."

Angelike knows that. She speaks up when she feels it's important to our relationship. But I was never good at talking because of what I mentioned, the male pride thing. I imagine some of you men reading this are the same way. By nature, we don't take well to criticism or correction, especially when it comes from our wives.

Driscoll addressed that too, though, saying, "Men, you're often the teacher, never the student. Always right, never wrong." And that's when I realized, this miscommunication (or lack of communication) is killing marriages. There needs to be a revival or transformation to turn the tides.

And that's where the final piece of Pastor Driscoll's sermon came in; information doesn't necessarily lead to transformation. In this case, Angelike informing me what I had done did nothing to improve the situation; it just made me defensive. However, information in the context of a loving relationship does equal transformation. It wasn't that she wanted to scold me or check the box that she was right and I was wrong, it was that she loved me and cared about our future. She took the time to explain that to me and made sure I understood that this was about US winning and not her being right. I'll repeat that so that you get it, to her, it was about US winning and not her being right.

Angelike used her words not to control, but to connect in a loving way. She stood firm but stood in love, explaining to me why she felt the way she did and how our relationship would benefit by putting our phones away. Whether we are with our spouses or with our children, we must know it's not what we say but how we say it. Anybody can get mad and vent, but a student of human interaction, a disciple of love, knows that words matter. Tone matters. Nobody keeps score in a loving family. It's not about winning because even the winners in a spousal or family argument end up being losers. It's a lonely victory. Always think first, how can I say this in a loving manner, not to win but to come to an understanding.

Throughout this book and in our Turned On Live events held across the country, you will hear Angelike and myself continue to say, "We are hardwired for connection." In other words, God gave us the tools to be in communion with one another. He equipped us with the parts to be experts at it in fact. And science only backs that up. In a University of Arizona study, researchers showed that people were generally happier and more satisfied with life when they spent less time alone and more time interacting with other people in social settings. A research team, led by a psychology professor named Dr. Matthias Mehl, also found a tendency for happy people to have more meaningful and substantive conversations and less small talk. (For you single men, *small talk* is a term you'll one day become very familiar with).

If you agree with this study and know that your goal is to be happier and to find more meaningful and substantial conversations, then it would appear logical that you are figuratively raising your hand right now saying, "Yes please, I'm all in to learn more." I call these moments "Yea Duh" choices. Rhetorical questions in which we say sure, of course, we want to be happier. Who wouldn't?

So if these "Yea Duh" choices are so obvious, then how come so many of us struggle with them? Is it because we are not always as in control as we think we are? The tendency to go back on cruise control is a strong one. It's a seduction by way of technology which you've heard me say a lot. Your phone, social media, and other menial distractions are associated with a dopamine response that we have to acknowledge. Dopamine is a neurotransmitter, a chemical released by nerve cells to send signals to other nerve cells. They play a major role in reward-motivated behavior.

If we feel a reward for consistently checking our phones or social media, then the desire (even subconsciously) is hard to break from.

In one particular study done at the University of Bergen in Norway, researchers found that almost 75% of people reported feeling anxiety or panic when they misplaced their smartphone. The study also suggested that smartphones, to a certain degree, are incorporated within the individual and could be regarded as an extension of the self, and being restricted from one's smartphone causes more negative effects than having no restrictions.

I can personally recall being in the back of a large conference room once and seeing a woman who was obviously panicked. It worried me so much that I felt compelled to approach her and ask, "What's wrong? Are you OK? What can I help you with?" She responded frantically with, "I've lost my cell phone, and I don't know what to do. I'm trying to just stay calm." My internal response was, "Whoa, overreaction party of one, your table is ready," but then I had to put myself in check because I'd recalled feeling the same way for the same reason on a couple of different occasions. That odd-end-of-the-world reaction for the temporary loss of an electronic device should be a huge clue that our priorities are out of whack. HELLO!

The choice we are presented with, if we wish not to be slaves to distraction, but rather have balance in our lives, is one that simply requires one thing—PRACTICE.

It's the same way you might approach going on a diet. We know in simple terms, the difference between good choices and bad ones. Of course we do, and the same pleasure responses we look for in say chocolate are similar to those we get from social media and our electronic devices. You go on a diet; you fall off. It requires constant course-correcting and practice. You don't just say, "OK, I'm giving up sweets," or "I'll leave my phone at home." Of course not, you have to always be vigilant and go back to a healthy practice of balance.

Again, the path of least resistance is one which most of us seemed to be hardwired to take (i.e., the stairs are right there, but you'll wait for the elevator, or you don't like the television show you're watching, but the remote isn't right at your side so you'll watch a double episode of *Matlock* or a 45-minute infomercial. You have lean turkey in the fridge but cold pizza on the counter.)

Life is typically most gracious and rewarding to those with the ability to exercise one single attribute above all others. Do you want to know what that is? Delayed gratification. The ability to put off something easy in order to reap the benefits of something perhaps a bit harder. When it comes to our physical health, it's things like taking the stairs over an escalator or choosing to cook at home versus going through a drive-thru.

When it comes to our mental health and communication decisions, the same pattern of choice is in effect; do we go to bed angry or talk it out? Do we take the iPad away from our children and have them do something more productive or just relish in the fact they are being quiet and not bothering us? Is it better to call your customer or pop off an email or text?

The more we can do to make human nature natural again, the better we will be.

BEING PRESENT

Growing up in America and being raised in western culture and religion, I was never exposed to eastern philosophies or culture. Exploring one's inner self in my culture was something for shrinks to do. That changed one day when I was suffering from terrible shoulder pain. I'd tried just about every modality western medicine had to offer with no luck. That's when a friend of mine suggested acupuncture.

On my first visit, I went into the room, took my shoes off, and was like, "OK, let's put some needles in this shoulder and get to work." The therapist was not of Asian descent but studied diligently over the years in Chinese medicine. He said in a very calm voice, "Not so fast. Sit and relax. Let's talk about what's been going on in your life."

My experience up to that point had all been with Western medicine which amounted to; sit, where does it hurt, and here is a pill or a shot for that. Not to mention, I quickly realized if I'd never had a conversation with somebody who was a 180 of my personality, I was about to.

He immediately began to ask questions about my mood and my mindset, to which I told him, "Well, I'm especially on edge today because I got really angry and laid into my daughter last night and couldn't sleep well because of how awful I felt."

When he probed the issue further, I explained to him that it was late, past her bedtime, and she was playing with a little magnifying glass and wouldn't go to bed when I asked her to. When she failed to listen a third time, I really yelled at her. Then the therapist said something that I'll never forget, "Children are presence machines; they are forever curious and live in that moment. At six years old, she's not worried about what time she has to wake up tomorrow morning or what's on her schedule. All she knows is that she's fascinated by that magnifying glass and being present in the moment." He then added, "Wouldn't it be nice if we as adults had that same capacity?"

Boom! Light bulb moment. He was so right. The situation had way more to do with my adult ego (and her not obeying me) and my forgotten memory of what it's like to see through the eyes of a child. And this was a turned-on moment for me. How many times, as adults, do we miss the wonder in life's simple moments because we're so focused on the future, what we have to do tomorrow, or the past, reliving a mistake we made yesterday?

If you want a perfect pop-culture example of this, look no further than Clark Griswold, the loving but bumbling father in National Lampoon's *Vacation* movies. If you are familiar with them, you'll remember that Clark was always preoccupied with his agenda. He always had a list of things to do and see while on vacation all in the spirit of helping his wife and kids enjoy themselves. One problem though—his zest for getting it all in almost always backfired on him leading his wife and children to ask, "Why can't we just enjoy the present?" In his quest to do all and please all, he did nothing but create frustration, missing all the moments he was trying so hard to create.

Perhaps you've felt that way? Have you ever taken the family to Disney World or the zoo and had so much you wanted to pack into the day, a list of list of must-do things that in your rush to create the perfect experience, you instead created the perfect anxiety? Sometimes even our best intentions can disrupt the quality time as it did with me, until I finally realized that it's not a matter of doing all the things on the list, but rather being present in things we do get to do.

So the challenge set forth for us is to be presence machines like our children. Meaning the toddlers. It seems we may have already lost an entire generation, call them X or Y, or whatever. You know them, they are the ones you see at a concert who appear to be way more occupied with filming it for social media than actually being there to enjoy it themselves. When "Look what I'm doing" becomes more exciting than what we're actually doing, that's a problem.

For instance, I attended a business conference, and the guest performer was the Hip Hop artist Flo-Rida. We were all pumped as he was within a stone's throw of us singing his hit song "Low." A few minutes into it, he began inviting people up on stage with him. One by one, my co-workers went up the stairs, making their way toward him and his giant State of Florida gold piece that hung around his neck. But then something else happened. Nearly every single person on stage began taking out their cell phone and began shooting videos selfies of themselves dancing next to him. They were definitely less aware, I'd say borderline oblivious even, of the actual star and more dialed into the reflection of their selfie screen trying to connect with their social media audience. Little by little, they began desperately jockeying around stage determined to find which angle best included them next to Flo-Rida.

It's hard to make a judgment here. Those are my friends, and I'll admit it, I've been guilty of doing similar things I suppose, but when you're in the audience, seeing it from an observer's standpoint, it glaringly odd. So here is this famous performer, singing and dancing, he calls you up to the stage and you're really not even present? Your greatest concern isn't to live out this amazing encounter and soak it in; it's not to look at a live audience of 15,000 people in front of you (like you'll have many opportunities to see how that feels). No, it's to make sure that your social media followers see that you're on stage with Flo-Rida. Social validation at its worst.

It's strange, very strange indeed to see it from the outside, but it's not just that particular instance. This type of behavior has become the new normal. You can't watch a concert or live show without seeing an enormous section of the audience whip out their smartphones to record it rather than live it.

When I think about how far we've come in such a relatively short time, in terms of presence, there's one stellar example which I'll present to you. In 2002, I had an opportunity to be in the press box at Super Bowl XXXVI in New Orleans. Now for a frame of reference, this was about four months after 9/11, so the world was on edge. In the days leading up to the game, I explored The Big Easy for the first time. I went to bars and restaurants and saw fans and iconic images I'd only read about before. And I took some photos.

Finally, the day of the big game had arrived. The Superdome was larger than life. Some 24-year old, sixth-round pick finagled his way to the big show to face-off versus the golden arm of Kurt Warner and the Greatest Show on Turf. We'd soon learn Tom Brady was about to become a household name. The halftime show was headlined by the greatest rock band of the era, U2. Their performance was equally exhilarating yet sobering as a screen behind the band scrolled through the names of all the Americans who'd lost their lives on September 11th. Bono and the boys played the song *MLK*.

As the second half ensued, those in attendance quickly realize the 14-point underdog Patriots weren't just happy to be there, they intended to win. With under a minute to go in the game, the second-year quarterback out of Michigan completed a 23-

yard pass to Troy Brown putting New England within striking distance of a victory. With 7 seconds left, Brady spiked the ball setting up an improbable 48-yard field goal attempt from kicker Adam Vinatieri.

IT BECOMES SURREAL

Here I am, a nobody in the world of sports, standing in the open-air press box of the New Orleans Superdome on the 50-yard line watching one of the greatest games in NFL history, during one of the most tumultuous times in world history. To my left, within arms distance, is legendary Hall of Fame coach Al Davis, an NFL icon. To my immediate right is one of my all-time favorite players and Florida State alumnus Deion Sanders.

The snap is down, the kick is up, a hush comes over the 72,922 in attendance, and the ball sails through the uprights.

History is made, and I was an eyewitness to it.

So, what does that have to do with being turned on and being present?

My friends, do you know I don't have a single photograph of me in that press box or of the game itself? Not one shot of U2, not one selfie of me and my childhood idol Primetime or the legendary Darth Raider. The odd thing is, I had a camera with me. I had a cell phone that took photos, too. But not one memory of that amazing moment exists except those remaining in my head.

That was only 18 years ago. How different would that be today? And when is an experience worth just experiencing versus having to record?

I'd say presence is probably the number one thing that's in jeopardy in many of our lives today. We're trading real-time experience for digital memories.

LIVING FOR THE DAY

Why are we, as a culture, on the rise with anxious and depressed people when "Fear Not" is said to be mentioned 365 times in the Bible. It tell us, *Therefore, do not be anxious about tomorrow, for tomorrow will be anxious for itself* (Matthew 6:32). We're always told to live like a child, but we can't grasp what living for the day, in the present, truly means.

I tell my four-year old we're going to Disney World for Christmas, and she says, "Yeah," but within 60 seconds, she's back to focusing on her coloring unfazed by the future. If I show her a picture of Disney World from the year before, she smiles, then (you guessed it) back to the task at hand. And if she was swooped up in a Disney parade by Mickey Mouse himself and placed on his shoulders, the last thing she'd be thinking of is getting a selfie with him.

My acupuncturist, whom I mentioned, made me aware to just how much presence is an awareness and a goal of Eastern Asian cultures. Chinese philosopher Lao Tzu wrote, "If you are depressed you are living in the past. If you are anxious, you are living in the future. If you are at peace, you are living in the present." So why aren't we as Christians more thirsty in our yearning to pursue a peace in where we are at the moment? Jesus himself said, *Peace I leave with you, My peace I give to you; not as the world gives do I give to you. Let not your heart be troubled, neither let it be afraid.* (John 14:27).

If it is indeed peace in your life that you are looking for, being with being present in the moment.

CHAPTER SIX

TURN ON
YOUR HOME

"Home is the nicest word there is."
– Laura Ingalls Wilder

In the Norrie house, the pinky swear is bond. It doesn't get any more serious than that. When it occurs, both parties know there's no turning back; you MUST follow through on your promise.

And while I crack up every time my daughters go to the pinky swear, I'm reminded how important commitment and follow-through is to children. And more importantly, how significant good communication is because it all begins with communication.

Joe Rogan, who hosts one of the most popular podcasts on the planet, is a guy who is very outspoken. He doesn't hold back, and from time to time, he speaks about things which I may not always agree with and in a manner which some could easily find offensive; however, he does make valid points on many topics. One such point really hit me in the gut as a father. He said, "I want my kids to say, 'My dad did what he said he would.'"

So simple, but oh so powerful.

Words have meaning—we know this. But how many times do we back them up as we should?

As a working parent, I know all too well how difficult it can be to turn on and communicate effectively with young children.

When things get hectic, and I feel like I'm being pulled in ten different directions at once, it's easy to brush them aside and give them lip service with things like *wait a sec, hold on,* or *Ok, later.* We think to ourselves 'They're just kids, they don't understand' or 'they don't care' or 'they'll forget', but that's often not the case. Young children, even toddlers, are almost always able to understand and feel beyond what we perceive they can speak or communicate to us.

In this current era of busyness, technology has blurred the lines between work and home. As more and more parents work from a home office, there is a growing stress and uneasiness on children who feel neglected, abandoned or less important because the concept of a home office isn't always clear to a four or even an eight-year-old. As a father, I've used the aforementioned phrases to buy time, promising that we can do it *later*. But what happens when the game of catch or the reading of the book doesn't come later because we've found a new distraction that popped up later. Then the child is left thinking exactly what Rogan said, "Daddy didn't do what he said he was going to do."

I understand that with progress comes complexity and learning new rules, so wouldn't you agree that this new wave of devices in the home requires a new type of education? It would seem as if we, as a society, have not gotten ahead of it yet for two reasons. First, this new tech revolution is moving at lightning speed. Second, we just haven't had the time to study long-term effects. What I see as a parent is a lot of my peers acknowledging something is going wrong but at the same time throwing their hands up saying, "I just don't know what to do or where to start." Then, they question, is it really even that bad anyway?

What I'm seeing is that education needs to come a lot earlier than we may think. When my youngest daughter was about three years old, I remember how we'd talk on the phone and use FaceTime with grandma and grandpa. When I asked her

"Phoenix, what does a phone do?" she shrugged her shoulders with a smile and said, "I don't know," but when I asked, "Can we see Grandma and Poppy on this?" she says, "Yes." How that conversation may vary among different three-years-olds isn't important, what is important is that at three, Phoenix knew that in order to have my attention, I needed to put the phone down. I remember her telling me, "OK, Daddy done. Put your phone down." Unfortunately, it's a painful reminder of where we are at today. Our flesh and blood are competing for our attention like never before.

Let's think about that. Think about how this has changed over the years. There may have been a time when I was growing up in the 70s when I tried to get my parent's attention while they were on the phone, but that was certainly limited to very specific times. In the pre-cell phone era, there was typically a main house phone located in the kitchen. Those of you who remember the spiral chord, it only allowed you to go as far as about midway down the hallway, but that was it.

Think about what our children have to compete with now. We have our phones on us at nearly every single moment of the day. So, they will compete for our attention in the kitchen, in the living room, on the front porch, on the walk to the park, at the playground at the park, in the car on the way to school, and just about everywhere we go.

So, let's go back to that Joe Rogan quote, "I want my kids to say, 'My Dad did what he said he would.'" When Daddy says he is going to put the phone away and play, will he? Can we watch a family movie or go to the park without checking our phone?

According to research, many of us can't. Some 40 percent of mothers and 32 percent of fathers admitted some form of phone addiction, such as being unable to resist checking messages or always thinking about incoming calls or texts. You might recall earlier in the book the story of NBA star J.J. Redick saying he checked it at every stoplight and how he couldn't resist the urge.

Researchers dubbed these interruptions "technoference," and the results are not comforting. Children are sulking, whining and throwing tantrums as a means to get our attention.

I'm going to assume that we're all good humans and try to be good parents. I'm going to assume that our intentions are pure and assume that when we say to our children, "Daddy (or Mommy) will put the phone away and come play with you" that we mean it. But I'm also going to assume that many of you reading this are like me and that when we put the phone away, it still has control over us. We still hear it ring, chirp or ding and interrupt our TURNED ON time with our children. Or there's just that one extremely important text or email that we just HAVE TO check to make sure we can fully relax and enjoy this playtime or story time. It's like a glowing beacon which, even when put in a drawer or placed under a pillow, seems to call to us. The anxiety of not knowing what the beep or chip is delivering is too much for us to resist.

Where is the congruence? Angelike always says, "How am I going to tell my children they can BE, DO, HAVE, OR GIVE anything they want in this world yet I'm over here being a slave to my phone, doing something I said I don't want to do?" We don't want to give a small portion of leftover time to our children. The scraps. That's not congruent.

How can we say we will make time for them if we don't? More importantly, what happens when it's the reverse? When you just want your child to put down the phone, tablet or iPad and spend time with you or come to the dinner table, but they won't. Hmm, who in the world could have possibly shown them that a device was more important than real-life interaction?

Maybe the most difficult part of this new encroachment on home life is that it's somewhat of a stealth intruder. Dr. Kushlev puts it like this, "I don't think the problem of constant access to a screen/internet indicates that we are doomed to be slaves to technology, I think now it's more dangerous because it's more subtle. In other words, I don't know what the cost is of what I'm losing or missing out on."

What a great point. How can we want we don't know? How can we miss something we've never experienced? It's like this, have you ever been to a great restaurant or beautiful park that was right around the corner from your house or neighborhood? What do you say? Where has this been all my life? How did I not know?

If you're a parent of a newborn or toddler, then you know the thing you hear most often from parents of grown children is "hold onto every moment because they grow up quick." They know what they miss, what they may have taken for granted. If we don't acknowledge this absentness or ability to be present in the lives of our children, I predict an epidemic of regret on the part of both the parents and children who feel robbed of the times they lost, or should I say forfeited, to devices.

THE SNUGGLE IS REAL

In this era of *work hard* clichés, I'm sure you've heard or read, "The struggle is real." But I like to flip it and say, "The snuggle is real."

There I was one day, rushing all over the house trying to do 50 things at once, make breakfast, prepare for my podcast, get my oldest daughter Ella off to school and look over a contract. It all just had me racing around in a dozen different directions.

Then I saw Phoenix, who was only three, quietly looking out the window with nobody paying attention to her. An overwhelming feeling of both sadness and disappointment (in myself) came over me. I quickly put on a slow song and asked her to come to me. She ran over and jumped up into my arms and put her head on my shoulder, and we did a little slow dancing.

She is my joy. My weakness? Patience and restlessness. I need to slow down. I need to slow down so much that I literally took a sharpie and wrote SLOW DOWN on a big sheet of paper and taped it to my office wall. Like many of you, my mind finds difficulty in slowing down for even a moment most days, but I remind myself to PRACTICE and to fully embrace the moment.

This day was different. I went to put her down, and she hung on tighter. And it hit me—she's teaching me a lesson in presence. Here is this three-year-old who is supposed to be the hyper one, and she's perfectly still with her head on my shoulder as we slow dance in the kitchen. I wondered in my mind, *Wow, she must really be content right now, and I'm allowing a precious moment to be cut short by what? A business idea? My work out? A return phone call? Shame on me.*

When you get stressed out about getting work done or growing your business, ask yourself does your two-year old know the difference between a George Washington and a Benjamin Franklin. How come it's so easy for us to get worked up about how much time we have left with our kids if they're not? Our children live in the moment while we, the parents, are often caught napping in the past or focused on the future.

We can become so preoccupied with what we will earn for our children (money) and provide for our children (clothes, toys, food) that we can lose sight of what they really want most, our attention. When I get caught up in overwhelm and worldly things, I always try to remember what author Chuck Swindoll once said, "Each day of our lives we make deposits into the memory banks of our children." I ask you to think back to your memories as a kid. Would you be fonder of a truck or a doll you received or the memory of your dad throwing you up in the air and catching you or your mother tucking you in at night? I know

I don't want to be so hyper-focused on the past or the future that I ignore the present.

There is no time like the present to reclaim your household, tell yourself you're not going to lose more precious moments. The decision is easy. Say I will foster a more balanced home/work relationship? I will make this a priority.

For each family that may be different, based on traditions or what region of the country you live in. Some fathers take their kids ice fishing while others take theirs to surf. It's not just about the activity. It's about being in the moment without distraction. It's about not juggling between work and play but making a stand to be present in the things which you have set specific time aside for, even the small things like tucking them in or being at the park. Those moments are sacred for children, I've seen when they get interrupted by a phone call or an email. It disrupts the flow of play and the happiness of the moment.

LEGACY

Legacy is defined as a gift of property, money or will. Part of being a turned on home is thinking about the legacy you will leave for your children. However I'm not talking about that type of financial legacy, I'm speaking of a spiritual one. Many fathers of past generations used work ethic and money as substitutes for physical affection and love. To provide for the family was a patriarchal role while the mother of the house was the one who provided emotional support. But that was then, the Leave It To Beaver era I'd call it. Our world looks radically different today.

According to the Bureau of Labor Statistics, in more than sixty percent of American families, both parents work full time. As parents, we know it's easy to say, "Well somebody has to clothe and feed these kids." Of course, but at what price? I don't have the answer for this, but I will ask how much is enough when it comes to work-life balance? Will more money buy our kids more happiness? How much will assure they'll be well adjusted? An extra 50K in our bank account? Or will praying and playing with them contribute more to their long-term well-being?

Our actions today set a foundation for decades to come. What will the repercussions look like if each generation gives in a little bit more to distraction and busyness?

We need only look to one of the greatest distractions of our time, the 24-hour news cycle, in order to find the answer. Cable news shows and television tabloids are quick to report stories of rich kids gone bad or privileged children going off the deep end, but where are the stories of the kids in rehab or committing suicide whose mothers and fathers prayed and played with them? I'm not saying they don't exist, but surely you have to like the chances of a better outcome with the latter.

A recent survey by OnePoll found that seventy-three percent of American kids would like more opportunities to bond with their families. Another study by Harvard's School of Public Health found that children raised with spiritual practices have better mental health as they grow into adults and were 33 percent less likely to do drugs in their 20s.

I know what you're thinking, "Well, duh, spending quality time and raising children with a strong faith is a no brainer. Of course, they will be better off." So if we know this, what's keeping us from it? If we have the information, then why aren't we using it? Because we're so hyper-focused on our money jobs that it's easy to lose sight and slack off on our most important job.

My daughter Ella may be the most persistent person I know. Once we make that pinky promise or she sets her mind to something, there's no turning back. And in many ways, she's helping me be a better parent. This is particularly true when it comes to our nighttime routine. Even on nights when Dad is exhausted and can't keep his eyes open, she says, "Get in here and do your job, Dad!" My *job* being to tuck her in and read a Bible story to her. And in my quest to practice being congruent, I made a commitment to her and myself that I would never say "NO" to that request regardless of the situation or how tired I was. I can always muster some energy for God and my children.

I ask you today to be what you say you will be. Do what you say you will do. Love how you promise to love. We don't have to be perfect; we just have to try. Our children depend on that example, and I guarantee it will affect you in a positive way just as much as it will affect them.

DISCIPLINE

Any talk of legacy must be paired with the word discipline. As I just stated in the previous chapter, we know what we're supposed to do, we have the game-plan, but we get thrown off our game-plan very easily in the age of distraction. As a former sports journalist, I saw the fruits of discipline and sticking with the game-plan on a daily basis. My easiest example of this is to go to the legends of the sporting world: Michael Jordan, Cal Ripken Jr, Wayne Gretsky, or Tom Brady. Each of these athletes will be remembered for centuries because of their accomplishments and performance on the field.

Every kid grows up pretending they're making that last-second basket, 3... 2... 1, he shoots, he scores! But if every kid wants that, why do so few achieve it? If every parent wants to be a good parent and create a turned on home, why do so many struggle? I say because although we have the ability (talent) we lack the discipline.

Talent goes a long way, but those legendary athletes mentioned above went way beyond their physical talent—all had incredible amounts of self-discipline. It's the same type of discipline that's required to achieve a successful marriage and family. What's ironic is we hear stories every day of disciplined athletes with undisciplined practices off the field. We have stories of disciplined businessmen and businesswomen with undisciplined social lives or bodies. It seems we can get caught in the practice of perfecting one area of our life (one hallway) but often at the expense of another.

A turned-on life requires attention to balance because balance is most easily disrupted by the distractions found on the path of least resistance. Being a leader in the home requires finding a new kind of strength to persevere and place our attention on those things which nourish and give back, not rob and take away. There's no greater reward than mastering our ability to enforce a schedule and exercise discipline when it comes to family time, even if it means we have to pass on that 8 p.m. video conference or miss that Saturday seminar. Simon Sinek said, "There is no decision that we can make that doesn't come with some sort of balance or sacrifice." Read it again and think of what that means to you. Yes, some sacrifice may be needed to provide for your family, but Angelike and I know too well that once you say yes to breaking family time once, it's easier to say yes again and again.

This reflects the importance of compartmentalizing what is work and what is not. We know when we get hyper-focused on one area of our life (career), other areas are likely to suffer (home life). Are balance and sacrifice directly related or polar opposites? When you do what you are called to do, what you love, it would certainly seem as if the prior applies rather than the latter.

I work from home, amongst my children, and make a very good living at it. That's balance. I'd be lying if I said my work didn't sacrifice because of my kids or vice versa. But that's life, and sacrifice is expected no matter how figured out you think you have it. To me, balance is a *course correction*. We do it with work, our finances, and certainly our bodies. To be on point 24/7, 365 is not realistic, so we strive to have more good days than bad.

I've found the most successful people are not those who go to extremes and full-out sacrifice, but rather those who see themselves steering off course one way or another, then course correct to get back on track. This is where awareness comes in. The ability to stop yourself in a moment and say, "Is this who I said I was going to be?"

CHAPTER SEVEN

TURN ON
YOUR FAMILY

All great change in America begins at the dinner table.
– Ronald Reagan

When I was 15 years old, I got my left ear pierced. That night, I frantically wandered about the house as evening approached knowing my Dad would be home soon. I couldn't help worrying what he'd do if he found out? I had to think quickly and said to myself, "Aha, I've got it." Off to the kitchen I went where my mother was preparing dinner as usual. I politely asked her to switch seats with me at the table that night, and she knew something was up. My entire life, I'd sat to my father's immediate right, and one look in my direction would mean that gold hoop would be staring him in the face.

My mother obliged, and there I sat, hurriedly eating my roast beef and peas. I asked for permission to be excused and walked back to my bedroom like Ralphie in *A Christmas Story,* gleaming with pride that I'd got one past the old man.

I hadn't stepped one foot into my room when I heard my dad yell, "Nice earring, David." My mouth dropped. Luckily, Pops was cool about it. He didn't like it, but he didn't flip out as I imagined. But this story isn't about my earring; it's about eating as a family. Looking back now, those days gathered around the table with my sisters and brother are cherished. And the family dinner is something Angelike and I both share the same passion for, and something we both agree is in need of a major comeback.

Don't just take it from me, most experts agree that gathering around the table for a communal meal is highly beneficial to families as it represents a pivotal time for children to express thoughts, ideas, and emotions—and the routine of doing such is said to be comforting to them. In 1943, the sociologist James H.S. Bossard wrote, *It is at the dining table, and particularly at dinner time, that the family is apt to be at its greatest ease.*

Other child development experts have added that meals around a table help children get used to conversations in close quarters, learn to facilitate eye contact, and also facilitates social, cognitive, emotional, and nutritional development.

The National Center on Addiction and Substance Abuse at Columbia University (CASA), reported a correlation between family dinners and good grades saying that children who ate five to seven family dinners per week were more likely to report receiving mostly As and Bs in school and less likely to report receiving mostly Cs. According to the American College of Pediatricians, over the past three decades, family time at the dinner table and family conversation, in general, has declined by more than 30 percent. One-third of families with 11- to 18-year-olds eat one or two meals a week at most together. Only one-fourth eat seven or more family meals per week.

Contrary to popular belief, a family dinner was not a common idea until the mid 19th century. Before then, early Americans took their lead from their European roots, and during the Victorian era, families of higher means and status reserved the dining table for adults and more formal occasions while the children often ate in the nursery. When children were present at the dinner table during this era, they were not expected nor encouraged to speak.

Over the next hundred years, that would change, and by the mid-1950s, the family dinner was an American staple and images of families gathered around the table filled newspapers and magazines. When televisions became commonplace, those images were then broadcast into our homes on a daily basis. If you grew up in the 1970s and 80s, then you're probably familiar with the iconic images of families like the Waltons, The Ingalls, Cleavers, Cosbys, and Cunninghams all gathered around a table sharing conversations about the trials of their days. This is the generation I grew up in, and most of my friends shared the same experiences.

But somewhere between then and now, things have changed, and I'd say changed drastically. The family dinner is on the verge of extinction, and along with it all of those benefits so crucial to child development and wellbeing. So, like President Ronald Reagan, Angelike and I agree that all great change starts at the dinner table, and our mission is to encourage families to get back to the table as a staple of American culture.

In my case, being at the dinner table with my parents and my siblings was a non-negotiable. We were expected to be on time, no excuses. And trust me, there were days when breaking up an awesome playground football game was tough, but the thought of drawing my dad's ire was tougher. And looking back on it, there's no doubt that dinner at home was a huge part of me feeling loved and cared for, and like the studies show, having a time and platform to voice my young thoughts and opinions.

Angelike, on the other hand, has a very important perspective on the family dinner as she's seen both sides. She says, "Some of the sweetest memories of my childhood were when my parents were still together, and we were at the table. But when my parents split up, and that stopped, there was definitely something missing. A huge void."

The rise in divorce rates is one of the main reasons family dinners don't happen in today's culture. It's difficult for single parents to make it happen as they struggle to work and play both parental roles. But there are bigger factors at play here that affect all of us regardless of status.

My family is no different from most in this day and age where planning meals around work can be difficult and the lure to use order-in food delivery services like DoorDash, Postmates and Grubhub is strong. When I was growing up, my mom made one meal for the entire family. It took sometimes hours to prepare and therefore we had little choice but to eat it. Angelike, remembers falling asleep at the dinner table because her dad said she couldn't get up until she ate her green beans.

Fast forward to the present, if your family is like ours, it feels like the house is in a constant state of chaos, with multiple devices turned on and noise emanating from all different directions. Choices and options are now part of the norm with the ability to satisfy each family member's different appetite depending on their mood, so planning and forming a routine seems almost impossible.

Does this sound familiar? Parent: "Kids, do you want pizza, chicken nuggets or mac 'n cheese?" Kids: "I don't know. What else is there?" I responded to my kids, "Next time Grandma and Poppy are visiting, ask them how many times they asked Daddy what he wanted to eat when he was your age. Zero."

I laugh because it's funny and I understand that times have changed, but we can't forget that routine is very important to children and, even for adults, more structure in the evenings is crucial to our sanity and cohesiveness. And it is written in the instruction booklet; 1 Corinthians 11:33-34 says, *So then, my brothers and sisters, when you gather to eat, you should all eat together. Anyone who is hungry should eat something at home, so that when you meet together it may not result in judgment.*

Recently, Angelike and I felt uncomfortable admitting to one another that we were falling short in this area despite it being something we both agreed that we wanted badly. We'd say over and over how important dinner time was, but then find ourselves with our laptops opened and the girls watching TV. And let me be candid—we were not always engaged in work. Many times, we were checking the news, ordering something on Amazon that had to be done right then, or maybe answering an Instagram poll. At one point we just had to take a long hard look at ourselves and agree to be more disciplined.

THE BIG A-HA

There comes a time in every family's journey when enough is enough and you reach a tipping point. When that happens, put away the laptop, place the smartphone in the other room, and turn off the television. Get an agreement from everybody present, that tonight, we eat without distraction, as a family.

Despite the temptation to check the phone, even when the kids get down from the table or ask to turn the TV on, stand firm. Because when you stand firm and wait it out, something amazing happens, your mind becomes at rest, the world slows down, and without the interference of technology, you become more in tune with the humanity surrounding your table. You're forced to think about things to talk about. Maybe it's your son's animal project on the Meerkat at school or your daughter's question about why Olaf can't play in the summer. Or maybe it's simply eating your food and looking at one another in peace. It sounds crazy, huh? Almost surreal, but it's a vibe you have to switch, a habit that takes time to make.

We had to muscle through an uncomfortable period to get to the other side, and along the way, we looked at one another as if to ask, "Are we really doing it?" Angelike laughed. Ella was smiling too, and Phoenix, well, she just beamed. One night we finished our meal and I could tell we were all having the same thought, "Wow, it's possible. We can do this!"

Here's the really cool part. After dinner, instead of turning the television back on or reaching for our phones, we had an impromptu dance contest. Who could floss the best? One round after another, three of us went and one judged. "One more time," the kids kept asking. It was like time slowed down and God winked at us as if to say, "You see, they want to hang out and spend time with you."

Since then, we have taken steps to make sure we protect this time. First, we redesigned our dining nook a bit, configuring it with new chairs and a table to make it feel more family friendly. Next, we agreed to cook at least three dinners at home each week and to include our girls in the meal preparation, so they felt invested in the outcome. But most important was the mandate that all devices, belonging to both adults and children, were to be turned off and left in another room. And nobody may leave the table until we all agree we can be excused.

That last one was the big one because one of the biggest issues with technology invading our homes is that we think boredom needs to be replaced with stimulation. This is a problem for today's kids, and I've often heard my daughter ask, "I'm bored, can I play on your phone?"

Kids need to be bored. Because when they are bored, they are forced to use their imagination, they gravitate toward other children, the outdoors or (if they're alone) grab their dolls or action figures and create stories. And stories are really what's important here. Angelike remembers her father emphasizing the importance of family stories as a dinner time tradition. "If we don't tell them, it ends here," he'd say. How true is that? We can't facilitate creativity and create a legacy without stories. Imagine in thirty years from now, when your children are sitting with their kids, what would you prefer their stories consist of, a YouTube video they watched or dancing with you in the living room?

As with anything else, resurrecting the family dinner takes practice and perseverance as situations will arise that beg for an exception. Our goal is to protect our ritual without being militant about it, and that's where we sometimes will have to be creative but steadfast. We're the parents. We make the rules. And while I believe to some degree in the "King of the Castle" approach, Angelike and I found that ruling with an iron fist doesn't always create loyal subjects. We see ourselves as parents first, but we're also coaches as we both come from sports backgrounds. That's why we call it HOME TEAM.

If it's important to you, and you put thought and energy into it, then it will be important to your children. So, if you long for connection under your roof, I highly encourage you to also make the family dinner a priority event. Try it for a month and watch the ripple effect it has on your family's wellbeing.

THE BLURRING OF THE LINES

When I was a kid, Dad got up in the morning and went off to work an 8-hour day at the office. When the work day was over, he came home, and family time commenced. It was pretty cut and dry. But that's not the case anymore, is it? Times have changed, and much of the population has been freed from the shackles of the four walls of an office thanks to those very things we just said are creeping their way into our family life, laptop computers, smartphones, and video conferencing.

But whoops! One small side effect. If your laptop and smart phone come home with you, then so does your work. This has become quite a predicament for the modern family. When are we on the clock, and when are we not?

With about eight million Americans now working from home at least part of the week, the blending of the home and office has taken off to new heights, and it's likely to keep going. The question is, where do we draw the line? Sure, we've tried to set boundaries, declare specific work hours and convert separate rooms in the home, but the call to do more and produce more is powerful, and I'm guessing like me, many of you who balance this space have found yourselves saying, "Ok, but just this once" way too many times. And it's when the exception becomes the habit that discord ensues. Angelike and I can attest, first hand, it's caused some of the most heated arguments of our marriage.

It's a legitimate Catch-22; we're no longer slaves to the 9-to-5 jobs, but we also see a lot more work during nights and weekends. Words like *hustle* and *grind* are now heralded as badges of honor, finding their way onto t-shirts, mugs, and wall art, and it's easy to see that now a house may no longer be a home in terms of sanctity.

As public speakers and business coaches, Angelike and I have spoken to hundreds of couples who, just like us, have allowed the lure of financial success to creep into their homes and impinge on precious family time. I'm sad to admit that one of the most common phrases our kids hear is, "Hold on, Mommy (or Daddy) is on a call." Not only do we see the expression on our children's' faces change, but there is a tremendous amount of guilt felt on our part. And I know this is not just some phase or made up problem which we feel because at nearly every opportunity Angelike and I have had to take questions or speak in public, by far the number one topic we're asked to address is Work/Family Balance.

CONNECTING WITH OUR CHILDREN

The greatest gift we can give to our children is our presence, something I've just pointed out that is being challenged in our homes today. In a large international study of 6,000 eight to thirteen-year-old children, 32 percent reported feeling unimportant when their parents use their cellphones during meals, conversations, or other family times. They reported that they felt they were competing with technology for their parents' attention. Over half of the children in the study said their parents spend too much time on their phones, and I'm ashamed to say, I would have to stand up and say I'm one. In the words of Abraham Lincoln, "There is but one way to train up a child in the way he should go, and that is to travel it yourself."

And it's not just business either. Parents are falling victim to the social media craze just as intensely as their teenagers. There's nothing like an eight-year-old saying, "I'll only (dance, sing, etc.) if you don't video it, Mom." How's that for a slap in the face to remind you that your priorities are being compromised? Kid's aren't stupid. They get it, trust me, they do. And that's why I paid the large sum to secure the TurnedOn.com URL because it's our intention to make the concept a rallying cry for families across the world.

If we teach our children to look both ways before crossing the street and not to eat chocolate bars for dinner, then certainly we can set the example and remind them when it's alright to be logged on and when it's not. The Reverend Billy Graham often spoke on the importance of leaving a legacy of character and faith. If the trend to relegate our children to electronics or television at every instance we parents need some time to think or need quiet, then we won't be leaving the legacy, what they see on television or the internet will.

Experts say anywhere from 60 to 90 percent of children's socializing these days is digital. Let that sink in and then couple it with the fact that there is a significant decline in the number of children 6-12-years old who are playing organized sports. What about the fact that the average child today is only spending four to five hours a week outside? A week? I'd spend four to five hours a day outdoors.

So there it is again, the cruise control button. Do we do some real parenting or succumb to easy street and allow our children to sit in front of a screen all day?

Here's what you need to realize and do your own research if you don't believe me, the record clearly shows that even the pioneers of the technology age, the giants of the revolution, who made and continue to make millions on it, realize the dangers it presents on the horizon.

BusinessInsider.com wrote that Microsoft CEO Bill Gates capped his daughter's screen time when she began developing "an unhealthy attachment" to video games. And he wouldn't let her have a cell phone until she was fourteen. It was also stated that the late Apple CEO Steve Jobs strictly limited his kids' use of technology at home and prohibited them from using the new iPad.

The Waldorf School of the Peninsula, a prestigious private school in Silicon Valley in which the kids of many tech giants attend, doesn't allow children under 11 to use electronic devices, instead encouraging them to cook, knit and make go-karts. And finally, in December 2017, Fox News interviewed former Facebook Executive Chamath Palihapitiya who said he would not allow his children to use the platform and he feels "tremendous guilt" over helping to "create tools that are ripping apart the social fabric of how society works."

There's your sign.

WHAT ARE WE MISSING?

I can use my smartphone to look up the weather, get driving directions, see a restaurant menu, watch a movie preview or take a yoga class. All on this tiny screen in the palm of my hand. But let's not kid ourselves, it's still a screen. What in the REAL WORLD are we missing out on to look at that screen? I feel like my generation, Generation X, has the best vantage point because we're old enough to know what life was like before this phenomenon, and we've had a front-row seat to what it's meant to our culture. It's the younger generations, the Millennials, Gen Y and Gen Z who grew up, dare I say, not knowing what they're missing. That scares me. You can't miss what you don't know, so at times it can be tough explaining to our kids that it really is better to go to the park and play real football rather than sit on the bean bag and play Madden for hours.

Case in point, my girls used to love YouTube reality shows like *Ryan's World*, *JoJo Siwa* and *Ninja Kidz*. How they find these, I have no idea. One day I sat and watched Ninja Kidz with them, and on the surface it's completely harmless, even educational, as a family of brothers and sisters talks about physical fitness, does chores, and performs martial arts skits. On the surface, that's great. I have no complaints with the content. But at the end of each episode, the kids in the video talk about their number of likes and followers, after which they solicit comments and interaction. If you're the parents of these actors, no problem, they're not only super active but they're getting paid large amounts of money in YouTube ads. Not so great if you're the parents on the other side of the screen, pleading with your kid to turn off the computer or TV and go outside to be active.

According to socialblade.com, *Ninja Kidz* has just shy of five million subscribers. On the day I looked, they'd had 99,295,500 views in the last thirty days and estimated earnings between $24.8K and $397.2K a month. According to *Variety Magazine*, Ryan's World pulled in 26 million dollars in 2019. Before you label me an angry or jealous parent, I'm in no way castigating these children or their parents as I'm in favor of their entrepreneurial endeavors. In fact, I don't mind my girls watching them in limited amounts. The bigger point here is that I'm trying to draw attention to is the bizarre fact that children are making millions of dollars off of having other kids watch them play. To me, that's a sign of a culture on the brink of disaster.

As parents, don't we have to take responsibility? After all, kids take their cues from adults, and what have we been teaching them? *The Bachelor. Survivor. Keeping Up With The Kardashians.* We've made binge-watching other people doing normal things acceptable. Rewind to the 1970s and 80s. I remember my parents watching maybe one or two television shows in an entire week, and if anything was a habit, it was Johnny Carson. Are you ready for this? According to a recent Nielson report, adults in the United States watch five hours of television per day. That amounts to 35 hours a week or 77 days in a year. And it's not harmless entertainment anymore, a study in the *Journal of the American Heart Association* reported that adults who watched more than three hours of TV per day doubled their risk of premature death compared to those who watched less.

Let's talk about the phrase binge-watching I mentioned in the previous paragraph. It's defined as the practice of watching multiple episodes of a television program in rapid succession, typically by means of DVDs or digital streaming. Is this even something we should feel comfortable admitting to? Being proud to be a couch potato?

It's not just television, it's technology in general. Experts say that more than half of the population now spends six or more hours in front of a screen each day—that's one-quarter of their day. Is all of that bad or frivolous? No, of course not, as I mentioned, these devices we use have become an essential component to our jobs, even providing some sort of freedom from a desk. I'm looking at one right now as I type. But is there something we're missing here? Sure there is. As a person gets older, they naturally realize how many things of their youth they took for granted. Great hair. Great skin. A smaller waist. A lot less stress. But will these next generations add to that list the regret of how much time they've wasted watching other people's lives through a screen? Is our population becoming more content to watch rather than live? Can we muster up the courage to take our lives back and reclaim some of our humanity, or will we only live to regret wasted opportunity? In the words of the immortal Dr. Seuss, "How did it get so late so soon? It's night before it's afternoon. December is here before it's June. My goodness, how the time has flown. How did it get so late so soon?"

WHAT ARE WE BRINGING INTO OUR HOMES?

It's not just that we're watching more; it's also what we're watching. At the halftime performance of the 2020 Super Bowl in Miami, we witnessed Jennifer Lopez dangling from a stripper pole (that's what it was) in a barely-there bodysuit as dozens of dancers below reached up and groped her sliding down. Not exactly what I'd hoped to see with my daughters sitting on either side of me that game. But what really lowered the bar was J-Lo's own 11-year old daughter taking the stage with mom moments later. The next day, when I picked my second grader up from school, without prompting, she said that the halftime show was the talk of the elementary lunchroom today.

So now the Super Bowl is something I must question watching with my family?

What's left? What barrier of decency is there to be conquered by television or the internet? How did we sink so far so fast? It wasn't that long ago that Elvis couldn't dance in a suit on Ed Sullivan or Jim Morrison couldn't sing "Girl we couldn't get much higher." Seems less than petty by today's standards, and if we look at how television has changed over the last couple of decades and what satellite or the internet has brought into our homes, we'd have to be crazy to question what the future holds.

Again, call me old fashioned, but I want you to pay close attention to how even the names of the shows we watch have drastically changed, then tell me if I'm overreacting. I remember not too long ago, there was; *Happy Days, Family Ties, Cheers, Love Boat, Good Times, Family Affair, Friends, Highway to Heaven.* Do you see a theme?

Today, we have shows like *Secrets and Lies, Criminal Minds, Scream Queens, American Horror Story, Ice Cold Killers, Homicide Hunter, Evil Lives Here, Murder Calls* and *Lucifer* (yes there is a show named after the Devil just in case those other titles were too subtle or benevolent).

And we have the audacity to wonder where we're going wrong and why we live in a violent culture. Should we be that surprised when we are inviting it into our homes?

And second only to violence is the newfound obsession with fame. The seemingly innocent shows I watch with our girls on television all have a weirdly common theme—they are centered around attention, popularity, and fame. Two Disney Channel shows, *Liv and Maddie* and *Coop and Cami Ask the World,* that my girls love, are both about famous kids. Liv is a teen pop star/ actor, and her twin (played by the same actress) is a regular teenager who loves basketball. Coop and Cami are a brother and sister team who also revel in notoriety at a young age. Wikipedia says the show "centers on two middle school siblings who make nearly all of their decisions in life crowdsourcing opinions from their millions of followers on Cooper's online channel 'Would You Rather?'" So, we're tackling the growing depression problem among our youth by sending them the message that you're really only relevant if you have millions of followers and people know who you are.

THE MISSING LINK

Is the family under attack, and can we turn things around? Is this a small problem that will work itself out? Is our mental health at stake? Remember the quote by TD Jakes where he points out that people feel alone even when they are around other people these days. It's like watching a balloon deflate in slow motion. It seems as if we just don't know how to patch it up and get it floating again.

We can make the biggest difference by prioritizing our sense of presence when we're in the company of others and by pouring affection into our homes. Do you need a television or computer in every room of the house? Does everybody at the restaurant need to have their phone on the table? Remember, our spouses, our children and our friends experience anxiety knowing at any second the conversation could be interrupted.

WHAT ABOUT LOVE?

A 2018 study by researchers at Penn State University concluded that small gestures, such as hugging, holding hands, and random acts of kindness all top the list of how the majority of Americans feel loved and appreciated. In short, physical actions, as opposed solely to verbal expressions, were greater indicators of love among participants.

I'm big on physical affection with my wife and girls, but it's not something that was bred in me. As a child, I grew up in a house with a tremendous amount of verbal love, yet very little physical affection amongst the family. Over the years, I realized it was mostly a generational thing. Remember, twentieth-century fathers were bread earners and disciplinarians, not so much huggers and kissers, and, unfortunately, my Dad got more open hands to the face than open arms around the waist when he was a child.

As I mentioned earlier, it's hard for a child to miss what a child doesn't know. No big deal for most of my life. But then something happened to me when I was about 19 that led me to question if I was missing out on something.

While a friend's house one day, we were shooting hoops in the driveway when his father pulled up in the car. A second-generation Cuban, having come to the United States just after Castro assumed power, he was a rather large man of broad stature. As for us, we lifted weights like it was our job. We were both bearded and muscular. I say this because here comes this big burly guy about to walk by his bigger, burlier son, and what happens? He embraced him with a huge hug and a kiss on the cheek. To me, this was shocking. I'd never in my life seen a father and son display that type of physical affection for one another. It was so foreign to me, yet so natural for them.

Nothing was mentioned at the time, but I couldn't stop thinking about how easy it was for that father and son to show their love. I knew my father loved me with all of his heart and would do anything in the world for me, yet affection was extremely uncommon in our house, even amongst my brother and sisters. Kory Floyd, Professor of Communication at the University of Arizona, says his research has shown that, in general, men are more likely to communicate affection by doing something supportive rather than making verbal expressions, which makes sense to me.

He goes on to hypothesize that a father's lack of affection "is complicated by the need to negotiate a complex tension between masculinity and intimacy." That also resonates.

Two weeks after that incident, my family was gathered in the living room watching old 35-millimeter film of a childhood vacation—you know where everybody looks like they are moving in fast forward and there's no sound. Very awkward to watch but a treasure, nonetheless.

So here we are on the couch, Pops on one side, Sis on the other, Mom going back and forth from the kitchen to the living room as we share a few memories. We're laughing and giggling it up for the first few minutes, and then everything changes. The scene showed me, about two years old on a family vacation, with my father as he picks me up and starts bouncing me up and down, tickling my belly and kissing me on the cheek. Waterfalls. I instantly became 190 muscular pounds of sobbing teenager, the kind of crying in which you can't catch your breath.

Immediately, my eyes closed, and my head went into my hands. Half embarrassed and half in disarray, it seemed like forever that nobody was asking what was wrong. I remember counting the seconds in my head, thinking, "Wow, nobody thinks this is weird? Anybody gonna come to my rescue?" Finally, my mother put her arms around me and asked, "What's wrong?" I tried to catch my breath to speak but couldn't. I just kept sobbing. Three decades later, and the tears are flowing even now as I'm recalling this.

Finally, I calm down enough to get a sentence out. I said, "Here we are this big beautiful family where everybody loves each other, and we feel like we know it, but we don't show it. We don't hug. We don't kiss. We don't show any affection. I know we feel it, but what good is it if we don't show it or say it?"

It was a watershed moment in more ways than one.

The next day, I decided to take a bold step. I called everybody to the living room and I said, "We can't do this anymore. From now on, this family is not just going to assume we love one another. We're going to show it and say it, no matter how uncomfortable we are doing it." Then, we did a long group hug, everybody said "I love you," and we all cried.

The family came together that day like a scene from *The Wonder Years*, and there were still times after that when we struggled and it felt awkward. But it got better and the payoff is that today in my home, with my children, we never let a moment go by where we don't hug, kiss, caress, and say we love each other. More often than not my daughters are like, "Okay, Okay, Daddy, you can let me go now."

The importance of physical affection between parents and children can't be overstated. Research shows Oxytocin, known as the bonding hormone, is released during times of close physical contact. Affection has also been shown to lower cortisol levels for both parent and child, thereby leading to improved immune system functioning.

If you were raised in a home or during a generation where physical touch and affection between parent and child was rare or nonexistent, this very instinctive act may not feel so natural, especially for fathers. It may take time and effort. As our culture becomes more and more inundated with technology, and it tears into the bonds of a family, physical affection within the home is now more important than ever.

Turn on the switch that makes a difference. Fathers, lead the way. Show your wife affection in front of your children. Love is infectious, and daughters need to see how to be treated while sons need that example of how to treat. Then hold, hug and kiss them too. Our sons and daughters can never get too old or too busy to give mom and dad some love. As families, we can't afford to take the humanness out of our households.

HE WHO CHOOSES TO LEAD MUST BE NOBLE

Author and radio host David Jeremiah says, "A girl's father is the first man in her life, and probably the most influential." Being a father makes you a leader, but it is a responsibility to be earned. It doesn't mean you have to be perfect as I fall short quite often. It means you have to be accountable to the office.

If anyone aspires to the office of the overseer, he desires a noble task. Therefore, an overseer must be above reproach, the husband of one wife, sober-minded, self-controlled, respectable, hospitable, able to teach, not a drunkard, not violent but gentle, not quarrelsome, not a lover of money. He must manage his own household well, with all dignity keeping his children submissive, for if someone does not know how to manage his own house, how will he care for God's church? (1 Timothy 3:1-6)

That's a long checklist God provided us Dad's with, eh? A lot to live up to. And being a father today is more difficult than what our parents or grandparents experienced. On top of the desire to succeed in business and the call to fulfill our own personal desires (golf, football, cars etc.), we must find a way to be more present (there's that word again) in the lives of our wives and children. And by present, I'm not just talking about in the physical sense. Hey, I'm in the same room as them. That counts as being present right? Not really.

You see the role of the father is under attack as well. Hollywood and the Internet have punked us out, portraying us as buffoons, pushovers and dweebs. Again, I know this because I'm highly in tune with what my girls watch on networks like Nickelodeon or the Disney Channel. I find myself frequently asking, "Where is the husband in this show? Why do I never see the dad? Where are the Steven Keatons, the Philip Banks, and Tony Micellis of today?" They're missing.

In many of the shows my girls watch, the father is either absent or a man who possesses no authority or backbone and has no clue about what's going on in the real world.

If we step back and take a zoomed-out view of what's happening to the family, both in real life and through our devices, it's simply being influenced and transformed by encroaching technology. The bandwidth with which our parents operated is out of date and insufficient by today's standard, and I don't mean that literally. If we, as parents, aren't highly in tune and on top of what is being brought into our homes, chances are we will be shocked by who or what is influencing our children.

Again, the answer isn't clear yet. Information is too new. We're stuck between a rock and a hard spot. Balance is the call of our generation.

Millennial women are most likely the first generation virtually immersed in technology. It's estimated that nearly a million millennial women become mothers annually, and more of them are competing for equal, if not, primary bread-winner roles in the family. They are also working from the home a lot more compared to their mothers who proceeded them.

A *Today Show* survey found that 63 percent of working dads envy stay-at-home dads, and about one in five (19 percent) said they feel guilty about not being present enough with their children. Seventeen percent said they suffer from dad guilt about working too much. But I thought technology was supposed to free us up to have more time with our kids? Wasn't it supposed to make like easier? Maybe it has, but we're just obsessed with finding ways to fill in the gaps by doing more stuff in the name of the "Hustle."

Recent research shows the average working father spends 35 minutes a day with his children, only seven of which is actually spent talking to them. Good when you consider it was just five minutes in 1974 but still, you cannot shape the character and form the mind of a child in seven minutes a day.

15 THERE'S STILL TIME FOR YOU

If you have had or were a teenager, then you know that this is the time when boys get a bit of hair under the arms, their voice changes and they get zits. Girls start to develop breasts, begin their menstrual cycle, and get blemishes. It all happens around the age of 15, and in Spanish cultures, when a girl turns 15, she celebrates her Quinceanera, a religious and social event marking her passage from girlhood to womanhood. Similar cultural rituals occur for boys, most notably the Jewish Bat Mitzvah at age 13. This is said to be where the passing of responsibility for a child's actions (law, tradition, ethics) are given from the parents and into the responsibility of their son.

I draw attention to these years because of the transition they represent, and even though a son or daughter at these ages may have three or four more years under their parent's roof, by this time, most of the important parts of their identity have already been formed. Their sense of self-awareness has taken shape as their values, behaviors and judgment have been developed and pruned in large part in the home, by the parents. This is also about the time the heavy-duty influences of the world outside the home take aim, when junior high and high school cliques form, and children attempt to fit into some sort of social hierarchy.

Looking back on what I remember about those years, it's pretty scary to know what your child is about to go through. Being involved in the self-development world, I know many parents wish there was a personal growth program for kids.

To which I say, there is.

CAN I KICK IT? YES YOU CAN

"I promise to be a good person, with knowledge in the mind, honesty in the heart, strength in the body. I promise to make good friends and to become a black belt leader."

I want you to imagine a chorus of about fifteen to twenty little munchkins, age four to six years old, yelling this at the top of their lungs. As a parent, this Tiny Tiger oath was music to my ears. When I first heard our daughter Ella, at four, echo this in unison with the other kids in her class, my eyes welled up with tears of joy.

It's been proven over and over again that kids who participate in extracurricular activities and sports associate better with other children and have more discipline in their scholastic activities, however, the American Tae Kwon Do Association (ATA) is so much more than a sport, it's like a blueprint for kids to stay on the right path in life. They teach life skills like discipline, honesty, belief, communication, respect and self-esteem. All things which I'm confident that most parents would love to instill in their children. In fact, on their website, it states that part of their mission is to develop more than just winning athletes.

I happen to be partial to and know a great deal about the ATA because Angelike is a third-degree black belt and taught at ATA schools for nine years. But now, as a parents, watching the Tiny Tigers perform from the outside, Angelike says she's become aware of things she couldn't see as the instructor.

"I know how hard it is for a parent sometimes just to get our kids to sit still and listen," she said. "There's something about this forum that crosses that barrier and promotes, obedience, self-control, and self-awareness."

From my own perspective, I noticed how the instructor, Master Mark Burns, was teaching the same principles we'd been learning as adults in self-development and I came to a realization that rings true for both adults and children, people need some type of accountability from another person who isn't related to them. That was the hardest thing about Angelike and me going from employees to entrepreneurs—there was nobody to report to or clock in, it all boiled down to self-discipline.

The second commonality we noticed in both our teaching and martial arts was the reality that we are in a softer time and place where people seem less resilient and less likely to want to work through the difficult parts of life. There's this notion where people feel like they deserve credit for simply showing up. When I discussed this thought with Master Burns, he shared an interesting opinion.

"I constantly see kids being rewarded for things they should normally do," Burns said. "And they are being rescued too quickly by their parents when adversity arrives. If we're going to build strong minds and bodies, we have to be willing to let our children fail and not be in a hurry to try and fix it for them.

Yes, we can be there to build them back up, but as mentors, we adults need to practice the patience and discipline to tell them what they did wrong and how to correct it rather than just taking the blame away from them and fixing it as quickly as we can. That's life, and it's how we grow."

That's what I would call a Turned-On philosophy. Tae Kwon Do has taught my wife and my girls that we can't rush through things just because they are a little bit uncomfortable or because we want immediate results. If we do that, we skip over so many other opportunities that need to happen in order for us to grow. The divine order of life and an order in martial arts, they mirror one another. There is no entitlement. If you fail the test or don't show up for classes, you don't get the next belt.

When she was coming up through the ranks, Angelike took a blow to the face from her instructor. She says she immediately got angry and blamed him for her bloody nose. Her instructor responded by saying, "Ms. Psoinos (her maiden name) rather than blame, you should bow and say thank you for the lesson as your nose shouldn't have been where my fist was." Sounds a lot like a lesson that Mr. Miyagi would've given Daniel in *The Karate Kid*.

It's also a pretty tough lesson for many of us to try to digest especially in these times of the snowflake mentality, but to this day, she insists that he was right, it was not her instructor's fault, and had she been doing the form correctly, she would not have been hit in the face.

Life and life lessons have become a little softer, can we agree? We've lost a bit of our edge, our toughness as a people. Look around our college campuses, there is no shortage of safe spaces for those who have had their feelings hurt by something some- one said. Personal responsibility is no longer taught as a virtue, and that is a recipe for disaster for the future our children will inherit.

In today's virtual world, for the most part, losing or getting punched means just hitting the reset button, no harm done. But that's not reality is it? Master Burns ended our conversation with something so relevant to our times, saying, "Children need to learn real character, not characters in a video game. They need to know real people do really amazing things when given the opportunity and that it's more important to level up yourself, rather than level up your character on a game."

CHAPTER EIGHT

TURN ON YOUR NEIGHBORHOOD

> *"If you don't know the guy on the other side of the world,*
> *love him anyway because he's just like you.*
> *He has the same dreams, the same hopes and fears.*
> *It's one world, pal. We're all neighbors."*
> *— Frank Sinatra*

Funny Farm is a 1988 comedy starring Chevy Chase who plays Andy Farmer, a writer craving inspiration and a simpler life. He and his wife move from the city to a small town in Vermont that resembles something right out of a Norman Rockwell painting. Once he gets there, though, he quickly realizes it's not all he thought it would be and longs to go home.

I reference this because not too long ago, we made a similar decision, moving to the suburbs of Tennessee into what they call a porch community. The reason? We craved a simpler way of life and truer sense of neighborhood like those of the days we grew up in. With all of its history and tradition, the neighborhood has played a pivotal role in the establishment of America's story, but it seems as if it's not just Americans who feel as if the neighborhood, with and all of its charm, has fallen victim to the modern pace of life.

Mark Perry, Chief Executive of VIVID, a London-based home development company, said, "We need to think harder about how we build new homes and neighborhoods, and create the right environment for communities to thrive. Our research shows that the most crucial part of the home is the social fabric of the neighborhood in which it's embedded. The social value of tenure mix and giving people the opportunities to interact with each other and reduce neighborhood tension."

Notice the use of words *mix* and *interact*? In our neighborhood, all of the houses have a big front porch, and the garages are back loaded, very similar to how communities were originally designed in the 50s and 60s. This was a time and era in America's history when there was a substantial shift in the way people worked. The affordability of the automobile and the construction of a vast system of highways offered people an ability to leave the dense population of the city yet still commute back and forth to work from something called suburbs. This was a time when the single-family home started to become the new standard, and developers intentionally constructed neighborhoods to foster a sense of community and a greater sense of belonging.

A return to that same concept is why we chose to move. We fell in love with the nostalgia of living on a street where everybody would know each other's names, and we could sit on the porch each evening petting the family dog while sipping lemonade and waving at neighbors. I knew it was perhaps a lot more nostalgia than reality so we asked ourselves the question, are we searching for utopia or just an image of what we think it should be?

Our hopes were especially high considering that in the five houses we lived prior to this one, we never truly felt at home. We hardly ever saw or talked with the neighbors at our previous homes and had this notion that the next move would somehow change that. But with each move, we just experienced more of the same, neighborhood cliques, people too busy with their own lives to make time for others and seasonal neighbors who were only there parts of the year.

Leave it to Beaver it was not. It had the right look, and we definitely did a lot more waving to people. One neighbor even gave us a Hallmark card and a $50 gift card to Target as a welcoming gift. But guess what? The big revelation was that nothing really changed at all. After the first couple of months, we were still craving connection and feeling isolated, and other than the occasional dog walk and hello, had very little interaction with the people who lived around us.

As you might imagine, our first inclination was to cast blame on everybody in the neighborhood. We levied the same recycled complaints and excuses from our previous experiences, i.e., these people aren't friendly, nobody here wants a relationship. These people are hermits.

But then something shifted. We did something we hadn't done before. We turned the mirror around on ourselves and experienced this "ah-ha" moment that told us that regardless of how many times we moved or how the community was designed, real connection always comes down to the human desire to take action and be proactive. Maybe it's not our neighbors? Maybe it's us? You see, our house, our garden, our new SUV or alma mater flag hanging over the garage isn't going to do the talking for us no matter how appealing or interesting we think they are. It comes down to being intentional about deliberately fostering the connection we desire in a world where, let's be honest, most everybody craves it but has just become either too bashful or too busy to go after it.

Shortly after this epiphany, I began to realize that despite us never really feeling content in a home at the time, we always looked back at each one with very fond memories and a strong desire to go back and play in this yard once more or go on that boat again. It was just another indication, further validation, that we take our current state of being for granted, never truly appreciating the present. Does that feel familiar to you? Are you one of those people who always thinks that something is missing, some clue to unlock true contentment, that you can't quite put our finger on?

If you take anything away from this part here, let it be this; don't live your days in a constant state of daydreaming of what could be. Be content where you are, with what you have, for someday, surely, you'll look back on it with fond memories and long to go back.

THE NEIGHBORLY NEIGHBOR

I have a question. Be honest here. Have you ever found yourself at the grocery store and ducked back out of the aisle because you saw a neighbor that you may be trying to avoid? We've all done it. Or how many times do you see a neighbor and say, "We gotta get together soon," only to have it never happen? Then you run into them again a month or so later and say with a certain degree of guilt, "Hey, we've just been so busy, but we really do need to catch up." And again, it doesn't happen.

Are we really too busy, or are we just afraid to be a little uncomfortable? Cultivating connections and friendships in your own neighborhood is important, but there are a few challenges holding us back these days.

The first is, we're just too impatient. Like everything else in our "I want it now" world, if it doesn't happen quickly and easily, we're likely to slough it off and move on, not willing to put in the work.

Angelike and I moved six times in our first eight years of marriage, twice for work and twice to care for her mother who was sick. The other two moves were just throwing darts trying to find our happy place. A year after moving to Tennessee, we contacted our real estate agent and asked her to start showing our house. But then something happened, we slowed down, we became way more intentional about getting out and connecting. We used technology for good, actively searching out community on social networks and on local websites. We went to street fairs and rodeos, new churches and restaurants. We took action and sought connection and what do you know, we found it.

I feel like I'm one of the most outgoing people you'd ever meet. Literally, I talk to everyone, everywhere I go. So, while connecting wasn't new for me, the patience, follow-through, reconnecting and putting the devices away when it was time to go out was. That was the game-changer. We realized that in order to live in a great place, we have to "be" in the right place, and not physically but mentally, meaning state of mind.

That brings me to the second point, one that should be painfully obvious, and that is that we (human beings) are just not getting out of the house enough. If your idea of going outside is peeking your head out the front door is to see if the UPS driver dropped off a package on your porch, then I'm speaking directly to you.

We've advanced our way of life so much that we've eliminated the need to leave home. Almost every necessity can be brought to us, therefore, we've somewhat become hermits without even realizing it. Food, groceries and clothing are delivered to our doorstep with the touch of a button. The in-home opportunities for entertainment in the form of television, movies, and video games allow us to hunker down in the living room for hours, even days. Simply put, it's hard to hang out if you don't go out.

Do you know your neighbors? Do you even know their names? When I was growing up, we knew who lived behind us, beside us, and across from us. We knew what they did for a living and shared stories and pleasantries on almost a daily basis. I remember taking my bike as a child and riding it five or six blocks in either direction with a bevy of houses I could stop at to ask kids to play. And we looked out for one another.

Now, in many neighborhoods, that's not so. There is a mind your own business, don't worry about us attitude. There were even many instances in our porch-friendly community, where we got the initial "Hello, you must be the new family" welcome and then boom, ghost town.

Occasionally we'll peer out the window and see a neighbor going from their car into the house and go directly into mischievous curiosity mode like Tom Hanks in the movie The Burbs, "I wonder what they're up to." We're always curious as humans it seems, but never quite enough to seek out an answer. For the most part, we'd rather just speculate. And speculation is often a road you don't want to go down.

KICK IT ROOT DOWN

Over the course of my life, I've lived in Fort Lauderdale, Charlotte, Scottsdale, and Nashville, all very different types of communities and all on Forbes 2018 Top 20 list of fastest-growing cities. Why? What's the common thread you ask? Well, what you might expect—mostly the economy, amenities, taxes, and weather. Those are the big ones. People with the ability to live anywhere want to move to these popular locations for those reasons.

But that provides another problem, with our 21st-century mobility comes more choices and more deliberating. Just like the dating apps we spoke of earlier, except this time we're taking the adage *The grass is always greener on the other side* to an almost literal meaning. If it's not the ideal weather, the ideal restaurant scene or the ideal traffic situation, looking fondly at another state will always be a tiny tug preventing you from making a solid choice to hunker down and make a permanent home.

And while the ability to move freely sounds like progress perfected at first, consider this observation that I feel is rather telling. I have many good friends in the Midwest, Illinois, Wisconsin and Minnesota. I think they'd be the first to admit it's not on anybody's top list for weather, and Wisconsin and Minnesota are among the top ten states with the highest state income tax rate. But despite the frigid winters and government constantly picking their pockets, many of my friends with the means to move don't. It appears to be for one huge reason, community. Heck, even when I was just visiting those states, I felt like I was home. It took one visit to Lambeau Field to make me feel like the favorite son of Green Bay. There was a sense of community, dare I say humanity, that I'd not really experienced in some other parts of the country. It was palpable, and, in addition, the family bonds often ran very deep in these places. It was generational. So I could understand why they'd stay.

One thing I've learned about laying down roots over the years is that these days there is a good chance you'll probably be picking them up as well. The trends show a population on the move because the economy is changing so fast and the marketplace is often is the greatest predictor of movement. According to a survey by the Census Bureau, the average American will move 11.4 times during his or her lifetime! Even if you haven't been forced to relocate yet, it's likely to happen in your future.

Born and raised in Miami, Florida I can tell you it's 180 degrees from Franklin, Tennessee. Founded in 1799 and taking its namesake from Ben Franklin, this little Civil War town is lined with battlefields and cow pastures. There's an old theater with a classic marquee out front and locally owned country boutiques by the dozen. But even here, in my little slice of utopia, I quickly began to see cracks. Among the southern charm, there's still a keeping-up-with-the-Joneses mentality, still crime taking place, and still an increasing feeling of disassociation with one another. I guess I was naive to think that cultural phenomenons like Real Housewives of Beverly Hills and Keeping Up with the Kardashians wouldn't infiltrate the way we think and treat one another even in the smallest towns of suburbia.

The funny part is everybody points the finger at someone else. Nobody wants to take accountability for being the problem because it's easier to deflect. We even have a Facebook page for our neighborhood intended for community, but it's more like a sounding board for everybody's displeasure with something. It was so hostile and so divisive that I had to get off.

That leaves us with the bigger question; do we even want a better relationship with our neighbors? Is it important? Sure, our children go to school with one another, and we run into one another occasionally at the grocery store or park. But we don't need or rely on a community like we did in the past? It's not essential for our survival as a race like it once was. Admittedly I ask, or say this, without a real clear cut answer. I'm really just trying to poke the bear and suppose only time will tell.

It does feel like the pendulum will come swinging back, though. I can't imagine that a body which was hardwired for connection wouldn't grow tired of being locked up and alone inside. If the pandemic of 2020 taught us anything, it's that when something is taken away, you realize you took it for granted. Not being able to go to our local bar or restaurant, visit our favorite store or movie theatre was something we all missed. But we also found out something that was a blessing in disguise; that when forced to stay home, we did get outside more often, we did thirst for community and crave human connection. And that's why I feel like a neighborhood revival is around the corner. The question is, how do we start it on our block first?

WE DON'T NEED A CIVIL WAR

My father began dating my mother when they were 16. But it was no easy task. My grandfather (my mother's dad) didn't like Italians and forbade my German mother to see him. There was just one problem with that... my dad had absolutely zero Italian in him. He was Scottish. He just happened to look very Italian.

The great melting pot has come a long way since the 1950s, but we're still melting. America is still the light of the world, a city on a hill. Land of the free. And despite our differences in skin color and language, we are more alike than we are different, and so I ask, where else does *love your neighbor* come as close to being true than right here? Despite what the news tries to tell us, we're good people for the most part. Remember the Sinatra quote at the top of the chapter, we all have the same dreams, hopes and fears. We're all neighbors.

It doesn't mean we're perfect or there isn't quite a bit of tension in our lives today, but the truth is, there has always been strife in the world, and the good old days weren't always good for everybody. Each generation has had its unique and scary set of problems.

In our little slice of Tennessee, there's a historical battlefield within a two-minute walk from my house. If you know anything about history, the Civil War was one of the bloodiest and most savage wars in our country's history. It literally pitted neighbor against neighbor, brother against brother. The stakes were high, and the issues grand. It's hard not to ask the question, why couldn't the Civil War have been handled more civilly? You might be familiar with philosopher George Santayana's famous quote, "Those who do not learn history are doomed to repeat it," and right now, more than ever, technology has afforded us the opportunity to learn history. Real history.

But history can be distorted, and fake news occurs on both sides of the aisle. The fact that young people actually have a favorable outlook on socialism tells us that schools aren't doing a good job teaching history either. Penetrating D.C. or public education is a daunting task, so let's stick to the neighborhood here and ask what we can do to affect the right kind of change. Allow me to pose this question to you: during the last election, did you ever drive past a political yard sign that actually influenced your vote? Did you once stop and say, "Oh look, honey, Mr. and Mrs. Johnson want Candidate A, we should vote for them, too!"

I'm guessing, like me, your answer is no.

While politics has always been a hot button topic, traditionally neighbors either kept their views to themselves or handled them with some degree of decorum. That went out the window with social media. Gone. The prevalence of expressing personal political ideology on social media has become one of the greatest inhibitors to real community of our time. It's placing a black eye on generations of people (across the globe) that habitually and often intentionally attempt to ruffle the feathers of their neighbors with uncivilized and unbridled attacks. I have struggled with voicing an often strong and polarizing opinion. At one point, I had to ask myself, what good is it doing? If somebody doesn't agree with your ideology, you don't have to be best friends with them, but you can certainly be civil.

Getting back to the yard signs... during the last election, they were littered all over our neighborhood, and I'd estimate a quarter to half of all homes had one. Many houses had two or more. And for what? In my opinion, it only accomplished two things: (1) it made me wish for the election to be over quicker and (2) caused more division among people sharing a community, schools, and churches. So now every two years, I feel like it'll be a mini civil war in neighborhoods across America with none of it actually moving the needle. These yard signs might as well have just read, "THIS IS WHO I AM FOR; CONSENT OR BE GONE WITH YOU."

Yes or no—in our neighborhoods and on social media, we've become less social, less cordial and less tolerant? Is anybody really debating? Anybody actually listening? That needs to be addressed and addressed in a mature way. If not, what kind of neighborhood or community are we leaving to our children? Can't we learn a lesson from our past?

I know some of the greatest minds of the 20th century were a great deal more effective in making a statement. As evidence, take a look at this passage from a famous American writer and really try to absorb what it means.

From start to finish, I found no strangers. If I had, I might be able to report them more objectively. But these are my people, and this is my country. If I found matters to criticize and to deplore, they were tendencies equally present in myself. If I were to prepare one immaculately inspected generality it would be this; for all of our enormous geographic range, for all of our sectionalism, for all of our interwoven breeds drawn from every part of the ethnic world, we are a nation, a new breed.

Americans are much more American than they are Northerners, Southerners, Westerners, or easterners.

That passage is from *Travels with Charley*, a book by the aforementioned writer John Steinbeck. It depicts Steinbeck's thoughts during a road trip with his dog Charley. In it, he asks, "What are Americans like today?" It was published in 1962, but here I am in 2020, asking the same question. And honestly, I feel like I would provide the same answer. We're more alike than we are different, and if I were to criticize anybody, I would have to look inward and make the same judgments of myself. The latter part is the hardest to do for me, and I think most of us. "I'm right and you're wrong" or "I know better than you do" typically gets us nowhere but more frustration, anger and ultimately division.

The outliers and instigators are really given a bigger stage than they deserve and that's why most people's opinion about the state of cordialness in our country is low.

If you think America is in a bad place, it's because each of us in America is in a bad place. Think about it, are we communicating civilly or with dysfunction? Are we using our words to connect or to control? Are we listening to who our neighbors are or assuming the worst? Before we can improve communication and discourse with others, we must improve it with ourselves (intrapersonal communication). I believe that is where hope lives, in our spirit. Hope lives in the fact we all have the same maker and I believe, intrinsically, the same goals; to make a living, marry somebody you love and raise a family in peace.

We'd be fooling ourselves though if we weren't aware that in today's culture many people are more than willing to just blame others for their lack of happiness. And when that fails, then they blame God. Do you or somebody you know question God first when things look bad, when nobody seems to be able to get along? He's an easy scapegoat for our human deficiencies. People will ask, "How can a loving God stand by while such things happen in the world?" Guess what? That's the plan, and it's the world, not God, that has us fighting one another rather than finding common ground.

The Bible specifically says do not conform to the pattern of what? This world.

It suggests instead that we be transformed by the renewing of what? Our mind.

How is that possible, I wondered. I live on this planet 24/7. The world (aka Culture) shapes me, does it not? How could I possibly transform?

Just when I asked this question, I got another word from Pastor Driscoll that made me see with new eyes. He said, "Our citizenship is there (pointing to Heaven), but our residence is

here (on earth).... and as citizens of that kingdom and residents
of this culture, we want to ask, 'how do I live in light of my
citizenship and bring the kingdom to the earth', because
ultimately that's best for all the people."

Go back and read that again. It's liberating because it's true.
Whether you believe in God or not, it's hard not to agree that
biblical principles like love, compassion, and kindness wouldn't
make our homes and neighborhoods a better place, yes? Of
course, they would, but that doesn't sell cable news spots. It
doesn't sell the fear of being on different ends of an issue that
we're told to fear. It doesn't make cash.

Driscoll also said, "Your biggest problem is not political; it's
moral and spiritual. And the biggest conflict is not between you
and someone else. It's between you and God."

If ever I've been in church and felt a mic-drop moment, this
was it. That made a ton of sense to me because only I can control
what I see (turn off the news). Only I can control what I do (talk
to my neighbors). And only I can make a difference, and that is
what I must do (make a difference).

Going back to the Steinbeck passage, "What are Americans
like today?" Would you say we're better or worse than our
parent's generation? I think we have our own unique fixing to
do. It begins with a look inside of ourselves and right outside
our front doors, in our neighborhoods. It requires intention.

We spend hundreds of thousands of dollars to buy a home.
And once we've spent the cash and planted ourselves there,
we're just going to put up an imaginary fort? One of my favorite
books is *Grace Notes* by Alexandra Stoddard, and in it, she writes,
"We all have neighbors. Greet them on the sidewalk or in the
elevator, but try not to peer through their windows. Windows
are to look out from, not into."

TWO TINY ADJUSTMENTS

I suggest the easiest way to make your neighborhood better is something we can all do with little to no effort... a smile and a wave. This is something I'm super intentional about, so much so I've figured out a way to make it a fun game with my daughters. I've challenged them to see who can get the most points. Each time they wave and say hello to a neighbor, they get one point. Whoever gets the most points that week gets frozen yogurt. I know it's silly, but it works. They see the value of going first, and conversely, they also see how unattractive it is when somebody doesn't reciprocate the smile or wave. Like Ella said, it's just a simple "Oh, they aren't turned on yet."

The second recommendation I'll make is borrowing from another recognizable phrase of our time. However, I'm going to take it from a fairly negative feel and put a positive spin on it, and that is, "If you see something, say something."

I think I speak for all of us when I say it's not fun to have to be on such high alert for things like terrorism or public shootings, and that's where *If you see something, say something* stems from. But imagine taking something so frightening and flipping it on its head in this way; if you see a neighbor outside, at the grocery store, or at your kid's school, even if you don't know them, make the effort to engage them. Say something! Don't allow the perceived busyness of your schedule to forbid you from slowing life down for a second to foster community.

Turn yourself into a master connector and watch how new friendships and opportunities blossom while misconceptions and stereotypes fade away. Remember, there isn't much difference between introverts and extroverts. Extroverts just act on their instincts more often.

Allow your neighbors grace. Stop judging others by standards we wouldn't hold to ourselves. You don't have to like your neighbor's taste in politics, fashion, or wine to still reap the benefits of their proximity. As we get older, it's healthy to realize that some things are better left either unsaid or just in the peripheral. In fact, it's healthy to be around other people who don't share your opinions on everything. That's why they don't have a separate high school for athletes, a separate one for academics, for band members, or the alternative kids because even at 16, we can get along, so why not at 40, 50, or 60?

CHAPTER NINE

TURN ON
YOUR CONFIDENCE

> *"Do not accept the roles that society foists on you.*
> *Recreate yourself by forging a new identity,*
> *one that commands attention and never bores the audience.*
> *Be the master of your own image rather than*
> *letting others define it for you."*
> *— Robert Greene*

Having worked as a journalist for almost two decades, I interviewed some of the best athletes and musicians the world has ever known. I'm also what you may call a documentary junkie, watching just about every biopic on musicians of the 60s, 70s, and 80s (John Coltrane, Nat King Cole, Eagles, Chicago, Miles Davis, Van Halen, and Fleetwood Mac) as well as athletes (Eric Dickerson, Kurt Warner, Walter Payton, Michael Jordan, and Larry Bird).

Gathering from my interviews and from what I learned watching documentaries, I began to see that every musician and every athlete who desired to be successful typically has one thing in common—they worked in and practiced their craft every day. These individuals determined who or what they wanted to be and then made it happen. So regardless of your chosen field, the fact remains, if it's possible in the world and somebody has done it before, that means it can be done again?

When we eliminate the popular excuse—*that's impossible*—then the only question left is, what will it take to get there.

History tells us, that in order to get there, we need to go to school to learn math, science, and English and then go to college.

I ask for what—more hypothetical learning in lieu of practical experience?

I want you to consider what you do now for a living and then think of all the other things you had to do in your classical (typical) education that contribute absolutely nothing to your current situation or income. The point isn't that basic skills in math, science and English aren't necessary; it's that our specific talents are often overlooked by an outdated way of looking at education. What are we doing with our valuable time when it comes to really honing in on our gifts? In other words, are you lingering in a job or career that you know isn't yours because you wasted a lot of valuable time focusing on skills you knew you'd probably never use? Then one day, somebody or some situation told you, "Well, this is all you know, so you must continue to work it."

A wise man once told me that clarity in life is really about a restoration of your consciousness, and a revival of your spirit. Because when your spirit is right it speaks to your mind and when your mind is right you see it manifest in your body thus making us capable of everything that we were put here to do.

Keep that in mind while I briefly tell you the story of Norman Cousins. The author and professor was given a 1 in 500 chance to live in 1964. Doctors said he had a few months left. What did he do? He went out and got a film projector, gathered up the funniest movies he could find and laughed himself to life. That was his protocol. Cousins did eventually die, in 1990, 26 years after initially being diagnosed with his life-threatening heart disease. Here is what he said, "Death is not the greatest loss in life. The greatest loss is what dies inside us while we live."

I can't tell you how many self-development seminars I've attended where there was a room full of middle-aged adults in tears over the path in which life had led them. Somewhere along the way, they died a little inside, and they were there in a desperate search to find meaning and contribution in their life. And that is where I feel confidence is king. Learning is not just about math, science and English, it's about how to write, speak and interact with confidence, therefore, you can assert your mark on the world. Something somewhere in regard to that is being lost on our youth.

The next thing we need to ask is when and where are the real-world and self-development skills being taught? If we're speaking of being TURNED ON and what it takes to gain confidence and make connections, wouldn't you agree that one of the primary things our children need to be up to skill on is communication? Of course, yet take a look at the younger generations, again, they're being lost to an existence of holding a device in their hand, to look another in the eye and speak has become awkward. Gerald R. Ford, the thirty-eighth President of the United States, once said, "If I went back to college again, I'd concentrate on two areas: learning to write and to speak before an audience. Nothing in life is more important than the ability to communicate effectively."

To that, I say, why wait until college? Why aren't we teaching children to be experts in communication in primary school? Why, then, aren't we teaching our youth the basics of human interaction? Why aren't they being led to discover their passions and gifts more intensely at an earlier age? I feel it is because we're stripping their confidence and putting them in cookie-cutter type curriculums. A one size fits all mentality that seems to be headed nowhere but backward.

Educators will say that all communication and self-development takes place in the periphery of the typical education, but I say that's not true. A lack of focus on team building and interactive projects seems to be hampering not only the economy but the way the younger generations interact with society overall.

By all accounts, higher education appears to be failing on a grand scale. A *Washington Post* article estimated that just 27 percent of graduates held a job that was closely related to their major. That means, like me, almost three-quarters of graduates have a very expensive degree sitting in their closet collecting dust.

One of the things neither college nor Google can teach is confidence. That comes from the streets and from actually doing, not hypotheticals in a classroom. If we're nurturing our youth to consume a seemingly endless amount of learning without the actual doing, spending a majority of their 20s in a classroom, how can we expect them to learn and fail faster?

Like me, you probably have spent a large portion of your youth sitting in a seat, taking notes from people who were classroom professionals, college professors who were tenured, telling you what to expect and how to act in the real world. Only one problem: it's not the real world.

We end up with notebooks full of theories, some valid and others outdated. We learn a lot of hypothetical situations and laboratory studies, some applicable and some frivolous. But in the end, the student ends up having very little real-world experience. Then you have the chicken or the egg dilemma. If you apply for a job, they want real-world experience, but how can you get real-world experience if you can't land a job?

One of my favorite t-shirts reads, "I could've Googled everything I learned in college." I love it because I made it up. And this brings us to a point of positive nature when it comes to advancing technology, and that is the ability to have a library in our homes.

Up until the last ten or twenty years, people went to a university for one main reason—geography. It was where all the knowledge resided. The books were in the libraries and the professors in the classrooms.

So, what's changed? Technology.

Today's classroom is no longer bound by geography as we now possess the ability to have any book ever written available to us almost instantaneously, anywhere we like, at home or on the beach. As for the teachers? They're teaching from all over the world, with real-time video chats and virtual classrooms that give them the freedom to continue actually working in their field, rather than being tenured at a campus.

So who needs college? Sure, it's right for some. Don't get me wrong, there is a time and place for higher education for the right people, doctors, lawyers, engineers, professionals of the sort, but should college be an assumed rite of passage for every 18-year-old on earth who just isn't sure what to do next after high school? Hardly.

Mike Rowe, host of *Dirty Jobs*, says, "Of the three million jobs available today, less than 20 percent require a four-year degree. We're lending money we don't have to kids who can't pay it back to train them for jobs that no longer exist."

The idea that a four-year degree is the only path to worthwhile knowledge and true happiness is an insane, elitist idea.

With student loans crushing our young people entering the workforce, why not pick a more streamlined and financially viable option of higher education? Why not save thousands on room and board? Why be forced to take, and pay handsomely, for a lot of classes that you'll never use but the universities cash in on as requirements? Required by whom, I ask.

We're streamlining every other aspect of our culture yet the thought of a University system as the only means to a higher education appears to me to be stuck in the stone ages for the most part.

Sure, there are those who will argue growing up is a part of the college experience, "Our kids needs college because it's a place for them to learn independence, responsibility, and maturity." I suppose, if being told what to think, living on borrowed money and delaying adulthood fits that bill. But I know, from my experience, that it takes a lot more to succeed in the real world than what's learned within the four walls of a university classroom.

I understand that this may be the most controversial part of this book. This is a somewhat polarizing subject. But I know you could find several of the world's most successful CEOs who would agree with me that college may be overrated because many of the best either dropped out of college or never went at all. Names like Bill Gates, Michael Dell, Richard Branson, Steve Jobs and Mark Zuckerberg. How about Ted Turner, Russell Simmons, John D. Rockefeller, Dave Thomas or Henry Ford. Let me be clear, I'm not saying college is bad or unnecessary, I'm saying that we must get past this notion that it's for everybody and it's the only path to success. That is false.

I'M EXPRESSING WITH MY FULL CAPABILITIES

The greatest asset we can give to a young person is confidence. The question is where does confidence come from? Is it intrinsic, meaning we're just born with it, or is it extrinsic, stemming from the outside?

I'll answer that but first, I have to ask one more question. Who do you have more belief in, yourself or God?

When I ask this to my clients, it's typically a split decision, with 3/4 of them saying they have more belief in God than themselves. When I ask them which voices in their lives they need to quiet the most, it's often their own voices of doubt and insecurity. This illustrates and overwhelmingly prevalent human condition of our culture today. We lack self-belief.

However, both sides are wrong as it's a mutually binding alliance. To prove it, we needn't look at any modern era self-development book but rather the oldest, Exodus. The story of Moses is the greatest in history when it comes to a lack of self-confidence.

Even though he was privileged to something most of us aren't, physical evidence of God, Moses was the quintessential example of insecurity. He saw the presence (burning bush) and heard the audible voice of God. He watched God turn his staff into a serpent and made his hand turn leprous and then healed. Yet despite all that, he cowered and found another excuse not to follow his calling.

Please, Lord, I am not a man of words, neither formerly nor since you've been speaking to your servant, because my mouth and my tongue are clumsy. And Yahweh said to him: Who made man's mouth? (Exodus 4:10)

Modern translation: Love to help God, but I'm out. I'm not a public speaker, so I can't do it. I stink. I'm just not qualified for the gig.

God to Moses: Pump the brakes on those thoughts son, you are forgetting I made you, so I know your mouth works perfectly fine.

Now consider how much we ourselves often act like Moses. We get drowned in self-doubt and overtaken by fear, unwilling to take a step in the right direction even when it's clear that's where our freedom is. And that is why I say if you're not succeeding in your mission here on earth, it's not because you don't believe in yourself, it's because you don't believe in a God that is big enough. You don't believe as much as you say or raise your hand that you do. And there's the gap.

This is why secular self-development programs are filling up, and books on self-help are popping up on every post. They gush the word *Belief* in nearly every sentence while often casting the burden of it solely upon the reader or ticket holder, i.e., you're not doing this, or you're not doing that, and this is why you lack belief in yourself. In other words, your self-limiting beliefs and subsequent lack of action are the culprit to your woes in business, marriage, weight management, so here's my 10X system to get you going in the right direction.

Man says vs. God says.

I'm not saying they can't help. There is definitely something to those books and seminars which have helped a tremendous amount of people move the needle. However, they are either copies or counterfeits of the original self-development book, the Bible. And of the 66 books of the Bible, Exodus is the one which most illustrates the one critical ingredient to belief and accomplishment that surpasses all other—that of The helper. The intercessor. The Creator. Or as was explained to Moses, "The Great I Am."

This means that we never walk alone, even when the yoke of accomplishment in this 21st-century world of hustle and comparison is great. A lack of confidence and feelings of insecurity are commonplace today, but remember, it's just as it was nearly 3,500 years ago when Moses was tasked with convincing the most powerful ruler on earth to let his people go. He didn't need to read another book or do more chin-ups, he needed to know he served the one true God, and that was all he needed to know.

Like Moses, when we get scared, we begin looking for the return policy or manufactures warranty. Something is obviously broke in us, which can't be fixed, and cannot be overcome. Nonsense, that's as false of a cop-out today as it was at the burning bush because He (God) wrote the manual. He's got the patent on us. There are no recalls; there is no fine print at the bottom of the page.

Hear this: the problem is neither with the builder, nor the product. The problem is that WE haven't taken the time to read the GUARENTEE on the box; *I will never leave you or forsake you* (Deuteronomy 31:6). *Greater is He that is in you* (John 4:4).

Let's not be mistaken, the Word doesn't promise that we won't have hiccups or even stutters, but Exodus reassures us that we are capable of great things if we have faith. It proves beyond a doubt that God uses broken people to do amazing things. We don't need a square jaw or a million IG followers to move mountains, and we don't need to wait for perfection in order to move forward.

While Moses found his confidence and completed the assignment, leading over a half million people out of Egypt, his is one of thousands of examples of great leaders both born and made. When it comes to a turned-on life, the real question is do you have the confidence to take control of your life and mold yourself into who or what you want to be even if it's not anywhere near who or what you are right now? I say a resounding yes, and that's why I chose to include a chapter on confidence because it's essential to everything we do.

Confidence has played a central role in the formation of the United States of America, a country of immigrants who wanted to be free from the hierarchy rule of England. Think about it, farmers and blacksmiths with little to no fighting experience don't rise up and take on the strongest army of the time without a ton of confidence.

And in America, for generations, we've held onto this belief that our children (the next generation) would always possess the confidence to believe they would do better than their parents. The term most often associated with that belief is *upward income mobility*.

For example, my grandfather was born in Glasgow, Scotland, at the turn of the 20th century. At the time, Scotland was still what you would call a hierarchical society with a series of ranks and marks of status. Grandpa, who was born into the same poor, or masterless, as his father, my great grandfather, would have had little to no social status or apprenticeship. My great grandfather worked as a simple cook on a merchant marine ship, spending nine months of the year at sea.

At the age of 17, my grandfather knew he wanted more, so he got onto a boat, crossed the Atlantic Ocean, and stepped foot in a new world. College or any type of higher learning wasn't within his grasp, so he went to work in factories and eventually began to do asphalt work, paving roads and rooftops. While he couldn't log onto a computer to learn a new skill, there was one thing he could develop without anybody's permission or special schooling—confidence.

My father took the best and left the worst of what his Dad was, and that good part was, you guessed it, a boatload of confidence. To make a long story short, my Dad did better than his father who did better than his father. Confidence begets confidence begets confidence.

Now let's go back to that term upward income mobility and the belief that we can and will have a better life than our parents. I know my generation, Gen X, held this belief, but a 2018 poll conducted by The Associated Press-NORC Center for Public Affairs Research and MTV found that only about half of the current 15 to 26-year-olds in America think they will be more financially successful than their parents. While reasons for this may vary, let's just look objectively at how a turned-on philosophy for life, in general, can bring that belief back.

Two of the biggest reasons people aren't as optimistic about living an abundant life anymore are (1) because they've been told to tone it down, not to dream big and (2) they've been raised in such comfort with a bounty of provisions that the desire to work for it doesn't exist like it once did. The hunger to achieve has been stripped for a large segment of the population.

Here is something I'd like you to think about when it comes to obtaining that hunger and getting proactive about turning on your life. Being born on this planet at this particular time in history is the greatest advantage any generation has ever had. But at the same time, we're seeing it can be a detriment in many ways. For a majority of the world, food, shelter, and safety are more commonplace and more abundant than ever before in the history of mankind. Those are the three things for which man has always had to work.

So, to be honest, we're reaping the spoils of our success as a species. If our basic needs (for many people in America) are somewhat of a given, then just being, or taking up space, becomes an option. To use a sports vernacular, if you have a guaranteed contract and spot on the roster, why take extra batting practice? How many of you got excited by your football team's latest free agent only to go sour on him when his performance didn't live up to the contract. Not all, but most, need that carrot dangling in front of us. We need to be motivated or inspired by something because on the other end lies apathy, the path of least resistance, which is afforded to us by a culture that, for the most part, can make things just OK for us to get by most of the time. It will be our downfall as a society, the epitaph on our grave, if we allow it. The couch potato culture will sink us.

I'm going to assume, however, that if you're reading this book, you do intend to get ahead and you are willing to put in the extra BP to achieve more. It's no secret that practice goes hand in hand with confidence. The more reps, the better you get. I'm sure you're familiar with the saying "Luck is when preparation meets opportunity." So, let's talk practice. How many swings are you taking a day? How many jump shots or slap shots? It's easy to see practice in terms of sports, but what about those of us in the business or the entrepreneurial space. What can we do to get better?

I say improve your personality and people skills which is an area many people don't feel the need to practice because they are under the assumption that you either have it, or you don't. You're born with it, or you're not.

Not the case. You couldn't be further than the truth.

A *Take me or leave me* or *Hey, this is my attitude, if you don't like it, tough* approach will get you nowhere and the type of people posting these type of memes on social media are most likely lonely or unemployed because that attitude may make you seem cool on Facebook, but it's a strikeout in the real world.

It's my experience that negative attitudes toward practice stem from two things, laziness (lack of work ethic) and/or fear, the latter of which is an easy fix. Lazy, however, is not. Lazy is an excuse we find in abundance in our current culture, and that's why so many people are choosing the autopilot button. And the consequences you get from laziness (from the Lemony Snicket quote earlier) are things you never asked for and don't always like.

The easy excuse we substitute for a lack of effort is that it's easier to say, "I just can't do anything about the hand I was dealt. Things are the way they are." Tell that to my wife who was raised by a single mother working three jobs. As a child, Angelike ate cheese sandwiches for lunch and cereal for dinner most days. At 19, she had to drop out of college to care for her sick father. She kicked and punched her way to a national championship in Tae Kwon Do before entering the corporate world.

Once there, she battled sexual harassment (she won a settlement because she refused to date her boss) and a low hanging glass ceiling, ultimately beating out 25 (male) applicants with Master's Degrees for a management position at the top orthopedic device company in the United States. She knows how to take lemons and make soup.

By her example, Angelike taught me more about grit and work ethic than I had ever known, and I took that knowledge and found effective ways to remind my coaching clients that skipping practice is no way to approach life. Again, I went back to my days as a sports reporter for the perfect example.

Each class of clients that came through my program was shown the viral video of NBA star Allen Iverson ranting about the importance of practice (or lack thereof). The video was recorded in 2002 when Iverson and the Philadelphia 76ers were coming off a season in which they barely finished above .500. This was in drastic contrast to the year before when he'd won the scoring title, was the league MVP and came within three wins of leading the Sixers to an NBA Championship. The struggle to repeat that success the next season boiled over into frustration from Philly coach Larry Brown, ultimately leading him to question his star player's desire to do what he (Brown) felt necessary. Brown griped publicly to the press about Iverson's lack of commitment to practice, and at one particular press conference, the All-Star guard finally had enough of people questioning his desire and went off:

"We sitting in here. I'm supposed to be the franchise player, and we in here talking about practice," Iverson said. "I mean, listen: We talking about practice. Not a game. Not a game. Not a game. We talking about practice. Not a game. Not the game that I go out there and die for and play every game like it's my last. Not the game. We talking about practice, man."

Yes, that is what everybody was talking about and while you (the reader) may care very little about basketball, you do need to care very much about practice. Iverson was undoubtedly one of the most gifted players to ever step on the court, a once in a decade type talent. He earned the Associated Press High School Player of the Year award in both football and basketball and won the Division AAA Virginia state championship in both sports.

After high school, Iverson played basketball at Georgetown for two years, where he set the school record for career scoring average (22.9 points per game) and won Big East Defensive Player of the Year awards both years. He played 14 seasons in the NBA, was an 11-time all-star, and his playoff career scoring average of 29.7 points per game is second only to Michael Jordan (33.4).

But here's the lesson: while his raw talent may have brought him a high school title, Iverson never won a collegiate or professional championship. Now some will argue he may not have had the right coach or players around him. Valid points. However, others, as well as me, will say it all points directly back to his 2002 press conference, and the fact he didn't feel practice was important. Sure, that's just an opinion and can't be proven, but it can be postulated to a high degree.

If you take two equally gifted athletes of the game, Michael Jordan and the late Kobe Bryant, they have 11 NBA titles between them. When you begin to dig into their views on practice, well then, my case is not hard to understand.

It's well-documented that Jordan would practice at his house prior to regular Chicago Bulls team practices. So much so that his teammates saw this and often joined him. Kobe's trainer tells a story of his phone ringing at 3:00 am and being asked if he could come over to help with some conditioning work. When he showed up at 4:30 am, Kobe was drenched in sweat practicing by himself.

Let's bring this conversation back to you. You have talent, God-given ability to do something at a high level. Are you going to simply rely on that, or do you have the work ethic to nurture it and groom it to get you to the next level? Are you hungry enough to put in the extra practice? I can tell you for sure that if we're not turned on in a way that makes us aware of our potential and all the possibilities that lay just beyond our vision, then we will fail to get there.

You either possess the power to change your life for the better, or you acquiesce to the mercy of fate. And I don't know about you, but I don't want to rely on the wind as the only way to cross the ocean. Throw me some oars and I like my chances a lot better.

YOU ARE WHO YOU THINK YOU ARE

Norman Vincent Peale, an American minister known for his best-selling book *The Power of Positive Thinking*, wrote, "Believe in yourself! Have faith in your abilities! Without a humble but reasonable confidence in your own powers you cannot be successful or happy."

Over the course of my coaching career, I cannot tell you how many times I've heard self-deprecating comments along the lines of "I just can't talk to people," "I don't know what to talk about," or "I have nothing interesting to say." I tell my clients that is simply not true; you just aren't willing to dig your heels in and do the tough work that is needed. You're allowing fear to create a story in your head rather than faith (like Moses) to take root in your heart.

I mentioned it earlier in the book, but it bears repeating, there really isn't that big of a difference between an introvert and an extrovert; it's more that the extrovert is simply willing to go with their instincts more often. If you feel that you fall on the side of being an introvert, if you shy away from people or conversation, go back and ask yourself if you often feel like you're suppressing a voice in your head, if you're going against your internal instincts.

I consider myself the ultimate extrovert and, in my case, 99 percent of the time, it means saying what I think, when I think it, without really second-guessing it. Ask my wife, and she will tell you it's my greatest gift, but she will also tell you that it's definitely caused me to insert my foot in my mouth many times.

But that's a risk we take. Play it safe, and you get a nice safe, often boring life. But to be bold is to seek connection and to search out opportunity that would have otherwise never come your way. In my life, it was confidence that begot confidence that begot confidence. It's like a steamroller—once you get a little bit of it, nothing can stop you.

THE BIG DREAM KILLER

I wasn't always an extrovert. But it became a part of me. It's who I am. My most authentic self. Now raise your hand if you're tired of hearing phrases about being authentic, such as *I just want to be authentic,* or *Show them your authentic self,* or *Show up authentically.* I applaud the term and everything it stands for. I strive to be the definition of authentic; original, not false, true to one's spirit or character. The problem is that we've overused the word so much that we're all becoming numb to it and nobody really knows what the heck it means anymore other than to just to use it as often as possible in your self-development journey.

If we try to get past the popularity of it and see what sticks, I have two ideas as to how; First, we must stop worrying about what we think it means to be cool or successful. An old school example is Johnny Carson. He was a nerdy magician as a kid. But he never tried to be anything other than Johnny. He was authentic and ended up being one of the coolest men to walk the planet. A more up to date example for me would be singer Lauren Hill. In an era where the diva ruled, she stuck to her roots and chose the road less traveled. She might have passed up millions in the process, but to this day, on the rare occasion she takes a stage, the entire music industry bows.

The second way to be truly authentic in who you are is to benevolently and politely declare your values and follow up with an integrity check on yourself. In other words, what are those things about you that you stand for even in rough weather when the seas are high and your stance might not be that of what's trending on social media. These are what we call I AM statements. For instance, I am God-shaped and God-fearing, I am committed to my wife, I am a father to my children, I am compassionate, I am fun loving, I am deep thinking and yet I am flawed. At times in my life I've tried to be too cool, too macho, too smart, and too opinionated and let me tell you, it didn't work out well because you can only fool some of the people some of the time but eventually, the real you always surfaces.

NEVER MIND THE OUTSIDE, SHOW ME THE INSIDE

Trying to be and keep up with something you are not is a 24-hour-a-day job, and it's exhausting. Imagine walking outside each day thinking, "Don't let them catch me with my cool off." Sooner or later, you have to go out without makeup or let your stomach relax. People will see you without a filter. You're going have to admit you're human.

As a music and nightlife reporter in Miami, I covered an up-and-coming band who sang a song called "Never Mind the Outside." The song was ahead of its time as it spoke about the huge divide between our authentic (inward) selves and our outward (public) perception, urging listeners to never mind the outside (what people think), show them the inside (who you are.) As I got deeper in my coaching career, I came upon a term that I felt really helped my students define that gap and better explain the divide—metaperception—which refers to our judgments made upon ourselves derived from what we perceive others think about us. Essentially, it's how we internalize a conversation in our head based on perceived (be it valid or invalid) actions of others to us.

Of course, I felt the need to simplify this concept beyond a definition and perhaps even to put a face to it, so I went back and searched the pop culture reference drawer in my head and said BINGO! I have the perfect example—George Costanza. Jerry Seinfeld's fictional sidekick on the sitcom *Seinfeld* was the epitome of a man who was all about the outside and never showed the inside. He consistently battled his way through his perceptions (most often misconceptions) he felt others had of him. So much so that he made up fake names, fake occupations, fake girlfriends, fake hair and fake accomplishments because he lived in a world of negative metaperceptions.

In my class, I play a particular scene where after a double date with Jerry and his girlfriend, George asks, "Well, did she like me?" but not even pertaining to his own date, rather Jerry's.

George says, "She didn't like me. Why didn't she like me? I tried to be nice. I wasn't nice? Was it because of the thing I said about her sister?"

It's pretty easy watch George and cringe as he succumbs to an internal pressure of gigantic proportions which he places on himself. It's looks and feels absolutely exhausting. The façade he puts on day in and day out, the lies he has to stay on top of, all in the effort to get everybody to like him. And while there are dozens, if not hundreds, of clips from his work on the show I could've used to showcase this, I chose this scene because of his obsession with the word LIKE. Is there another part of our current culture where the term *Like* has placed an enormous amount of pressure on us and our metaperceptions of ourselves? Let me jar your memory. Ever heard somebody, or maybe even yourself, ask, "Why didn't you like it?" referring to a post, photo, or video? In our social media-driven world, we've turned up the volume on metaperception to such an overwhelming degree that we now have a button for it.

Seinfeld filmed 180 episodes over ten years, ending in 1998. Facebook wasn't born until 2004. But I can imagine if the two had overlapped that there would be an episode where George overly obsesses about a post he made that would go something like this:

Did you read my post, Jerry? You didn't LIKE it, did ya? You couldn't take two seconds to press the little button of validation to say you liked it? It offended you, didn't it? Tell me, I know it did. Or no, you didn't think it was clever? I was too casual, right? Not clever enough for the funny Jerry Seinfeld. I knew it. Jerry doesn't think George is funny.

Then comes a pause, Jerry thinks he's done, but then George starts up again. *Was I too blunt, I knew I should've toned it down. Or wait, did I confuse you? Was I too coy, too political, too WHAT JERRY??? Tell me why you didn't like it!!*

Jerry then calmly responds with, "No, George, actually I did not push the LIKE button because I did not see the post that you made an hour ago because I was having a tooth pulled, under heavy sedation, at the dentist!!!! I have a life outside of social media, so perhaps if you could just give me some time to stumble upon it. For the LOVE OF GOD, what are we doing?"

Does that sound like a *Seinfeld* scene or what? Obviously, I poke a bit of fun here, but like all good comedy, we chuckle because we see the truth in it. Did you see yourself or somebody you know a little bit in that dialogue? Sometimes when the ridiculousness of a situation is pointed out to us all we can do is laugh.

But what are we going to do about this, seriously?

MY TIME HAS PASSED

As I close this chapter on turning on your confidence, I have to wonder how many of you read it, maybe nodded in agreement a time or two, but then in the back of your head said, "You can't teach an old dog new tricks." Or, maybe you said, "I'm too broken to pick up the pieces of my life and confidently go where I wanted to." To that, I say, nothing could be further from the truth. Whatever was lost can be found. Whatever was down can go back up. What was destroyed can be rebuilt. Whatever was turned off can be turned back on.

Confidence is the key to every opportunity I've ever had. In fact, I'll ask you to do something that a mentor of mine encouraged me to years back that changed the way I saw things.

He asked me to make a running list of 100 accomplishments that I've made in my life. One hundred things that you've done, that took you saying yes and then following through.

Like me, you may be saying, "What? A hundred things? You can't be serious; I don't think I've accomplished fifty." But, of course, you have, you just aren't giving yourself credit for all that you've achieved. Taking every yes for granted and selling yourself short.

Start like I did. I wrote down the first five: (1) graduated high school (2) got a college degree (3) got my first job (4) moved out of my parents' house (5) got my first loan... blah blah blah. But as the week went on, little by little, things in my past began to pop up in my head, and I was like, "Oh wow, yea," I took a role in that play that one time or I married a couple. I baptized my parents. The next time I met with my mentor, he said we do this exercise because most people forget their little (sometimes big) achievements over time, and that leads to a lack of confidence. Next time you need a boost, go back and read anything and everything that took even the slightest bit of courage, all the little confidence builders that got you to this spot today and use them for fuel to make the next leap.

I began doing this same exercise with my own clients, often having to nudge them to give themselves more credit. Hey ladies, if you gave birth to another human being and that's NOT on your list, are you crazy? Or I'd say to a guy going through a midlife crisis, "You have fed your entire family of four for the last twenty years and you don't see that as a worthy accomplishment?" Remember confidence begets confidence, and the fuel we need for tomorrow is tied to what we did yesterday.

JUST SAY YES

When you begin that list, begin to think about the things to which you've said yes and no. Remember, Moses was an 80-year-old stutterer when he was tasked with going to the Pharaoh to demand his people be set free. The great King Leonidas was said to have just 300 elite Spartans to square off against Xerxes Persian army of nearly two million. So, neither lack of skills (Moses) or lack of odds (Leonidas) were excuses for either not to be brave and say yes. What they both had in common was a massive motivation. Slavery and invasion provide an incredible impetus in getting people to answer a call to action, and while I'm fairly sure you won't be waking up tomorrow morning to take on the Pharaoh or Xeres, I'm certain you will be called upon to love your spouse, play with your children, and perform better at the gym and at work.

We can be slaves to NO. Slaves to monotony or fear. Part of being Turned On is being unafraid to say yes even when you're unsure. Even when you're scared. Life is about experience, and you can't get that sitting on the sidelines—you need reps. So, if it's a new skill or new opportunity that just adds one more checkmark to your life's resume, then say yes.

I was asked to host a Hip-Hop Poetry slam at 25 and said yes, asked to interview Super Bowl champ Kurt Warner at 35, and asked to speak in front of 16,000 people at 45. Each time I had massive butterflies, but I said yes before I could talk myself out of it.

Motivation in life is critically important, but words are just words unless you combine them with the essential element—a brave and bold "Yes." So next time you're faced with a tough decision, look in the mirror, put blinders on and don't allow fear of failure (like Moses) scare you out of pursuing your assignment in life. Gaining confidence is not hard, in fact, it's free, and you can start today, right now, by talking to new people, signing up for a new course, or volunteering for new adventures.

It's important, even comforting, to know that others are struggling with the same things that you do and that you're not alone. But if you're waiting on others to boost your morale or lift your spirit, you'll be waiting too long; you need to give it to yourself by taking small, consistent action.

CHAPTER TEN

TURN ON
YOUR OPPORTUNITIES

The pessimist sees difficulty in every opportunity.
The optimist sees the opportunity in every difficulty.
— Winston Churchill

Chances are you've heard of the show *Star Trek*, but you may not know how it came to be or who took a chance and catapulted the iconic show to fame.

Early in 1965, NBC executives nixed the idea for a *Star Trek* pilot, but a spunky red-headed gal from Jamestown, New York who ran a company called Desilu Productions thought the futuristic show about space travel just might have something to it and decided to take a chance on it against the advice of others, including her board of directors who thought it was a bad idea. She overruled them and gave the project the green light. That redhead was none other than Lucille Ball, and the rest is television history.

This is important because business is all about vision and recognizing what others can't or don't see. We all have this vision, it's just that some are just more in tune with it than others. An element of luck can play into our success, but again, the old saying rings true, luck is when preparation meets opportunity.

Star Trek could've very well have just been the right idea at the right time with the right cast, but when others said no, Ball said yes. Magic in a bottle? Perhaps, but the risk was there as well. We may have never heard of The Enterprise and its adventures had she, like others, said no, and the world wouldn't know any different. Lucille Ball and her husband, Desi Arnez, were turned on, open to new things, and willing to take chances and follow their intuition where it took them.

For the better part of the last nine years, I've done business coaching and helping people to find and articulate their gifts, ideas, and assignments. I'm encouraging you to find that same spirit of entrepreneurship that America's favorite redhead possessed. It means stepping into the freedom that sees with new eyes and using a mind that is always curious as to what is coming next.

VISION

My father was a traveling salesman in the late 1960s, and he covered the entire state of Florida. One day, he was heading to catch a flight out of Orlando, and he saw a sign advertising the Future Home of Walt Disney World. Curious, he drove down a pebble road and stopped a trailer, went inside and saw Walt Disney's plans to build an enormous amusement park right where he was standing. Having three kids at home, he was obviously excited. At the airport bar, he struck up a conversation with some fellow passengers saying, "You'll never guess what I just saw. Walt Disney is planning on putting a huge park right here a couple of miles away."

Dad told me the one man looked at him with a grin and said, "Yea, like that'll ever happen."

Seems funny now, doesn't it? But Walt Disney was without a doubt turned on in a big way. He possessed a vision like no other, and that is exactly what turned on means when it comes to business. Being aware, not just of what's hot or what you're currently doing, but what next, what's on the horizon. Disney himself seemed to put it into words better than I ever could, saying, "We keep moving forward, opening new doors, and doing new things, because we're curious and curiosity keeps leading us down new paths."

Being a student of human interaction, I began to write this book because I was curious. I saw and felt things that made me think I couldn't be the only one seeing and feeling. Indeed I was right, once I started to vocalize my ideas and vision, I saw that almost everybody I spoke to was feeling the same and I knew I was onto something. But I didn't stop there; I had to look ahead. Was this just a flash in the pan, this feeling of people missing real connections? Was the next five or ten years going to make it better or worse? All signs pointed to the concept of being turned on as a game changer.

NOSTALGIA OR NECESSITY?

In the book *Globalization of Technology; International Perspectives*, author Umberto Colombo writes, "The world is in the throes of a technological revolution that differs from the periodic waves of technical change that have marked the progress of the industrial society since its origins 200 years ago." He says that as the demand for new jobs and skills increases, the old activities disappear or lose their importance in the marketplace, and many shifts, like the human-free factory and integrated workspaces, are already here.

Again, I feel like I have to reiterate this point, especially to a younger generation—I'm not one of those old-timers longing for the good old days. I see the future, and I'm excited about the future, but I want to embrace it with the right mindset.

I've written many chapters of this book you're reading in shared workspaces and coffee shops. I've purchased the food to sustain me during the process from automated checkouts at the grocery store. I've outsourced the entire logo, fonts, and marketing resources from online marketers I've never actually met in person and probably wouldn't recognize if I were talking to them at a party. So, I know where the market is moving, and more importantly, how fast it's going there. If you have any sense of curiosity at all, surely you wonder where those jobs like checkout clerk, travel agent, and others are going, and what is coming next to the workforce.

I'm not a techie but let me open your mind to being turned on to the opportunities. When I graduated from college, I took the first job that I applied for, believe it or not it was selling pagers (aka beepers). I applied after seeing an ad in the *Help Wanted* section of the newspaper. I know I'm dating myself with both the newspaper and pagers, but my bigger embarrassment is who spends four years in college in hopes of selling beepers when they graduate? Nobody. But hey, it was a job, and it paid real money.

Around this same time, my father was making a killing selling fax machines. They went from a luxury in the early 1980s to a necessity by the end of the decade. So, what you're seeing here is the first wave of the technological revolution playing out in my family. I was selling beepers and Pops was selling fax machines. Would anybody pursue either of those jobs now? Hopefully not. But it really wasn't that long ago when you look at it.

Fast forward twenty years, and here we are on the cusp of yet another technological revolution, completely different than the first one which was heavily influenced by the dot com boom from 1995 to 2000. Consider again that nobody owns a pager, facsimiles are typically sent via computer, and just about every genius dot com URL you've thought of in the past decade was already taken by somebody else. In other words, the speed of business is moving much faster now than ever before, and if we're not anticipating what is around the corner, we will miss the wave entirely.

So, what does being turned on in business these days look like? Uber. DoorDash. Amazon Prime. You've seen the trend. It's about speed and convenience. How can we make everyday tasks like eating, driving, or shopping easier?

It begins with what I've told you several times already, turning on your perception to see with new eyes and listen with new ears. Because only those who have turned on will see and recognize a need for something. If you're just a consumer, simply consuming 24-hour news, 24-hour sports or social media, how can you observe what society will need next? Seeing into the future of business doesn't mean you have to be clairvoyant, it just means you have to be alert.

Business has always been that way, sometimes you see an opening and sometimes you make one. Let me give you an older example and then a modern one.

Jack Ryan. Many of you have never heard of him, but I know you are familiar with his work. Ryan was a Yale graduate with an engineering degree who worked at an aerospace company helping to develop the AIM-7 Sparrow and the MIM-23 Hawk missiles. He was your typical nerdy rocket scientist. What do rocket scientists do? They make rockets, right? Or do they?

In the mid-1950s, a woman named Ruth Handler made dolls, but there was something missing, and they weren't selling as much as she knew they should. In one of the most unlikely part-nerships ever, she met Mr. Ryan and asked the engineer if he could help. She needed a new design and felt he could assist. If you're a logical thinking person, right now, you're asking why would a missile maker make dolls. Good question.

To add to the equation, Ruth was strapped for capital and couldn't pay much. Being a sound businessman with an open mind and vision, Ryan offered to help with the agreement that he would get a 1.5 percent royalty on the product. That intellect would pay off handsomely in the form of a doll the world would come to know as *Barbie* of which approximately 350,000 units were sold in the first year. Had Ryan been turned off to the idea and said, "No, how dare you, I'm a rocket scientist," we probably wouldn't be talking about him here. In his time with Mattel Toys, he went on to design *Hot Wheels* and *Chattie Cathy* as well. As for his contribution to Barbie, she lives on as the most popular fashion doll ever produced. There are more than 100 dolls sold every minute, and a Barbie Dream House is sold every two minutes.

Of course a more modern version of this story should be more familiar. If you've had a heartbeat in the last decade, then you've heard the story about Facebook CEO Mark Zuckerberg and how in 2003 he invited five people to his Harvard dorm room to discuss a business opportunity, but only two people showed up, and today they're billionaires. Yadda Yadda Yadda. If somebody uses that story to pitch you to join their company, run. It's so worn out and overused.

My point is that, like Ryan, Zuck was a science geek who was willing to look at life with fresh eyes, open to possibilities that were slightly outside his zone of genius. While Ryan focused on giving Barbie a new face in order to appeal to a popular buying segment, Zuckerberg focused on giving college students a new face to pick from in order to appeal to other co-eds. His initial creation was called Facemash, and it helped students to pick the best looking person from photos.

Dolls or dudes, Barbies or babes, a turned-on entrepreneur is a glass half full, open to all possibilities type of person. When we limit our minds to what's already been done or how much we can make doing something, we turn off or shut down our possibilities. Did Travis Kalanick and Garrett Camp (Uber) know they'd change the way the world travels and become billionaires? No.

Did Phil Knight ever think people would pay upwards of $3,000 for a basketball shoe? Doubt it. Did Matt Groening envision his troublemaker cartoon character becoming the longest-running U.S. primetime-television series in history? Doh!

Nothing is too silly or too trivial. You simply don't know until you try.

THE LITTLE THINGS THAT COUNT

A niche is defined as a distinct segment of a market. The world is full of thousands, if not millions, of them. There's a new one popping up each day, often making us ask, "Why didn't I think of that?"

You might be able to picture a coffee niche, a yogurt niche and a Mexican burrito niche. Over the years in my Speak Up program, I began to develop a bit of a niche. I saw myself helping more and more people succeed in industries where personality made a difference in customer satisfaction and/or sales. I became proficient helping people turn their personality into profit.

Month by month, year by year, I was noticing more people in service-related industries were hiring me; real estate, beauty salons, hotels, hospitality, etc. Wanting to make sure I gave them the value they were seeking, I went back to doing what I do best, observing. I began to ask myself, what are some of my favorite businesses that I patronize, and what separates them from their competitors? This is a very simple exercise to conduct in your own life or business because again, going back to the theory that we're all more alike than we are different, it begs that if you find something really impressive or valuable, there's a good chance your neighbors/customers will too. If you find something that creates value that doesn't add to your overhead, then it's double the value.

So, in observing, I found three separate businesses that each did one tiny thing with zero extra overhead that made my experience better and made me want to come back. When I reveal these to you, you'll find they are so simple, it's almost like one of my "duh, yea" moments, but again, it's always the simple things, the littlest details, that make the biggest impact in the long run. So here they are.

The first company is a staple of the south. Anybody who grew up in Florida most definitely knows and probably shops for groceries at Publix Super Market. Founded by George Jenkins in Winter Haven, Florida in 1930, the chain now has over 1,200 locations throughout the South in Georgia, Alabama, South Carolina, North Carolina, Tennessee and Virginia, in addition to its 800 plus locations in the Sunshine State. It's one of the largest retail grocery chains in the United States and was ranked No. 12 on *Fortune* magazine's list of *100 Best Companies to Work For* in 2019.

Growing up in Florida, this was all I knew. It wasn't until Angelike and I moved to Arizona and shopped elsewhere that we discovered how privileged and spoiled we were. While Publix has succeeded for many reasons, there is one tiny thing that they do that makes them a perfect example of a Turned-On company in my book. You see, my wife's not like other wives who send their husbands to the grocery store for milk or bread. No, my wife sends me to the store for things like pureed pumpkin, chickpea flour or cashew butter.

Each time I go, I pull out a little bit more of my hair, and in other grocery stores, when I ask an employee where something is, they point and say things like "I think it's over there on isle 12 or 13" or "Try looking by the pasta." That's when I sigh and realize I was spoiled by Publix whose policy is, no matter who you are or what you're doing, when a customer asks where a product is, an employee is to stop and walk them directly to the item. It's one little thing that makes a huge difference to the customer and makes me feel valued.

For example No. 2, we'll shift to a retail chain that everybody is familiar with: Nordstrom. In addition to having high-end merchandise and clean, modern stores, this retail giant is ranked 183rd on the Fortune 500 list of the largest United States corporations by revenue. But there is one very tiny nuance its associates perform, which costs absolutely nothing, that separates them from most of their competition. When you purchase something in their stores, their sales associates place it in a bag and walk it around the counter to hand it to you personally. Again perhaps silly and somewhat trivial to some but people like my father just think it's the greatest thing in the world. It's just a little something extra that many customers take for granted but adds to the overall experience.

Example No. 3. In today's very tech-savvy world, competition is at an all-time high. If you're anything like me, your email inbox and Facebook messenger is flooded with people who can grow your following, expand your reach, and increase your sales. In fact, sometimes it feels downright yucky, and it's incredibly hard to sift out the legitimate offers from the used car salesmen. Even getting people to open an unsolicited email or message is hard. But I was thoroughly impressed recently when I opened an email and there was a video attached. To my surprise, when I opened it, it was a personalized video of a social media optimizer making a personalized pitch to me. It showed up in the bottom left hand of my screen, with my business home page as the main image. He proceeded to navigate my website and tell me first, the good job I was doing (very smart) and second how he thought I was missing out on traffic by not doing a couple of simple things. He ended the 5-minute video by edifying my business again and telling me that if I had a staff, he suggests they incorporated these changes.

As a former salesman, I immediately recognized the soft sell, but as a discerning businessman, I truly appreciated the time he took to not only make the video but do the homework on my company and personalize his message. In a hi-tech world, that was a high-class effort.

The larger point all three of these examples make is if you want to be successful in today's market, you must think outside of the box, pay attention to the experience, and pursue your customer's heart. If that's not plain enough, let's again use the antithesis to explain the point. It's been my experience, in over a decade of using one particular airline in America, that they just feel so large that they've abandoned all customer service. But since they were so big and were often the cheapest, I continually went back to them even after swearing them off time after time. But eventually, they broke the camel's back, and I swore that no matter how convenient or how inexpensive I would never use them again. And I meant it. Once you break the client's heart and trust, it's almost impossible to get it back.

TYING IT ALL TOGETHER

Where are you right now in terms of your career? Are you an employee, manager, or entrepreneur? The tuned-out person will nestle into a comfort zone, become lackadaisical in their approach, and ultimately burn every bridge or element of success they have. To be Turned On means you're always looking to see what is working, but more importantly, what can be improved. Price is always a great concern for consumers but doing one little thing that makes a footprint in the memory of your boss, customer or client is even more important. Don't get beat out because you're unwilling to go the extra mile, or even inch, to succeed.

CHAPTER ELEVEN

TURN ON YOUR BUSINESS

> *"The beast in me is caged by frail and fragile bars."*
> *–Johnny Cash*

In Nashville (also known as Music City), there is a saying, *When the music you live to play becomes the music you get to play to earn pay, that's gratification.* Translation? The adage *when you can do the thing you love to do to make a living, that's the definition of success.* Considering we all can't sing or play an instrument— it's good to know the same premise bleeds into any career. If your desire is to make your passion your work, you'll be successful. How do you go about doing that, though? Well, it takes a little bit of digging, soul searching.

Using what I call *The Turned On Method*, we try to figure out where the client is at and how to be happiest making a living by asking four simple questions:

1. Where am I currently?
2. What are my gifts?
3. How would I explain my passion or purpose?
4. What is the first step (or steps) that I can do now to close the gap between where I am and where I want to be?

You could go to Zig Ziglar, Robert Kiyosaki, or Dale Carnegie books and get answers, but let's go back a few years prior to those. In Genesis 3:9, God calls out to Adam, "Adam, where are you?" Now remember, we're talking about the creator of the garden, the creator of the universe, so why would he need to know where Adam is located? God is all-knowing after all. Well, he wasn't asking where Adam was physically. He was trying to get a read on Adam's mindset. Like, what were you thinking?

I love correlating the first step of any career move to this verse and question. Where are you? What are you thinking? In other words, let's get an accurate read on the current situation. Are you in a job that's a 180 from what you want to do? Do you have current responsibilities other than yourself (wife, family, employees)? Do you have the funds, training or connections to make a leap or transition? It doesn't matter if the lay of the land is close to, or far away from, the desired destination, you just have to make sure you know what you're working with.

The next step asks us to position ourselves in another type of inventory situation, this time with more of a focus on our tools, the gifts we have to work with. Again I go to the book and look at Psalm 139, "We are all fearfully and wonderfully made…all the days ordained for me were written in your book before one of them came to be." Translated it means, we have a specific calling and gifts we're supposed to use in life.

Later in the chapter on faith, I'll touch on where this verse was first explained to me and how it opened my eyes to so many things, but for now, let's just ask ourselves what we are good at. I typically have my clients write out these gifts, both the obvious (I'm good at math, work well with my hands, I connect easily with people) as well as the not so obvious (I'm a good host for guests in my house, I have a knack for feeling people's heart or I'm good at jigsaw puzzles). In other words, nothing is off the table; we must explore all areas of our capabilities.

Once we know where we are at and what our gifts are, then comes finding out exactly how to use these things to our advantage and then convincing people of what it is we do. Remember Moses told God that he couldn't ask Pharaoh to let his people go because he was afraid that his mouth didn't work well, that he wouldn't be able to articulate the vision with authority. Well, he was onto something.

In his book, *Lead Like Reagan*, Dan Quiggle, who worked as an aide for President Ronald Reagan, asks this crucial question, "If you asked those who are closest to you what your vision is, would they be able to articulate it?"

It's a simple question, but ask yourself this, "If somebody spoke to my neighbor, my child, my co-worker or spouse, would they be able to say what I'm most passionate about and have a general sense of what I'm doing to get there?"

For many people, it's a no. We have no problem articulating what we don't want or don't like to do, but when it comes to our ambition or passion, we kind of stutter because often we don't truly know ourselves. We know something is brewing inside of us, a desire to do work that doesn't even feel like work when we're doing it, but if we ask the people closest to us, they might shrug their shoulders and say, "I'm not sure what he or she does." Further muddying the waters is our current culture, which seems to embrace ambiguity and allows, even encourages, fluffy or woo-woo answers like *Nancy is a thought leader, Steve is a life coach,* or *Lisa does women's empowerment.* They sound great but don't say much, they are very obtuse and overused.

Quiggle says, "Without vision, you drift at the mercies of a constantly changing environment, pursuing day to day business with nothing more than a repeated series of activities." To which he makes the comparison of walking on a treadmill but getting nowhere. People go to more seminars, read more books, and bang

202 · DAVID NORRIE

their head against more walls, asking themselves what's missing. Often the answer is the details. The plan. A target.

Be it in Moses' time or in our present day, we have to have the same details and the same confidence speaking our vision in order to target what we intend to do. It's crucial to the implementation of the plan and probably one of the most challenging parts of success. The process is often gritty, time-consuming and frustrating, yet it's one of the most important tasks we can do, especially in today's short attention span world where being clear and to the point is critical.

That traditional 30-second elevator speech our father used has really dwindled down to what I call an "8-Second bull ride." Being in Tennessee, I've become a big fan of the rodeo. The bulls have one job, to buck off the cowboy. If the cowboy stays on for eight seconds, it's a successful ride. Today's quick-to-click social media attention span bares a similar feel; you have about eight seconds to stay on, make an impact, before you're bucked off by the consumer.

That being said, we need to be equal parts dynamic and specific in a short amount of time, if you miss either one, you risk being overlooked and will probably get swiped online or an "Ok, that's nice" moving on type of statement in person.

When I began talking about my vision to turn people on, you can imagine the assumptions people made with just the title. That was by design. I felt I needed something that would immediately get people's attention in a very noisy world. But then came how do I explain this? It had a lot of moving parts and endless possibilities but knew that if I couldn't zero it in and get people to understand the gist of it, then it would just be a novelty name. If I were at a coffee shop, church, my kids' school, business meeting or a mastermind, how would I answer the question WHAT IS IT YOU DO? Before I could move forward with my vision, I had to be able to clearly explain what it was. I went back to my newspaper days, remembering my first editor and the litmus test he used for the headline of a news story; if you met an eighth-grader in the street, would they be able to understand it?

That's when I said Turned On is about doing the easiest thing you can do to initiate change. It's like flipping a light switch and putting excitement (giving light) back into the areas of your life which are boring (went dim). That's my 8-second pitch that an eighth-grader could understand. My goal after that is simply to get the client (prospect or person) to ask themselves and answer me, which area of their life needs a little excitement or a wakeup call. Now it's about them and how they can be happier. Who do you know who doesn't want excitement or a wakeup call in some area of their life? It's a conversation starter and when you can get into a conversation, it's good, your foot is in the door.

The last part to getting started, No. 4 in your turned-on business, is best explained again, from a journalist's perspective. In this case, let me go from the Bible to baseball. Let me dig into the sportswriter in me. Here's the situation:

It's just past midnight on a chilly October night and the home town fans are distraught. They're down three games to none to their most hated rival. There's very little light at the end of the tunnel and it looks like their season will end the same way it did the year before, losing to the Yankees. The Red Sox faithful are wearing despair on their faces as the game's all-time best closer Mariano Rivera is on the mound. He's been lights-out, 6-for-6 in the postseason in save opportunities versus Boston. It doesn't look good.

At this point, you may be wondering what this has to do with turning on a career. Well, you see, time and time again, sports prove that all it takes to gain some momentum in your favor is one small step, one tiny, perhaps seemingly minuscule step. One small victory begets another victory, then another and another. If you're a school teacher, and you want to open up a bakery, it may look like that dream sits miles away. If you're a mechanic and you want to be a motivational speaker, that's not in a different zip code but a different planet. If you dropped out of college and the opportunities look bleak, how can you get out of the hole.

It's kind of like this situation, when the Red Sox, 86-years removed from a World Series, were down to their last three outs versus the best closer the game has ever seen. It was hard to see the light until one small victory, a lead-off walk by Kevin Millar, providing just the slightest bit of momentum. Millar was replaced at first base with pinch-runner Dave Roberts. After several throws to first by Rivera, Roberts took off and stole second base. Another small step in momentum. The crowd erupted as the Fox television camera's scanned Fenway Park, the shift in momentum was palpable. Remember, this was not a home-run, but back to back small victories. The next batter Bill Mueller singled past Rivera into centerfield, and Roberts rounded third and slid into home tying the game.

The Red Sox not only went on to win that game in extra innings but completed what many call the greatest comeback in Major League Baseball history, beating the Yankees in seven games then riding that momentum to sweep St. Louis in the World Series and in doing so, breaking the infamous 86-year curse of the Bambino.

This story doesn't just reflect how quickly momentum can shift in sports but in all aspects of life, including your career. It seems commonplace to look at successful people and assume they either made it overnight (one big home run) or that they just have more talent than us (Mariano Rivera) when the fact is, most successful careers and businesses are built one walk, one stolen base, one small victory that gained a bit of momentum at a time.

Know where you're at. Know what your gifts are. Learn how to articulate the plan then ask what step can I take in order to get one base closer to making my dream come true.

SEEING AHEAD OF THE CURVE

One of the hardest things to do in baseball is to hit a curveball. One of the hardest things to do in business is predict the future. But that doesn't mean we can try to see ahead of the curve.

In addition to covering a lot of baseball in my time, I also did stories on more leisurely sports like surfing. If you've ever tried surfing, then you know it's one of the hardest things on the planet to do. And it's not so much the standing on the board and balancing part of it but rather everything leading up to that point. Ninety percent of surfing is in the foresight and preparation, and I see the same parallel in business.

Anybody who has ever spent time on a board in the water can tell you that you have to think ten steps ahead. You're looking out to the horizon, watching for ripples, seeing which ones have momentum, and will turn into waves and which ones will lack the necessary timing and elements and fizzle out.

To the novice eye, the waves all look the same at first, but experience and time in the water helps sift out which have the most potential. When you're in the zone and spot it, you know it, and you start paddling ahead of it. If you sit on your board, overthink it, and get a late start, then you've set yourself up for disaster because it's too late, and before you know it, you're thrown off saying, "But I thought..."

Preparation + experience + timing. That's the best equation there is. A little luck doesn't hurt either.

Ask yourself this question, is there a need for what you want to do right now and in the foreseeable future. How can you prepare yourself for this need and what type of experience do you need. Like surfing, you're going to have to do a lot of hard work (paddling). Expect you'll get some saltwater splashing in your eyes and for your arms and back to get exhausted. If you've attempted a startup then you know it often feels like a solo sport even when you have partners. Every day you're paddling like crazy, and sometimes you think you're there, you think you're ready to ride, but you fall off your board and you're back on the beach at square one.

The thing that separates the winners from the losers, the riders from the posers, is perseverance. In the Word, or Christian vernacular, perseverance is defined as *continuance in a state of grace til the end.* I love that definition because it inspires me. Like Moses, we must know that we aren't walking alone. We walk in the grace of God, therefore, we must persevere.

Perseverance is also synonymous with words like stamina, grit, tenacity and doggedness. Remember earlier how I said, you have to have a little bit of dog, or grit, in you in order to succeed? After I tried surfing, I had a newfound respect for surfers as athletes. Watching onshore, it looked easy. It's not.

Much the same way, I watched entrepreneurial icons of our day make it look simple. Most of you have seen the photos or heard the stories of entrepreneurs like of Jeff Bezos or Steve Wozniak and Steve Jobs in their garages when they first started and thought, *see, I can do that, they're just like me, I have a garage too.* But photos of them in their garage don't begin to explain the long days and years of trial and error, being tested and still persevering. Each great entrepreneur not only has a great idea, but they have a little something else that's not so common, fortitude.

THE WALKING DEAD

It's that same technology those pioneers crafted that is making life easier. It is easier, would you agree? So, is the ability to succeed by using it. Perhaps easier now than ever before in the history of the world, but that doesn't mean it's not still hard. Do you get that point? It's not a contradiction. In other words, there are tools like this MacBook I'm using, which make writing a book way easier than 50 years ago. Still hard to write a book, though. Most of you reading this book pressed a button to order and had it appear on your doorstep or on your device. Easy yet it still requires some man power and logistics. In other words, anything worthwhile requires effort and determination. And those are two things that technology won't be able to replace. There will always be a choice to be made; ramp up and take responsibility for your business or coast working for minimum wage or for somebody else's dream. The difference in the two outcomes often comes down to one thing, how much energy, or juice, will you bring to the table each day?

Let me explain it better this way. Energy, in the form of oil/petroleum is the most valuable commodity in the history of the world. Annual production is valued at around $450 billion with the supporting infrastructure to produce, refine, and distribute it valued at over a trillion dollars. Without it, the world as we know it shuts down. Where does it come from? The earth. It's deep inside, and you have to dig for it. It's not easy. Fortunes, I'm talking generational fortunes, have been made from finding it. The same goes for you. Your energy will predict your future and your legacy. Like petroleum, you must dig for it, and when you find it, it helps drive everything else in your life.

That being said, perhaps the choice to be turned off is alright with you. You've been sold on the idea to take it easy, keep the lights dim and coast through each day doing the bare minimum to get by. Maybe this permeates into your personal life as well. It could very well be that you elect to befriend and congregate with others who'd be classified as lazy communicators or people who see no problem with giving the bare minimum when it comes to connection, communication, and effort.

No doubt you've encountered them before, the walking dead at their job. The discontent shows on their face, and they see no cause for alarm in being part of a society void of much personal contact. They don't go out of their way to acknowledge or interact with people unless it's absolutely necessary. Hey, it's a free country, and if your shell is where you feel most comfortable, then, by all means, retreat into it. But hear this, there will be consequences.

Don't be surprised when your inability to communicate and share thoughts and ideas puts a dent in your wallet or kills a career opportunity. I don't know of any Fortune 500 companies posting job listings that read "Looking for massive introvert with an inability to interact with others in normal conversation and thought sharing who is just looking to skate by." That's funny, but it's not funny. To put it bluntly, if your head is looking down most of the time, then that's where your career and your future is most likely pointing as well.

Let's go back to school for a moment and look at the word charisma which is defined as: *compelling attractiveness or charm that can inspire devotion in others; a personal magic of leadership arousing special popular loyalty or enthusiasm.*

That last word, enthusiasm, is a lot like energy. Now ask yourself this, what do you remember your high school teachers or college professors teaching you about charisma and enthusiasm? I'm guessing next to nothing, if anything? Bueller? Bueller? How much time was spent teaching you how to keep your enthusiasm high and maintain a certain level of energy in order to get ahead? Anyone? Anyone?

I believe that the real reason most people don't get the job, land the deal, or receive the promotion is that the person making the decision just didn't like their personality. Most employers, managers, or buyers can't just be blunt and say, "Well geez, you have the right qualifications, but being in the room with you just drained me. I wanted to hit my thumb with a hammer to make sure I was still alive." No, of course, they don't say that, so they come up with some other lame excuse, and that's it, your chance has passed.

I teach connection. I teach charisma, and I've helped all types of people from all types of occupations either get the job or earn the promotion based on their ability to connect. I always say unless you're an underwater welder, chances are you can benefit from being more charismatic.

In the modern landscape of business, connection, communication, and charisma are valuable commodities. When you can find them in abundance, it's like striking gold. Don't believe me? Look at the last four presidents of the United States—two Democrats (Clinton/Obama) and two Republicans (Bush Jr./ Trump). None of them were dummies, but resume-wise, none of them were exactly Einstein either. And by top of their class, I'm not talking about college; I'm talking in terms of resume or experience. There was always a candidate with a better resume or political track record which they beat out.

So why or how did they win?

They were charismatic. They connected with the American people better than their opponents. The same can be said about jobs at all levels, personality and the ability to connect is a growing concern for employers as the technological revolution has stripped many people of their confidence and basic abilities to interact with other human beings.

Businessinsider.com writer Scott Huntington said, "It's taken a long time, but companies have slowly begun to understand that it's personalities that matter in the workplace, and not impressive resumes," adding that if the relationships inside the business don't work, then no amount of experience will matter.

Tina Sharkey, Co-Founder and CEO of Brandless, says, "People are craving human interaction. That's going to move the needle more than any technology you could ever dream up."

A wise man told me not too long ago, "We've arrived in the land of knowledge and skipped the encounter part," to which I couldn't agree more. For years, we've been told to go to school, study and gather knowledge, but we skipped, or should I say lost, the part on how to share it. And what good is knowledge if you can't communicate it? As much as we focus on teaching children an arithmetic equation or science formula, we should be putting an equal focus on how we can better communicate and share ideas.

When we gain the capacity to articulate our ideas and vision, we waste less time bogged down in confusion and stagnation. Instead of understanding one another better, we're growing farther apart and getting more confused. For instance, can you recall an incident in which somebody has taken a text message out of context, misinterpreted an email or failed to return a call, any of which resulted in a lost deal or huge misunderstanding? Have you had to ask somebody to speak up or repeat what they were saying because they lost you in translation of their idea? They couldn't, as Quiggle mentioned, articulate their vision.

"PERSONALITY IS TO A MAN WHAT PERFUME IS TO A FLOWER"

If I gave you 100 chances, you might never guess who said the above quote. Perhaps an actor, musician, or philosopher, you might suppose, but how many of you would say that quote belongs to one of the most successful business tycoons of all time? Charles Schwab understood the immense value of a personality when it came to prosperity. At 35 years of age, he became the president of Carnegie Steel, a company he helped negotiate the sale for a price tag of $480 million (equivalent to

$14 billion in today's market). How about a more recent example? In 2018, billionaire Warren Buffet said there was "one easy way to increase your worth by at least 50 percent." Can you guess what he said it was? Speaking and writing effectively.

"If you can't communicate, it's like winking at a girl in the dark—nothing happens," Buffet said. "You can have all the brainpower in the world, but you have to be able to transmit it."

Of course, I agree with Schwab and Buffet, that for a majority of you, some part of your job requires you to speak and write clearly. I'd also say that being a likable person to be around would help to advance your career in many ways, including financially. If that's the case, why wouldn't you invest in the skills to be better at it? I'll tell you why, because most people don't know where or how. This communication goal isn't just for the subordinate or person looking to climb the ranks, it's for bosses, owners and management as well.

Travis Bradberry, author of *Emotional Intelligence 2.0* and *The Personality Code*, said, "More than half of people who leave their jobs do so because of their relationship with their boss. Smart companies make certain their managers know how to balance being professional with being human. These are the bosses who celebrate an employee's success, empathize with those going through hard times, and challenge people, even when it hurts."

The world has changed and so has the way we do business. The traditional resume has changed. Fortune 500 companies are focusing on the person behind the paper, realizing that attitude is often harder to train than skills, so companies are looking for people with people skills.

In other words, are you fun to be around? Easy to carry on a conversation with? Do you articulate your vision in a way in which people clearly understand you? And are you likeable? Like Chris Harder said, collaboration is the new shortcut, and networking is the new currency driving the global economy.

We know that deals have been getting done on golf courses for decades, but we're seeing an even bigger shift toward mixing business and pleasure in this new gig economy.

It's time to wake up and get in the game. The old way of thinking put education at a premium and assumed character would always take a back seat, and that the world would turn a blind eye to a lack of personality. But Schwab and Buffet say differently, and I think you see it too.

I've always said personality "rules the day and directs our future." It's a huge point of emphasis I put into my courses, and certainly a huge part of what I would credit to my success. But the more I spoke about being Turned On, the more I realized that this was a major issue in all walks of life, regardless of the profession.

I remember a man coming over to give us an estimate for an expansion of our house. We began chit-chatting about what I did for a living, and I explained that I help people communicate better and turn their personality into profit. He explained to me how he'd just retired from a career in the Air Force in which he was a recruiter. He went on to explain in great detail and passion how the young recruits over the last ten years became harder and harder to communicate with and train because they all lacked the people skills that were once very common. He said he'd tell a recruit to do something, and they looked like they wanted to run under the table and hide because they weren't comfortable talking face to face and taking direction. He went so far as to tell me the Air Force began incorporating more public speaking courses into its recruit's training.

Contrary to what some may think (you just drive a tank, fly a chopper, or point a gun), being a professional soldier is one profession in which the ability to communicate seems essential, in my opinion. Any job tasked with life or death missions, in which a missed or failed communication could cost the ultimate price, needs to pay special attention to details of the messaging.

The communication of ideas, be it on the battlefield or Wall Street, is vital to putting together a successful plan, and Generals and CEOs know it. In my research, I was surprised to learn that even the jobs you would think could be performed by an introvert (computer programmer, video game designer) are given to people with good personalities. Why? Because everybody has to work on a team and share ideas and tell your story. And your story is where it's at.

Take the words of one of the most influential and successful men of our time, Sir Richard Branson. In a blog post, the British businessman who founded Virgin Airways wrote, "Today, if you want to succeed as an entrepreneur, you also have to be a storyteller. Of course, it is no use being a good storyteller if your product or idea is rubbish. But it is not enough to create a great product; you also have to work out how to let people know about it."

We're not speaking clearly, and we're not seeking clearly. And getting clear on what we are good at and how to say it are skills I feel are essential but often overlooked when trying to find our happy place.

When I teach my courses, one of the first things I do is poll my clients asking, "Those of you who are clear on what you want and what your mission is, raise your hands." I'd say 80 percent of the people don't. Why is that? I'm inclined to say because a majority of them spent their entire young-adult lives in a classroom obtaining knowledge somebody told them would be valuable to them before they actually sat down and took the time to answer the simple questions; (1) what do you like to do? (2) What are you capable of doing (3) What's separating those two things and (4) Where do you begin to close the gap?

Let's dig back in our pop culture reference drawer again for an example. In the movie *Rocky*, Adrian asks Rocky why he wanted to fight, to which he replied, "Because I can't sing or dance." If I had to guess, Adrian was probably thinking, "Wow, ya got a really good point there, Rock, how 'bout we lace up those gloves then and make some money?" While I poke fun at that, Rocky knew his gifts, and he saw that people would pay him to fight. He wasn't wasting his time trying to be something he was not, something others thought he should be.

The world is a big place. It's growing bigger and faster every day. If you don't stop and take a serious look at your skillset and where it can take you, then chances are you'll end up going to a job that you hate. That being said, please write these next two sentences down, circle them and highlight them - It's never too late to reinvent yourself. And if you have children, it's never too early to start asking them what their gifts are and how they are going to use them to earn money and be happy. Giving up on life or delaying life, only leads us to a place where we live in regret and are more susceptible to pain and disappointment.

WHAT THE WORLD SAYS VS WHAT YOU SAY

The business world is changing in one major way. Unlike the industrial revolution where people simply said I need work, people today want more. They want to find meaning in their work. Self-actualizing the landscape of your career, looking for a higher degree of reward rather than just a paycheck, is good; it's even noble, but it's not easy unless you pay strict attention to a couple of things.

This is where technology has affected our lives again. We've succeeded so well in taking care of the basics (Maslow's Hierarchy of Needs) that we can now look for a higher purpose. The next generation of workers is asking, or rather demanding, purpose in their toil.

Wouldn't you agree that it's important for people to find purpose? We want a happy workforce and a happy and content world. But then the question needs to be asked, are we serving our youth in a way which is helping them get clearer on their purpose or are we simply teaching them to shoot arrows in the dark? If it were up to me, Guidance Counselor would be one of the most important and highest paying jobs in America.

William Damon, Stanford University psychologist and author of the book *The Path To Purpose: Helping Our Children Find Their Calling In Life,* said, "There have always been kids that drift, but I do think we have a special problem today in the numbers of kids and the kind of trouble they're having in finding a sense of direction."

He said that in 2008. Do you think we've gotten better or worse since then? If I go back to the time I was in high school and college, I recall having awful encounters with guidance counselors who just wanted to push me through the system. I was like many young adults, lost in the mix and seeking direction. They volleyed me back and forth between offices and colleges like a tennis ball until one day they said (wow, this is funny) they found a degree that fit the kind of credits I'd amassed. Do you see what happened there? Nobody took the time or concern to find what I was good at or wanted to do; they had me take classes and then found a degree that scooted me out the door, diploma in hand, and just as clueless as when I'd entered.

Surely you sense my disappointment (maybe even disdain) for the educational system, but I've spoken to too many people with similar stories, living unfulfilled lives, because they were equally let down and forced through the factory by guidance counselors or parents who had predetermined what their kids would be. Neither of which serve the young person. To some degree I apologize to the dedicated counselor or educator out there, I know it's not all. But if the system is broke, lets fix it.

Instead of giving our youth lip service, let's turn them on to their passions at a younger age.

DON'T BE SCARED TO TRY

You've probably been asked the question, "What could you accomplish if you had no fear of failure?" It's an outstanding question, but one that's very hard to come up with an honest answer to, primarily because we don't live in a vacuum, and fear is the number one, most consistent, human struggle. There are some people who have tamed fear in moments, but nobody who has actually conquered it.

Fear is a destroyer, a destructive force that can get in the way of your true calling. Faith is the opposite of fear. We can all use more of it. Faith in our gifts. Faith in our ability to put them into action and faith in achieving our higher purpose. When you dig hard enough below the surface and question what really is the reason you aren't acting more in faith, what do you come up with? A fear of rejection? Fear of failure? A fear of man?

The fear of man lays a snare (Proverbs 29:25). Man will hurt you. Man will chastise you. Man will question your abilities and intentions. Man will attempt to get you to conform. That happens every day you step out of bed. People will try to tell you what to do, how to act, who to follow. You will be told you can't do this, or you can't do that, maybe not literally by a man, but the seed of doubt will be planted.

That seed of fear is of the Enemy, and it's carried out by his accomplices, some of which are willing, but many simply acting under the seduction of worldly things such as money and power. When you live according to the fear of man, you're held captive, a prisoner of your own potential.

Now flip that and choose to live according to faith, faith in God, and suddenly you are released from that prison of fear, freed by God who has told you time and time again, fear not. That's the best feeling you could have. True freedom.

I began this chapter with the Johnny Cash quote, "The beast in me is caged by frail and fragile bars." You probably didn't pay much attention to it but look deeper at it again and ask yourself what it might mean. It means it's very probable that you're not living up to your full potential because you're afraid. And the reasons why you're afraid are not really that strong; they're indeed frail. We could break out of the fragile bars holding us back at any time as long as we remember one thing. We have the favor of God.

Would you ever go into a fight with one arm willingly tied behind your back? Or enter a marriage and say let's only live under the same roof for half the year? Do you think you could open a successful restaurant if you were only allowed to use five ingredients to make the food? Or would Neil Armstrong have planted the United States flag first had John F. Kennedy said, "Ya know, one of these days, I bet we get to the moon."

The American poet R.H. Stoddard wrote, "All that you do, do with your might, things done by halves are never done right" Of course not. The biggest accomplishments in life are achieved when you go all out and use all your might. Can you see Ricky Bobby giving Armstrong a big fist bump saying, "Hey Neil, if you're not first, you're last?"

Will Ferrell's fictional race car driver was so lovable because of his zest for going all out and his passion for winning, but in real life, up until 2019, NASCAR made its drivers use restrictor plates, a device installed at the intake of an engine to limit its power. The official reason was to "limit top speed and provide an equal level of competition." Subsequently, drivers turned to forming large packs of cars that ran close together for a majority of the race, which ended up causing huge crashes and pileups.

Let's put this rationale into our own lives. What kind of restrictor plates are we putting on our spirit that's limiting our ability to separate ourselves from the pack and fulfill our own goals, be it in marriage, health, business, or faith? Are we sometimes playing life too close to the vest, only giving half an effort, because we're scared to go big?

Hall of Fame racer Mario Andretti, one of only two drivers to win races in Formula One, IndyCar and NASCAR once said, "If everything seems under control, you're not going fast enough." I don't think he means we need to be reckless. I take it to mean if we restrict ourselves trying to play it safe, we will never win. Another famous Italian from a completely different occupation essentially says the same thing:

> *"Somebody should tell us, right at the start of our lives, that we are dying. Then we might live life to the limit, every minute of every day. Do it! I say. Whatever you want to do, do it now! There are only so many tomorrows."*
> *– Pope Paul VI*

Let this be a wakeup call to get moving. To try and even fail if need be. I've learned a lot more from trying and failing than by passing up opportunity. The best way to get to where you want to be is by actually doing that which you seek to do.

SEEING TWO STEPS AHEAD

Turning on your business comes down to being ready and on the lookout for the changing tides in industry, technology, and entrepreneurship.

It's about looking through the windshield rather than the rearview mirror. Some people allow themselves to concentrate only in the here and now, and they fail to look four, five, or even ten steps ahead. Often when they do get around to getting Turned On, it's too late—the speed of business has passed them by.

Let's consider two travel-related industries: taxis and travel agencies. Over the last ten years, these two staples of American life have taken very drastic paths that only few may have predicted.

In 2013, I had just started in network marketing, and my friend Steve had some experience in the field. We met for drinks and spoke for an hour or so about the industry, and then he said, "I've got to get going to work for a couple of hours."

"At this time of night?" I asked. "Where are you going?"

"I'm going to drive my car and pick up some people."

The look of surprise on my face was so obvious, he just grinned.

"It's called Uber. I get notifications on my cell phone when someone needs a ride, and I pick them up."

"In your car?"

"Yes."

I wished him good luck and went on my way. When I got home, I told Angelike about what I'd just heard. I think the adjectives I used in that conversation were crazy, stupid, and nuts. Who in their right mind would ever drive their own car to pick up other people for money? That's what taxis are for.

Seven years later, how the perception has changed. "Who in their right mind would ever call a taxi? That's what Uber is for."

Right now, you're nodding your head. Why? Because it's painfully obvious to see. But in 2013, I'm guessing most of you would have been saying the same thing I did. The difference between vision and insanity is often the lens you're looking through.

In the 80s and 90s, travel agencies were one of the most popular businesses. During the last three decades, air travel has gone from a luxury few could afford to almost a necessity that is available to everybody. Throughout the 80s and 90s, the economy expanded at a rapid pace along with the airline industry. In 1974, airplanes carried 421 million people globally. By 2017, that number increased tenfold to 4.1 billion.

With more money in their pockets and more destination options, consumers provided a huge opportunity for somebody to help make ease of those options. Enter the Travel Agent. In one phone call, they could find you a flight, hotel, and any other arrangements needed to get you to your destination. If you're over 35, chances are you've used a travel agent before.

What about Millennials? Do they even know the job exists? CareerCast.com listed travel agents in its list of Useless Jobs as the number of retail travel locations has gone from about 34,000 in the mid-1990s to 13,000 today.

According to the Bureau of Labor Statistics, the number of full-time travel agents in the U.S. dropped from a high of 124,000 in 2000 to around 67,000 in 2017.

Online sites like Expedia, Trivago, Kayak, and Priceline have made it so convenient and easy for the consumer that the go-between has been phased out. And while I personally know, love, and still occasionally use travel agents, they will be the first ones to tell you it's not an industry that they'd get into now.

Here's where seeing with new eyes comes in. Just because their specialty has been phased out doesn't mean a need isn't there. According to the International Air Transport Association (IATA), in 2016, there were a staggering 3.8 billion air travelers, a number it predicts will balloon to 7.2 billion passengers by 2035—a near doubling of current levels. So, if we know that we will be traveling more than ever, the focus then becomes what's next? By being Turned On and looking ahead, one can see new opportunities where others don't.

THEY SAW IT

On New Year's Eve a couple of years ago, my friend Rob Murgatroyd sat down at the kitchen table with his wife Kimberly, and they asked themselves, "What do we want this new year to look like?" He wanted to leave his chiropractic business of 25 years and travel the summer and fall in Europe.

"After we laughed out loud at the seemingly absurd idea of executing this, we got serious and devised a plan," Rob said. "We asked ourselves a better question. What would reverse engineering this plan look like?"

And that gave the couple the idea for the Work Hard/Play Hard Mastermind, a unique twist combining amazing travel experiences with high-end business networking.

Here's how it came together: the Murgatroyds had always loved to travel and even had a very successful YouTube channel (Jet Set Life) as a passion project in which they toured parts of Europe and reported on their experiences. For the last several years, in addition to running a chiropractic clinic in Georgia, they've been involved in network marketing. Through those avenues, their eyes saw people who were highly successful and continually seeking to expand their businesses, but they wanted to do it in a more enjoyable fashion.

"We saw that most people were focusing on money and making more of it, but Kim and I felt people needed to be rich in body, mind, and soul as well," Rob said. "What we do is not just about unplugging, because anybody can book a trip on a computer, we had the idea to craft bespoke travel experiences that would bring entrepreneurs together and change people's lives."

The Murgatroyd's first trip sold out at 32K a pop, and the next two filled up as well. The saw a need, they saw that people were starving not just to go somewhere, but for memorable experiences. Knowing that anybody could book a trip online, they had to find, or in this case create, a niche for a certain type of customer. They took their old skillset and combined it with their new one to create something unique and lucrative.

Whether it's batting practice at Fenway Park with a personalized Red Sox jersey in your locker, or a vintage car ride through the French Riviera and a masterminding session at the Chevre d'Or hotel, the Murgatroyd's vision is to leave their clients with a more enjoyable way of reaching their goals. In that process, it helped them to reach theirs as well. That's a Turned On business.

A MINDSET IN YOUR BRIEFCASE

Working with entrepreneurs from all walks of life and even in our own business, Angelike and I have tried to anticipate where a need is going to be or when a bubble is coming.

Leaving the house Turned On is so relative to our careers that we've made it part of our teaching curriculum, emphasizing that the answers to what's coming, the trends, the technology, the ability to connect the dots, only comes when you have the ability to leave your eyes wide open ready to see the patterns, ready to see the people, and ready to ask open-ended questions like, "What do you see happening in our industry?"

A big influence in both of our lives has been the guidance of our good friends Chris and Lori Harder. We've watched them grow from very humble beginnings into what they are today—market influencers with multiple seven-figure businesses. Chris' podcast *For the Love of Money* offers a wealth of advice for both start-ups and established brands on how to see things coming and avoid pitfalls. He says, "We are in a really interesting time for entrepreneurship. It's never been easier to succeed than it is right now. All the answers you need, you can Google. The knowledge and information are out there. There is so much free content. You can listen to podcasts, watch YouTube channels. Everything you need is actually out there for free."

If we use technology in harmony with interpersonal relationship skills, it can bless our lives. But Harder agrees that information by itself without implementation gets you nowhere.

"If you are not 'Turned On' and willing to go find it and research it, watch it, listen to it, then you are going to be left behind. The reason it is so easy to succeed right now is the same reason why you can be left behind so much faster than ever before. Somebody else is doing the planning and putting it into action, and for some reason, others are not. In other words, the same reason why there is NO excuse for you not to succeed is the same reason why you are going to be left behind quicker than ever."

The challenge for many of us born in Generation X or prior is balance. We were raised in a face-to-face business world that our parents excelled in and now much of that interaction has gone digital. It's the same balance that the younger generations (millennials) are missing on the other end. They've been raised to rely so much on technology and digital communication that they often look and feel awkward when it comes to in-person communication.

The game changer right now, the reason why business travels so fast, is that people are incentivized to build an audience and teach them what they know at a pace we've never seen before. Information is distributed and changing so quickly, and there remains this allure of striking it rich quickly. That's where not being Turned On in the right way can sabotage you.

For those of us who grew up in the mid-90s (the Bill Clinton era), we remember the massive and lighting quick expansion of the dot com boom. It launched the careers and made household names of people like Jeff Bezos (Amazon.com 1994), Pierre Omidyar (Ebay.com 1995), Jay S. Walker and Michael Loeb (Priceline.com 1998), and Mark Cuban (Broadcast.com 1998).

And it wasn't just an American phenomenon; it was global. According to the BBC, in the year 2000, 63 dotcom millionaires appeared on the Sunday Times Rich List (a list of the 1,000 wealthiest people or families in the United Kingdom.)

But where there are winners, there are losers as well. Of those 63 millionaires on the list in 2000, a year later, there were just 26.

BBC writer Alex Hudson wrote, "It was a time when adding e- or dotcom to a company name could dramatically alter its share price, a time when investors were willing to risk vast sums of money on young computer-savvy entrepreneurs with little more than an idea and a catchy company name."

But bubbles always do what? Burst. And none came harder for our generation than the time that followed the dot com boom. Which brings us back to the get rich quick pitfalls of a person who is not truly Turned On. It comes down to having a foundation. Are you an exciting name accompanying an exciting trend, or are you a well-researched, well-positioned entrepreneur who has looked ten years into the future and possesses a well thought out and long-term strategy?

One question Angelike and I always ask ourselves is, "What can replace us or our product?" We've had many ideas over the years, and we'd be quite embarrassed if you looked at our GoDaddy URL ownership list. We dipped our feet in a handful of ventures over the last decade and joined forces with other entrepreneurs who we saw synergy with.

But, ultimately, it came down to two bigger questions (1) what are we good at? (2) who do we trust? The answer to both led us here. We knew we were gifted at coaching our passion, which is relationship and ministry and we knew it would all fall on our shoulders to make it or break it. We wanted no outside forces to factor into our vision. So, we put all our chips on the table, including the $10,000 price tag for TurnedOn.com. We wrestled with the need for it and purchased every $15 address that could be remotely associated with it. Ultimately, we felt this brand, and this concept would stand the test of time because the need for human connection would always play a factor in the happiness and well-being of our society.

While we called our Home Team our true team, it wasn't our only team. We knew, in today's business world, that connection was essential to making it. In early 2020, we walked away from a half-million dollar position in our network marketing company to go out on our own. Living in Nashville, I had a neighbor in the music business ask my why we'd do such a thing. Wow, that's a good question and hard to articulate, however, I answered with this: imagine you're a cover band skating by on playing everybody else's songs, eventually you want to play your own songs and see if you have the chops to make it big your way. No risk. No reward. We knew that we'd have to give up a comfortable position and work harder than ever but felt that was exactly what we needed to do.

WORK SMARTER NOT HARDER

Any parent will tell you that when you have a baby, the most primal instinct in the human body is to protect it. And any entrepreneur will tell you that the same holds true for their business babies (intellectual property). It's a cut-throat world out there, and trust is no longer a handshake and head nod.

A huge component of being Turned On in business is discernment, or the ability to judge well. Once you begin to make a name for yourself, people come out of the woodwork to either pitch you or recruit you. I can't count the number of next-best-things Angelike and I have seen placed before us. From Bitcoin to EMF protection, we live in an era of recruitment and get-rich, next-best-thing ideas. We've said no to most simply because we weren't knowledgeable enough to put our money on the line. At the same time, we had to look at one another and say, "We may be missing out on a fortune."

Angelike and I sought control and connection. The control part came from holding onto our intellectual property and not just asking for business partners in order to shoulder the load and make it easier. The second, connection, was a critical part of the new way we saw people doing business. Angelike and I knew nothing could replace good old fashioned sweat equity when determining whether your business fails or succeeds. True, but Chris Harder also told us we must also remember that collaboration is the new shortcut.

"In the past, everybody worked in silos. This is my information, and I am going to protect it," Harder said. "Now, that is what will get you left behind. Now, everybody is collaborating. They are doing books together, events together, starting companies together, podcasts together. They are guests on each other's show. They ghostwrite in each other's books. They are doing Facebook and IG interviews together. Collaboration is now king pen. And being Turned On means you are Turned On to the idea of collaborating with other people and seeking opportunities to collaborate with other people- whether they are sharing your information, or you are sharing theirs. And it should be an equal energy exchange."

Now think about how control and connection can be implemented into your business. It's like a do it yourself mentality but asking friends to help you out. The best of both worlds.

Remember, protecting what is important to you and what you work for is critical to success. If you super passionate about your work, you'll treat it as such. If you're not, and go about it haphazardly, it will get corrupted.

ALIGNING YOUR BUSINESS TO YOUR HEART

Not everybody is an entrepreneur. There are investors, managers, and workers who help shape the economy. Warning: the motherlode of great trends and revenue-producing machines can be thrown at you, but if it's not aligned with your core values, then it should be a no.

A lot of good ideas are out there, but they don't have to be part of your portfolio. That's why it's so important to know your mission and your role, otherwise, you will be diluting your efforts and chasing rabbits. The Bible speaks of King Solomon, who owned everything under the sun, who chased success and ultimately came to the conclusion that be it the most money or collecting the most accolades, neither, in the end, is very gratifying. *I have seen all the things that are done under the sun; all of them are meaningless, a chasing after the wind* (Ecclesiastes 1:14).

If we put our business in the same frame of reference as a romantic relationship, it's like courting a spouse (marketing) versus marriage (keeping your customers for life).

When it comes to romantic relationships, people are quick to say, "I'm bored, so I'm outta here," or "We don't have this in common, so it won't work." They give up when the going gets tough. If this is the same attitude you take in business, expect similar results. We know there will be disappointments and tough stretches in both, but a Turned On business doesn't fold for the same reason a Turned On marriage won't, because you're aligned with a higher calling. So, whether you're catering to your spouse or to customers, doing the right thing is not always easiest but is best in the long run when your goal is success. That means communication is the key that holds the bond together, as is being vulnerable, course correcting and listening to your conscious.

In a relationship world, single people or discontent married people are always quick to judge those who are doing well. *Why are they always so happy? Nobody is really that way.* We see the same thing happening in the business world. "Why is that business over there thriving? Everything they touch turns to gold." In both the relationship world and business world, it's because they worked at, did their due diligence, and didn't just jump on the first shiny object in front of them. In both circumstances, there was most likely a huge shift from being greedy and *what's in it for me* to being unselfish and abundant with a *how can I add value to them* attitude. Most importantly, it's because it came from a place of abundance, not lack.

WHO IS TURNING ON WITH YOU?

Social media allows us to clearly see the many different levels of success. Within a few swipes, you can see the newbie, the veteran, and the royalty of the business world. It's only human nature to, either consciously or subconsciously, judge yourself against those standards. In fact, among the people I've polled over the last several years, it's one of the things that is most stressful about social media—the comparison.

But remember our discussion about metaperception at the outset of the book. If you're constantly worrying about what others are thinking about you, it's the greatest recipe for disaster. Try as you may to ignore social media, you know it's a vital part of business today, and it presents two sides of the coin, people who you are trying to get to see the value in you and people who are trying to get you to see value in them. To say it can be a distraction is an understatement because we are being pulled in so many directions at the same time.

Entrepreneur Ty Lopez has an excellent rule of thumb: make sure that at any given time in your life you are adhering to the 33% rule—33% of the people you are interacting with on a daily basis are looking up to you, and you are helping them, 33% of them are your homies who are right where you are at and they understand you, and the other 33% are outpacing you and are your mentors that are teaching you. This 33% rule is is a good guide or rule of thumb in budgeting your time and influence.

The thing that I love about this concept is that you never get lost in terms of perception because you see in front, besides, and behind you. The other thing I love about it is that the role can shift. The person who was struggling along with you or behind you can catapult to success. If you were true to them, encouraged them, and shared resources with them, the chances they will continue to help are that much greater.

WHAT DO YOU DO?

A huge part of finding your circle of influence depends on how confident you are speaking in social circles. What we are allowed to talk about with strangers has shifted radically from the business landscape in which our parents or grandparents grew up. In the past, you were not supposed to talk about what you did for a living because it might be considered bragging. You were not supposed to bring up money or how much you earn or how much you charge for something. Most professionals kept that information close to the vest or in the board rooms. But now we share information freely, and what is considered an acceptable conversation (especially dependent upon what area of the country you are in) has radically shifted.

When you first meet someone, you generally ask what they do, how they do it, how you can help them do it, or how you could collaborate and help each other. What is accepted in our vocabulary and what we are allowed to talk about initially (breaking down walls) has changed.

If you're Turned On and looking for collaboration, you must be prepared to answer the question, "What do you do?" In the

230 · DAVID NORRIE

past, it was a simple answer: I'm a teacher, banker, or mechanic. Those were the days of defined occupations and single streams of income. Today's landscape is not as cut and dry. People are morphing and merging traditional occupations and juggling several ventures at once, with the goal to be bringing in multiple streams of income. It's very important, previously mentioned, to be as detailed and engaging as possible in exactly what it is you do, even if it isn't clearly defined as a traditional occupation.

Permission to have deeper conversations, ask people what they are struggling with and asking for collaboration are now acceptable on the first date to use a familiar term. If you are afraid to have those conversations, you are going to be left behind. If you are Turned On in the new way, then you are going to be able to keep up with everybody.

To wrap it up, Turned On means not being afraid to reinvent yourself. The old way of being loyal to a company and thinking that is going to get you from age 25 to 65 is dead. The new way is reinvention because the world is changing so fast that you are going to have to be open and Turned On to changing quickly with it. That might mean learning new skills, reading new books, and taking new classes.

When you've got that gut feeling that there is something else you would rather be doing, but you feel guilty because you have already put in so much schooling or you have already built a reputation in your current occupation, you must push yourself to move on anyways. Maybe the boss fires you, the company shuts down or robots take over (kidding, but not kidding). The reality is if you're hunkered down, comfortable and tuned out, the wake-up call will come as a shock, like a thief in the night.

Turned On is being alert, listening to your intuition, and understanding that tomorrow will not be the same as today, and that's ok. To use an old football term, you've got to keep your head on a swivel because you don't want to be blindsided.

THE PIVOT: WHEN YOU'RE DOWN BUT NOT OUT

Today's visionary entrepreneur or employee can benefit from learning to tell a good story. As consumers, we buy the story after all, and what do people like more than a good comeback story? My favorite example is the Active Faith sports clothing line founded by former University of Houston basketball player Lanny Smith. His dream of playing in the NBA was cut short due to a freak injury to his foot and subsequent surgeries.

He asked God how he could come so close to his dream only to have it taken away. Then, Smith says had a vision for a clothing brand and began writing down notes. He thought of popular taglines, wondering what his would be. He thought back to his playing days and his pregame ritual of saying a prayer before he stepped on the court.

I ended every prayer with, *'In Jesus name I pray...'* but this one particular game, I messed up and said, *'In Jesus name I play.' It came back to me, so I wrote it down and got goosebumps. I felt it was something God placed on my heart, and I pursued it with everything inside of me. I'm just as passionate about Active Faith as I was about basketball. It showed me a dream deferred is not a dream denied and God can bless you with a dream bigger than the one you had for yourself.*

Despite all his trouble and heartache, Smith was able to see with new eyes the new opportunities ahead of him. And he was able to collaborate his story into a $7 million business. I used him to illustrate a Turned On business philosophy for two reasons. First, because I love his faith in God, and I think the NBA and its visibility provide a divine showcase for such a revival. But the second is because Smith's story parallels my wife's so much.

Before I met Angelike, she was a professional martial artist. She was paid to kick, punch, and teach Tae Kwon Do to young children. One day while training for her black belt, she landed awkwardly and tore her ACL. Her passion and livelihood were at stake. Like Smith, she made a comeback, pushing through surgery and a grueling rehab eventually working her way back to form.

Two months after the injury, she was back and ready to test for her black belt. Kick after kick, the leg held up. She impressively went through all the tests and broke all of the boards until she was just two forms (kicks) away from her goal. When she landed after the first board, she immediately knew what happened. She injured the good leg, this time not just blowing out her ACL, but her MCL and meniscus as well.

She limped into the supply closet, closed the door, and began to weep uncontrollably. It wasn't the physical pain making her cry; it was the frustration. All that work, all that rehab, only to make it back and suffer a worse injury. How, she questioned like Smith, could God let this happen?

Her Master knocked on the door, and upon opening it said, "Let's get you to the hospital."

Not this time.

"Permission to finish testing," Angelike asked. Then, while two fellow classmates held her up using her belt, she broke the remaining boards with her fists, earning her blackbelt.

"I didn't give up, not because I was that intent at the moment, but rather I knew that this would be a defining moment for me," Angelike said. "Martial arts was not going to be a forever thing, and I could see the writing on the wall. My body was failing and just couldn't keep up that intensity. That was an indicator for everything else. I said, 'Ok, if I want to live the rest of my life broken and bitter, then I'll just stay here, but if I want a happiness that matches the fullness of God's grace then I'm gonna have to go out and do something else now, but this will be my catalyst for that.'"

This situation isn't as unique as it seems. Maybe it's not a physical injury, but one of the heart (divorce or death) or of the spirit (failure/bankruptcy). Everybody has moments when they must pivot one way or another, and it's not necessarily what's happening at the moment as much as an opportunity to prove to oneself that you are strong and capable of defeating adversity.

Both Smith and Angelike each had their time of doubt. It's during those painful moments, during the lowest points of our lives, when we are feeling incredibly insecure, unequipped, and unsure, that we question God. It's human nature, especially when the stakes are high.

But we don't see or can't understand at the time His path and the door that He will open when one shuts. He provides the power to turn the corner and help us find hope, find a new identity of sorts when we think ours has been stolen or ripped away. Angelike's physical gifts would pale in comparison to her spiritual ones.

It's a rough world, and today's business culture is bruising, cut-throat at times, and it's constantly evolving at the speed of light. Those who sulk after a big blow, those who feel sorry for themselves for too long, and chose to blame God rather than seek him, well, they may not be able to recover. But those who pick themselves up, abide by the spirit, and see the lesson will always be able to reinvent themselves and bear new fruit.

COURAGE

Be it a relationship, injury, or career change, picking up and moving on takes courage. I spoke a lot about courage and confidence at the beginning of the book and how important it was to unlock one's full potential. While our eyes always seem to be drawn to the mavericks of business, a lot of people today are playing it safe by sticking to those fluffy phrases that they know will get them a Like or make them sound smart and compassionate but in reality, they are just regurgitated fluff that don't move the needle.

I call it living vanilla, which is saying little fluffy things that just go in one ear and out the other and calling that work, allowing yourself to go to bed every night thinking you moved the needle of your dream. God calls us to be bold, not clones. Success calls us to come to love our uniqueness, our imperfections and failures, and be willing to lay it all on the line for our convictions. So, don't be a duplicate of somebody else.

Would you prefer to go first or to say, "Awe, that was my idea," in regret? What if it's your thought, your invention, your prospect, but someone else got their first because all you had was intention while they possessed the courage. Momentum loves courage and courage loves momentum, they both feed on one another. They are the steam that keeps your train chugging, that keeps you progressing from the little things to the big, eventually landing you where you never thought you could go.

If I were to put a bow on the Turned On business, I would say the first step is to step back, to observe, to take notes. What do you see? What are the trends in your industry? Where are the gaps? What is on the horizon? And where do your specific talents and passions fit into that? To put it succinctly, how can you take more of WHO YOU ARE and place it into more of WHAT YOU DO? There is definitely an intersection. You just need to go there.

Remember the words of John A. Shedd, "A ship is safe in harbor, but that's not what ships are for." And don't forget, they call the show *Shark Tank* not *Guppy Bowl* because tenacity is the one thing that cannot be missing from an entrepreneur's tool belt. As a former sports journalist, I compare it more to a base stealer in baseball. If you stay to close to the bag, you'll never get the jump you need to get to the next base. So, you play it safe and wait for the next batter to do the work and take the big swing that brings you home.

If you know anything about baseball (or ask someone who does), you probably know Ricky Henderson is the all-time leading base stealer or Barry Bonds is the all-time leader in Runs Batted In. But what you don't know, because there is no category for it, is the all-time guy who waited patiently and never took a lead or stole a base.

I don't know about you, but I would prefer to take that big lead, get that jump, and steal that base, keeping my fate in my own hands, rather than relying on the guy behind me.

What are you scared of right now? Can you be brave enough to triumph over it?

You either doubt your ability, or you doubt God. Neither of which are good. Considering there are at least 37 verses in the bible about being bold and courageous, you need to know God doesn't put doubt in you. In fact, one of my favorite verses is Romans 8:31 *If God is for us, then who can be against us?* Remember that and stop doubting yourself. Keep pushing and fighting until you get where you need to go.

CHAPTER TWELVE

TURN ON
YOUR BODY

> *"People are fed by the food industry which pays no
> attention to health and are treated by the health industry
> which pays no attention to food."*
> *— Wendell Berry*

Let's not kid ourselves. We want to look good. And I could tippy-toe around this section of the book with feel-good stories about weight loss and pump-you-up body transformations, but I won't because experience forbids me from doing that. You only need to look in a tabloid magazine or open social media to get a quick lesson on how important our body image has become and that we're paying a lot more attention to what the outside looks like than what's happening on the inside. But there is so much more to a Turned-On body than what you look like, so my primary goal or intention here is to help you gain some peace about your body as a whole and the role it plays in your happiness. I want to strike a balance between the physical and spiritual issues of how we deal with our bodies.

When I look in the mirror, I like to see lean muscle. I want to look good. At times I've been downright obsessed with it like most of the population. It's why in 2018, the weight-loss industry eclipsed the $70 billion mark. It's why Instagram pages featuring hard bodies and workout tips have hundreds of thousands, sometimes millions of followers. However, I would like to speak of the physical body here not as much in terms of being attractive to other people, but rather making it attractive and functional to oneself? Take it from a super skinny kid who grew up with body issues, how you feel walking around in your vessel is a huge part of who you are and your self-confidence. That's where I get Turned On, by giving myself and others greater posture and greater sense of purpose through taking care of our bodies.

I can pinpoint the exact time when I had my light bulb or ah-ha moment. For most of my twenties and thirties, I was a fairly vain guy who was obsessed with getting 20-inch biceps. There wasn't a photo I wouldn't flex for sad to say. But that all changed in a heartbeat, literally, as I can vividly recall the very second my first child was born. When I saw Ella, I felt an overwhelming sense of responsibility to take care of my body, this time not in a vain sense, but so as I could be alive and healthy for her as long as possible. The biceps instantly became an afterthought of my health. I needed to invest in my longevity.

Our bodies are investments, and like other investments, you want them to be an asset in your life—much like a house, a publicly-traded company, or a startup business would be. When we invest in something, we want to protect that investment and benefit from the equity or return, therefore, seeing an increase in worth. By the same measures, taking care of your body and what you put into it, will, to a large degree, predict your quality of life. Why then, with our most important asset, our health, are so many struggling?

Angelike and I have been in the health and fitness industry most of our adult lives, teaching, training, selling and educating. We've made a very good living from it, and we've always looked at it from one very important angle: what good is having all the money in the world if you don't have the body to spend it in, to take you places, see and experience things your wealth can afford you? And subsequently, what good is having a super healthy body if you can't acquire the financial means to go and do those same things? In other words, the health of your body and the health of your bank account are vital in this life. We can try to fool ourselves in either direction, but we're doing exactly that, fooling ourselves.

There's no doubt in my mind that I wouldn't be who I am or where I am in life had I not made an early commitment to taking care of my body. It has taught me discipline and given me the confidence I needed to open doors I know I would otherwise have not had the ability to open.

THE CREATION OF ADAM

Our culture has become obsessed with looks. Abs, buns, boobs, and guns are what sells. But I want to begin somewhere else for a good reason, and that's with the eyeball. The human eyeball has more than two million working parts; it can see 2.7 million different colors and has about 12 million photoreceptors. Next, I'd like to mention our ears, which contain the smallest bones in our bodies and never stop listening, even at night. Did you know that you can never turn your ears off? Then let's take our attention to what it takes to in order to speak, around 100 muscles in the neck, jaw, and tongue working in synchronicity. In fact, humans are the only species capable of speech. Why aren't apes, chimpanzees or other primates speaking by now? According to a study published in Frontiers in Neuroscience (2018), it's not because they don't have the right parts (larynx, vocal tract), but it's the lack of brainpower.

"The primate vocal tract is speech ready, but most species don't have the neural control to make the complex sounds that comprise human speech," says lead author Jacob Dunn, a zoologist at Anglia Ruskin University in Cambridge.

So, when we step back to look at the complexity of the eye, the complexity of the ear, and the complexity of speech, we cannot just look at our bodies as something to get us from the bed to work and then to the couch. An amoeba could almost do that. Humans, however, have been blessed with senses and abilities intended for us to communicate, interact, be fruitful and multiply. And I know most people have no problem finding the will to move their bodies in order to multiply. We have no problem getting up for that, do we? Yet, the statistics show we've become lazy. As you will read, our population is getting bigger and sicker despite our advancing sciences. Something has gone wrong.

If you believe in God, in intelligent design, then I'll have to assume you don't believe we were meant to sit for hours in front of a screen or that we were designed to isolate ourselves from one another, or that we should choose virtual activities over real ones. We are made to run, lift and move in unison with our spiritual goals. We're not designed to be relegated to a battery-powered chair or sofa. Quite the opposite, the bible describes our bodies as temples of the Holy Spirit, and that we should eat and drink for the glory of God. It's says a Proverbs 31 woman sets about her work vigorously (not lethargically) with arms strong (not weak) for her tasks. It says, *Therefore, I do not run like someone running aimlessly; I do not fight like a boxer beating the air. No, I strike a blow to my body and make it my slave so that after I have preached to others, I myself will not be disqualified for the prize.* (1 Corinthians 9:26-27).

Run, fight, breathe. Action verbs. That is what is described throughout the bible. The Word couldn't be any clearer on physicality and movement, yet when we look around our malls, grocery stores, and churches, we see just the opposite. We see the balance that God intended between our spiritual lives and physical ones has been skewered, thrown way off course. I could throw in dozens of statistics here to prove that, but you have eyes to see, it's become overtly obvious. We've gone off course.

Our bodies are quite possibly the easiest thing to Turn On, meaning that which we have the most control over, where outside forces don't determine as much to the success. Yet, it's the greatest struggle for most people, certainly here in America. To prove it, ask yourself if you've ever heard of an instance where anybody that you knew, as far back as you can remember, was force-fed. Think about that. Do you know anybody who said, "I'd really love to be in better control of my body, but these two big guys come over three times a day, hold me down and feed me cheese fries?" Or do you know anybody who said, "I woke up this morning with the intention of doing some jumping jacks and push-ups, but gravity wasn't having that. Gravity said, 'No, you just stay right there in bed and don't move a muscle.'" I can't think of any of those cases. Can you?

If I'm overstating the obvious, it's for the sake of making a point. A large percentage of the American population struggles with body issues that they know how to fix, but somehow choose not to. And while illness, injury, finances, and geography can play a role in our health, a large majority of the population simply suffers from self-control that is out of control. We're killing ourselves physically and mentally with poor food choices and a lack of exercise. Compound that with a growing prevalence to allow political correctness and apathy to overshadow the obvious and it's easy to see why this is a hotly debated topic. But I'll say it, I believe when we stop being politically correct about weight, when we stop feeling sorry for ourselves and begin taking real personal responsibility, that is when we can start making some real progress. And it goes much deeper than physical appearance; it goes back to the assignment we are all called to do that was mentioned earlier in this book.

Our bodies are the vehicles by which we carry our spirit's mission. I remember a wise preacher once saying, "Do you think God wants to put all his glory in you, all His knowledge in you, only for you to turn around and live in a body where you can't use it? Do you think He wants to invest all that He has into you for you to only be here on this earth for 50 or 60 years because you chose to neglect your health? All that He'd done in you would then go to waste."

I know of another man of faith, with significant influence, who had struggled with his weight for most of his adult life. One day as we were talking, he said to me, "I think people would take me more seriously, and I'd have a lot more opportunities to spread the Word if I wasn't so heavy. Do you agree?"

"Are we being honest?" I asked. "Then yes, I believe you are right. It's your vessel, and people will judge you by the way you take care of it, the same as if I were to give you a ride in my car and it were unkempt."

At the same time, we're seeing an issue with eating disorders and body issues in young adults, much of which is being traced back to unrealistic body images on social media. Be it overweight, underweight, malnourished or whatever the case, we all come to a time when we will decide how we will treat our bodies and subsequently, how much we want to accomplish with our time here on earth. I think it's fairly obvious that if you're in better shape, chances are you'll be more productive at work, have a greater sense of self-worth and be better suited to accomplish your mission in the face of obstacles and stress.

BOXING OURSELVES IN

Connection to other human beings is hugely important, not just in matters of proximity and meeting people, but in the physical sense, in terms of touch. It transcends species, as countless experiments have been done with both humans and animals with regard to the importance of physical touch.

Dr. Dacher Keltner, a psychology professor at the University of California, Berkeley, says, "To me, the science of touch convincingly suggests that we're wired to—we need to—connect with other people on a basic physical level." This confirmed the true centerpiece of thought behind Turned On—that we are indeed hard-wired for connection and touch by nature.

God gave us our senses, and we need to use them as often as possible. Your day will be considerably better when you embrace the physical components of our bodies and planet by experiencing an abundance of the five senses. And therein lies a problem, in our technologically advancing world, we are more often continuing to surrender opportunities to be in the presence of nature and other humans in lieu of doing something alone and indoors. We are surrendering our ability to use all of our senses and all of our faculties for the sake of time and convenience, and therefore not really realizing that we are also relinquishing much of what makes us human.

Earlier, I talked about how the statistics show we're not getting happier with innovation; we're becoming more depressed. We're feeling more alone than ever before. We're taking human connection and substituting it with virtual things, which brings me to my first point. As a sports journalist, I did an adequate number of stories about boxing. And I always found boxers rather interesting compared to other athletes. Although many of them were loud and boisterous on camera or in the ring, I noticed that because of the nature of the sport and the way they trained, that outside of the ring, they seemed to experience a deep sense of isolation and loneliness. Boxers ran alone, trained alone and sat alone more than any other athletes I covered. They seemed to have developed an ability to shut themselves off to the rest of the world, which seems fitting, a warrior stepping into a ring by themselves must have an accommodating mindset in order to be successful. Heavy-weight boxer, Frank Bruno, who twice fought Mike Tyson, said, "Boxing is the toughest and loneliest sport in the world."

Similar to boxing, other individual sports, like running or swimming, seem to have a component of isolation. I realize that people who gravitate to these types of sports or exercise often enjoy and look forward to the solitude, but it can also take a toll.

In an article in *The Guardian*, Andy Baddeley, a two-time Olympian for Britain, said, "I've often felt that I would be better suited for a team sport. What I enjoy most is group training, but the nature of distance running is that that doesn't happen every day." He said sometimes it's a lonely decision.

I point this out not so much to draw attention to the competitive athletes that choose these sports but rather what is happening to those people simply looking for exercise. Because now, the world is seeing an isolation of exercise. Should this continue, we have to ask what the consequences might be? If we persevere in the name of progress and continue to take the assemblage and the social aspect out of group exercise, what will our spiritual body suffer?

Allow me to explain further, and to shine some light on this with one particular example I am very comfortable speaking about. I spent two decades of my life teaching group exercise (weight training, Spinning, Zumba). I've taught at more than two dozen different facilities in a half dozen states, and so I feel I have a very good frame of reference for the dynamics of exercise and in particular, group exercise. It's about much more than getting the muscle stimulated or the heart rate up.

When I look at the rising popularity of the Peloton bike, I see it as a perfect example of where we're heading as a culture. The allure of Peloton appears to be in its convenience and the ability to save time and money. It gives us the ability to exercise in a virtual group-like setting in the comfort of our home. Notice I said group-like because I don't consider Wii Golf anymore like actual golf than I would consider a virtual riding class like real biking, and even I didn't do real biking (outdoors). It's great that Peloton has positioned itself to allow busy people to feel like they can partake in a real-time, high-energy cycling class with a real-time, high-energy instructor. But what are we calling real?

In my experience as a group cycling instructor, people often came early to class to visit with others. They hugged, laughed and shared stories. During class, they could not only see other people but, like it or not, they could smell others too. Some of you may be asking, "And that's a good thing?" Yes, it is a good thing. It's a sensory experience much in the same way I can look at a high-definition virtual video of a sailboat and enjoy it, but I can't smell the ocean or feel the water splash on my skin. Now while those two examples may not convince you to go to a real class versus a Peloton one, it's the third that's the most critical. The after-class in person, human experience.

When Peloton or any virtual exercise class is over, it's over. You power down, and you're out. And that's probably a huge reason why people take it. Congratulations, you're welcome, now tune out and turn off. You have other screens to get to at work or in the living room. You've taken one more step in isolating yourself from physical interaction. In all my years of teaching classes, I can't begin to tell you the number of stories, friendships and impromptu endeavors that happen in that magical 10 to 15 minutes after the music stops and the class is over. The walking around, hugging and smiling. Some people became best friends, business partners and one couple even met during my class and ended up getting married a year later. Why? Because we're human beings and after seeing, feeling and, yes, even smelling, other humans for 50 minutes, it's very natural and comforting to want to continue that human interaction. It was almost as though the fellowship was the anticipated reward of finishing the class.

Before Peloton fanatics begin cursing me, I want to remind you that I'm not saying it doesn't have its place or benefits. What I'm saying is that this, and other virtual training simulators, are replacing aspects of life that we are slowly relinquishing our humanity to for the sake of convenience. And eventually being alone leads to not having real accountability or incentive to show up at all.

Whether it's Peloton, DoorDash, or my wife ordering a pair of sneakers on Amazon, the fact remains we're not physically interacting often enough with other people throughout our day, and I think we're clearly seeing the effect it's having on our culture. This is a topic I discussed specifically with Dr. Kushlev who made a great point. He said, "I went to a yoga class recently, and it's not that I necessarily talked to anybody, I just felt like part of a community, and I think the only way you truly notice it's benefits, is that once you take it away and go back to it."

And therein lies the famous frog in the boiling water analogy. Maybe we just start with one online class because we're super busy that day. Later in the week, it seems to fit in our busy schedule again. The choice becomes more and more appealing as getting in the car, going through traffic, parking and (uh oh) having to interact with people begins to feel like too much trouble. The next thing you know, virtual exercise has become our new norm, and we forget what being a part of a real community feels like. Then it's gone. But it happened so casually that we didn't notice it. We couldn't point to a spot specifically. We just began to feel more out of touch. We began to feel like a part of our lives was lost, and then we're left scratching our heads on how to get it back. Remember C.S. Lewis? The safest road to hell is a gradual one.

Most people who feel depressed about their physical body or depressed mentally will struggle to give an exact reason as to why. They have difficulty pinpointing when something went wrong, and they started feeling different. All they can do is shrug their shoulders. Why? Because they've never been able to be an observer of their life from the outside. They were in the comfortable water before it began to boil. In specific language, nobody says to themselves, "HEY YOU, WAKE UP. YOU STOPPED BEING SOCIAL ABOUT SIX MONTHS AGO. WHY CAN'T YOU SEE THAT IS WHAT STARTED THIS?"

It feels like a warm blanket at first, just keeping us cozy in our house and not having to leave for anything. Let's face it, nobody ever starts out saying, I'm going to be a shut-in. I'm going to completely shut myself out from my walking in my neighborhood or going to the park to be around other people outdoors. Of course not, but somewhere along the way, something convinced us that having a 70-inch flat-screen tv and 840 channels was good for us. Somebody in your house said, "Let's not go on the walk today. Let's not go out tonight. Let's get the food delivered just one night." Somebody suggested it wouldn't be worth it to go out in the cold to the football game because you can see it on TV in high def. Somebody convinced you to skip the gym today and do the virtual class in your living room instead.

If this path of least resistance continues to dominate our lives, will we continue to report feeling more alone and more depressed. Will we realize what we're missing, or will it happen so slowly, over time, that we will just wonder why we feel empty, why we don't enjoy things that require physical movement and why we feel uncomfortable looking at ourselves in the mirror.

JUST ONE FIX

Once we have realized that we've stopped moving as much and we've isolated ourselves from the social aspect of movement and active socialization, then we can look at the next way we've turned off our bodies. We're looking for man-made answers to a God-made machine. Welcome to the pill-popper era. If there isn't a pill for it, well then, we'll make one. Once again, science has brought us so many comforts that we're willing to turn one more thing over to it, the trust in our bodies.

I worked for a bit in orthopedic device sales, and during that time, I'd say more than half of my patients were total knee replacement patients. If you know nothing about this surgery, it's basically the sawing off of the kneecap and replacing it with a plastic joint. It's brutal. The scar looks like a 10-inch zipper, and it's one of the more painful rehab processes imaginable. In my time fitting patients, it was fairly obvious most weren't just overweight, but morbidly obese. We even had rubber/spandex Velcro extenders for patients to which the normal device would not fit around their thigh.

According to a June 4, 2014 news release from the American Academy of Orthopedic Surgeons, weight problems accounted for 95 percent of the increased demand for knee replacements, and by 2030, total knee replacements are projected to grow by 189 percent to 1.28 million procedures. That's staggering.

At the time I was fitting these post-surgical patients, I was also involved in personal training and weight loss so naturally I'd ask the doctors I called on why they weren't talking to their patients about nutrition and exercise. Duh right? Do you know what most of them said? By and large, they said, "Don't blame us, we try to tell people to exercise, eat better and lose weight." Most of them just say, "Isn't there a pill you can give me?" So that's where we are. Not even the threat of massive pain and the sawing off of body parts will motivate some people to address their diet and exercise. A couple of my close friends and family members have been told if they didn't lose weight, a total knee replacement was imminent. Some listened, many didn't.

We've become a culture that, by and large, craves comfort over happiness. The cruise control button has invaded the kitchen, and many people are playing naïve, knowing that they are on a collision course with future pain and discomfort, even death. Currently, sixty percent of adults in America are obese or overweight. Obesity is associated with a higher incidence of a number of diseases, including diabetes, cardiovascular disease, and cancer. Obesity is the next major epidemiologic challenge facing today's doctors, with the annual allocation of healthcare resources for the disease and related comorbidities projected to exceed $150 billion in the United States. That makes it not only a health but an economic issue—one of significant proportions.

It's not just about weight loss. The pill for every ill phenomenon is creeping into every aspect of our health. This is the part where I could name a couple dozen of drugs or throw some more staggering numbers at you, but I won't. I'd rather just use common sense.

To be Turned On is to point out and acknowledge the obvious. So, here are two questions to help illuminate the problem. First, do you know anybody in your family who has an oversized Ziploc bag full of prescription bottles? Or maybe they have a cabinet overflowing with them? I'm guessing many of you are nodding your heads right now. I've seen this several times, with friends and family alike, and each time my jaw hit the floor. How can you even keep track of what you're taking? That looks like a full-time job. Common sense tells me that it can't be good to be putting that many prescription pills into your body each day. That seems like man playing God.

And my second question is, do you remember ten or twenty years ago seeing pharmaceutical drugs pushed so hard and so often on television? Of course you don't because they weren't. You can't watch television today without seeing commercial after commercial telling you what might be wrong with you, what you might need to take to make you feel better. Again, use your common sense here. Why is this happening?

The order has been mixed up. Ever since the beginning of medicine or healing, it's always been, "I don't feel good, something seems off, let me go to a physician or a specialist." You go, they examine you and then make a recommendation. Now it's "Let me watch TV, have a seed planted in my head about what might be happening to me, and then make an appointment with my doctor and tell him or her I need this."

Many doctors, not all, are wined, dined and solicited by the very pharmaceutical companies making and advertising the drugs. Again, not all, but enough, have been sold hard enough to go down their list and say here is the problem and this is the drug that cures it, script signed, next patient please.

For the record, this is an opinion I've made with my own eyes, my own family, and my own experience. Correct, physicians can't take kickbacks from pharmaceutical companies. And the mob can't own casinos in Vegas. What else can you tell me? And yes, by and large, most doctors chose to go into medicine to cure people. And most teachers go into teaching to help kids learn. But medicine and education are heavily influenced by the same thing—big government, big business and big money.

Doctors and teachers aren't bad, they're just human, which makes them what? Susceptible to getting turned off, taking the path of least resistance. So this isn't the point where you call me a conspiracy theorist or get mad at me if you're in that profession. This isn't the point where you placed me as a zealot in a political group. I'm just throwing out observations, things I've seen. Nothing is absolute, but if I'm seeing it, perhaps you are as well. So this is the point where I say AGAIN, let's get back to being more human, not more artificial.

WHATS THE ALTERNATIVE YOU ASK?

A Turned-On person takes their health into their own hands and, at some point, personal responsibility in terms of their body becoming a priority. They do their own research, question the status quo, and look toward preventative medicines (i.e., food, supplements, and exercise) as alternatives to pills and surgery.

Angelike and I are all too familiar with conventional medicine as we watched both her parents pass from cancer. We know specifically that my mother-in-law was not led in the right direction during treatment for stage four cancer. One night, we went to visit her in the hospital and asked what she'd had for dinner. Her answer—Spaghetti!! That's purely carbs. Do you know how they scan for cancer? They inject glucose into the body, and it goes right to the cancer. Cancer feeds off glucose, and this is what experts at the hospital were feeding a stage-four cancer patient. Furthermore, I was highly alarmed that the cancer hospital had three to four full-time valets outside parking cars. It looked more like a busy restaurant on a Friday night than a Tuesday afternoon of treating disease. Common sense tells me there's something very odd with that. No?

As people demand better answers and more alternatives, the world is finding out that in a rush to do things scientifically, we have overlooked the ability to do things intrinsically or intuitively. Once again, technology coupled with convenience proves it can sometimes get ahead of us. We should be thankful for science, thankful for research and medical advances that treat and cure diseases, but the question is when does the pendulum swing too far in the other direction? When do we stop doing what is right in lieu of doing what is easiest? When do we stop playing God?

Novelist and activist Wendell Berry grew up on a farm. His parents came from generations of farmers and, therefore, he was passionate about sustainable agriculture and appropriate technologies, or application of technology on a small scale being environmentally sound. This brings us to his quote I began this chapter with "People are fed by the food industry, which pays no attention to health and are treated by the health industry, which pays no attention to food." The fact is we're feeding more people, more food and faster than ever before.

With the rise in popularity of chain restaurants, fast-food franchises, and in-house dining delivery, we're not getting the home-cooked squares like our parents and grandparents did. We don't have firsthand control over what is being put into our food, so when is a green bean no longer a green bean? What could possibly be put into a harmless vegetable like a tomato? The human eye can't detect preservatives, GMOs and dyes that proliferate our food choices. The truth is that many of us go into the grocery store or restaurant with a blind trust that literally put our lives in the hands of those selling or preparing the food.

For the record, let me be clear, I'm not talking about the hard-working American farmer working the family farm. I'm talking about the food industry, the one in which dollars count more than quality.

In my 20s and early 30s, I never paid attention to nutrition or the food industry. I was always under the assumption you could out-train a poor diet and that my grocer and my government had my best interest at hand. It wasn't until my metabolism took a huge hit in my late 30s, and I met Angelike that I began to really look at what was going into my body. It was also about that time, around 2008, that I vividly remember being captivated by the documentary, *Food Matters*.

I'll never forget the part in the film where David Wolfe, a raw food advocate, says, "We, for what-ver reason, decided we were going to spray everything with pesticides, herbicides, larvicides, fungicides, suicide. We decided we were going to genetically modify things we don't know anything about. We decided for some reason that we were going to inject hormones into cows and then pasteurize that milk to death and then serve it to millions of people. We decided to go into this crazy world of the unknown and experiment on ourselves. But what's interesting is that experiment has led to an incredible discovery. And that is—food does matter."

I can almost recite that piece from memory because I rewound it so many times, watching it over and over again. It was a wake-up call, a slap in the face, which I desperately needed. And while I've never been one to hit the panic button, this may be the one time in my life I came closest. It was like, of course, this makes complete sense, we can't see what's being put into and on our foods but whatever it is, it's going to manifest or show up in our tissues, energy and thoughts. Like Wolfe said, "The food we eat creates the tissue of our body, it creates the quality of the energy of our cells and very deliberately affects the quality of our thoughts."

Twelve years later as I write this book, Angelike is lactose intolerant, we've lost three family members to diet-related diseases, half of my nieces and nephews have food allergies and it seems like every day I open social media to hear about a new person diagnosed with cancer, diabetes or some type of autoimmune disorder. I'm not a doctor, but something doesn't add up.

We're eating food-like things and there's seems to be a Starbucks on just about every corner of the country. The energy crisis is in our bodies, but the fact still remains we have control over what goes past our lips. Like Wolfe says, be it a horrid chemical soup or extraordinary superfood, it takes the same amount of work to get it into our mouths. Think about that.

As we've spoken about so many things in this book that need a spotlight shone on them, diet and nutrition is no different. We've also discussed the good and bad of technology, and I pointed out that we live in an era in which information has never been so readily available. In the world of health and wellness, though, it's pretty obvious there is information overload. We read something one week and forbid ourselves from a certain type of food only to read something else the next, which turns us onto the next great concern or next diet fad.

Five years ago, I was told to make sure to eat something every two to three hours. Now, that recommendation has completely changed to only eat during an eight-hour period of your day. This seemingly never-ending cycle of guessing what will make the difference takes its toll on us and, eventually, we just throw our hands up in frustration and ask how am I supposed to keep up?

But it doesn't have to be that way.

THE DIETING CYCLE ENDS

In my nearly four decades of exercise, I've seen every macro-nutrient become vilified. In the eighties, we were told to load up on carbs, then it was no carbs. In the nineties, we were told to eliminate fats only to be educated years later on how important they are. Proteins were the best, and then, too much protein wasn't good.

So, what are we supposed to think?

You're not. That's the problem. The diet industry has you thinking too much. It's a cash cow, and each year, a new celebrity with a new plan is touting the new trend. We, the public, eat it up and jump on board. It's time to turn on your common sense and stop the information overload. Stop the cycle of guessing.

Dependencies. Will Armijo, founder of NutriScribe, says, "The health and wellness industry is built on dependencies. If people can create a dependency, they know they can make money off of you. How do we have so many diets and so many prescriptions and yet obesity is at roughly 40 percent of the population and seven out of 10 adults are unhealthy. They are trying to confuse you. You have to do this if you want this. If you crave these results, this is the new way to get them."

I'm not saying they're all bad or don't work, many of them do, but the only way we can be free and do something that has long term sustainability is to become completely independent of bias and get more educated on the basics. Before you choose any program or confuse yourself with a ton of different theories and opinions, dial it down to these three basic components of your health; portion control, inflammation and toxicity. The Turned-On body looks for simplicity. It looks for what God intended for our bodies. These three are cut and dry, time-tested, principles that will not change with each new year or decade.

In America, we have a portion control problem. It is perhaps the greatest cause of obesity that nobody is really talking about. The evidence? Fast food commercials always talk about how much food you'll get. Chain restaurants often advertise *All You Can Eat* specials. Even in our homes, grandma said it was rude to leave food on your plate and always encouraged us to eat up or get seconds. The light bulb moment for me came when we had some friends from Australia visit. He was a miner with a muscular build and a handshake that could break a bone. She was tall and lean but by no means skinny. Here's why I mention that—they couldn't believe the size of the food portions in the States and told us that when they went out to eat, they would often share a meal or only order appetizers because of the overwhelming amount of food.

My second eye opener was again at Disney World. Angelike and I watched obese parents encourage their adolescent child to eat more food from the buffet. I said to Angelike that if it had been a parent putting a cigarette in that child's mouth, it would be a crime, but with food, somehow, even though it can be just as harmful, is OK. I'm not Mike Bloomberg; I'm not about telling people what they can and cannot consume, but I am about education, and again, self-responsibility.

A simple training or education on how much to eat would leave us with a great foundation for health. We know that too much is not good, but not enough isn't the answer because if you under eat, you'll lower your metabolism which will make you lethargic and keep weight on. In fact, studies show that if you reduce your daily calorie intake by 50%, your likelihood of binge eating increases by 50%. The answer, then, is portion control meaning the proper ratios of food to be eaten at a single meal.

The next two pillars, which are key to ending the dieting cycle, are toxicity and inflammation. Our bodies will gain weight and hold onto fat when we expose them to toxins and, therefore, become inflamed. The two go hand in hand. This topic could be an entire book in itself, but let's just cover the need-to-know part.

Toxins are harmful chemicals absorbed into the body which can come from household products (cleaners, pesticides, candles), beauty products (lipstick, foundation, deodorant), and food (preservatives, GMOs, added sugar, etc.). The liver can't process these things. They get kicked out and eventually get stored in fat cells. Inflammation then results because of these foreign substances being in the body causing joint pain, fatigue, brain fog, muscle fatigue, skin rashes, etc.

Without getting into too much on the topic know this, we can be deceived. If you walk into a room and there are two plates on the table, the first a juicy grilled chicken breast and broccoli and the second a fried chicken sandwich with french fries you might say, "Oh, that's an easy one." But what if the grilled chicken breast was cage raised, injected with hormones, and plumped up on genetically modified corn? And the broccoli was sprayed with pesticide. Meanwhile, the fried chicken sandwich was cage free, with no hormones or antibiotics and placed on gluten-free organic bread and served with organic potatoes fries baked using avocado oil. The second choice would be much better as it would be low toxicity and anti-inflammatory. Understand that often it's our perception of what's healthy that messes us up.

Lower inflammation and low toxicity are crucial to a healthy body because it allows the liver, kidneys, intestines, lungs and skin to go to work and perform how God intended them to. We experience disease symptoms, hit plateaus and underperform when we look for a quick fix and just do what somebody tells us to do without asking why. If you simply stick to the simple foundation of these three things, you're chances at looking, feeling and performing better will increase dramatically.

YOUR BODY AND YOUR BANK ACCOUNT

It's nice to have a good-looking body, but how many days of the week would you say you go outside shirtless guys? Ladies, how many days are you in a bikini? I ask because when I think of the benefits of a Turned-On body I think of the ROI (return of investment) when we have our clothes on, in everyday life.

I vividly remember taking my daughter to her first martial arts class. At the time, I was instructing people how to turn their personality into profit, and a large part of my course focused on body language. Watching these five and six-year-olds come into the class and stand there really opened my eyes even further as to the importance of how our bodies and our body language speaks for us.

Children, for the most part, are uncomfortable and insecure when they are introduced to something new. In the martial arts class, I observed that some students stood with their hands clasped together and arms held close to their chests. Others had their arms folded or their hands in their pockets. The instructor gave a strong command for them to stand at attention, and they all did quickly. But more than half of the children still kept their hands close to their chests or in their pockets. The instructor said, "Hands out of your pockets—that is a sign of weakness," and reminded them that when they received their uniforms, they would not have pockets at all.

According to body language experts, when a person stands with their hands in their pockets, it's a sign that they are uncomfortable with their looks or image. People will do this when they feel unsatisfied with their appearance, clothes, or their actions. It's a way the subconscious mind hides. Crossing one's arms is typically seen as defensive or negative posture, certainly one not conducive to being Turned On and open to new things.

The next time you're at a large gathering, stop and look around. Observe how the people nearby are holding themselves and then correlate that with how you judged them or thought of them. I'm not saying everybody who puts their hands in their pockets is insecure, or those with their arms crossed are defensive, but these types of body positions are definitely clues that can either help or hinder our ability to attract and communicate with others. When we are proud of our bodies, feeling strong with energy, it shows in our posture and our body language.

What I can tell you with absolute certainty, and from experience, is that if you take care of your body and pay attention to your body language, it will take care of you, and I mean financially.

Jennifer Shinall, assistant professor of law at Vanderbilt Law School and author of *Occupational Characteristics and the Obesity Wage Penalty,* wrote in a 2014 article, "A morbidly obese woman working in an occupation with an emphasis on personal interaction will earn almost five percent less than a normal-weight woman working in an occupation with exactly the same emphasis."

Even after considering differences in education and socioeconomic status, there seems to be no scenario where being overweight becomes an advantage for a woman. It is said that heavy women earn $9,000 less than their average-weight counterparts, very heavy women earn $19,000 less.

What about men? In a study of more than 12,000 American workers, Dan Cable of the London Business School and co-author Timothy Judge from the University of Florida found an interesting fact: skinny men seemed to earn less than those of average weight. And the men of average weight would also earn quite a bit more than those who were obese, upwards of $10,000-15,000 per year.

These studies beg the question, is it as much about physical weight or about what our perceptions are of people who stray too far in one direction or another? Are skinny men seen as weak or timid? Are heavier men perceived as being lazier or more indulgent? Do we compare women to unrealistic images from magazines or Hollywood movies?

These are touchy subjects that are difficult to talk about because we'd like to think in a day and age where equality is so stressed that it wouldn't matter. But no matter what laws are put in place, no matter how we attempt to put everybody on an equal playing field, we cannot get inside the minds of people and turn off their propensity to cast judgment.

Again, if you go to pick somebody up and your car is unkempt, it's fair to say that will make an impression on them. How much, who knows, but it does.

E.T. PHONE HOME

I can't think of another factor that contributes to our self-confidence more than our physical body. Why? Because most of the time, people see it before they can get to know your personality and before they know how smart you are or how much money you make. We are physical beings, and this is how we physically present ourselves.

In order to give you some perspective, I'll shed some light on my own health journey. For starters, my sister called me bird chest for most of my childhood, and for a good reason—you could actually see the bones in my chest. I looked like I could break in half from a high-five. In middle school, my classmates affectionately called me E.T. because I had a skinny frame and long neck, and this huge oversized head. And it all came to a head in ninth grade when my fragile body image took a huge hit.

For the first time in my life, things were beginning to change. I had been lifting weights all summer and was feeling more confident than ever. For the first time, my overprotective parents allowed me to play a contact sport—football. I struggled to gain weight. None of the cool clothes in fashion really fit me, and no amount of Ruffles Chips, chocolate ice cream or primitive raw egg protein shakes could put an ounce of weight on me. But I was absolutely committed to lifting weights, and after some long and patient waiting, I actually started to see my tiny biceps grow and the bones in my chest disappear. Finally, this skinny boy was about to be a man, or so I thought.

So, there I was in the high school weight room, feeling pretty good about myself on this particular day. In fact, I felt so confident that I looked at the bar with 25-pound plates on each end of it and said to myself, "Yep, today is the day I bench press that." All 95 pounds of it. It was the day I'd go from Screech to Slater.

There were only a half-dozen people in the room that after-noon, a few freshman friends, three or four seniors and the water girl who was prepping things for a later practice. I sat on the end of the bench, closed my eyes, and envisioned the weight touching my chest and going back up with relative ease. There were no mirrors in the gym, so I couldn't see myself in the school-issued grays that hung off me like they were still on the coat hanger. Nope, in my mind, I was as big and strong as Arnold Schwarzenegger in the magazines that scattered my bedroom. I was a muscular football player who saw the 95 lbs. as a piece of cake.

I gripped the bar extra tight, gave the old one-two-three count to my spotter and quickly lowered the weight to my chest with authority—where it stayed—with authority. My knees wobbled back and forth, my skinny butt lifted from the padding and my E.T. head went back and forth as my face contorted with every muscle it had. Nothing was moving that bar though. So, my spotter lifted it back up and racked it along with my pride.

Wow, I couldn't be any more disappointed or embarrassed. Or so I thought.

Remember the water girl? Nothing like getting pinned in front of the ladies to boost an already fragile teen ego, right? Wrong! Just when I thought it couldn't get worse, it did. The water girl came over and asked inquisitively, "Do you think I could give it a try?"

"Are you serious," I thought in my Fred Savage prepubescent *Wonder Years* voice. My humiliation wasn't enough. Now a girl had to take a little bit of what was left of my self-esteem and stomp on it? Yup, that's exactly what happened. She got down on that bench, lifted the bar off, touched her chest with it, and pushed it back up.

Check, please. I'll just be transferring schools now, preferably out of the state. Is there anything in Canada, perhaps a school in Iceland I could attend?

That day could've gone two ways. (1) I pack up my grays, turn in my pads, and go back to playing a non-contact sport like Frisbee or (2) I take that moment and use it to fuel and to motivate me to work harder. I chose the latter and what seemed somewhat insignificant at the time set in motion a chain of events that impacted me for the rest of the days.

This story is important to you and the concept of being Turned On because without me making that decision to work hard and stay physically fit, I'm not so sure I'm writing this book. In fact, I'm not sure I would have my wife, my children, or any part of my life had it not been for that moment. I feel like that moment may have been the catalyst that set off a series of events that led me to this moment right here, right now.

Now let's turn to you, turning your body on. While my plight was with lack of muscle in my youth, it still resonates with me today. Even in my 40s, that high school beanpole still holds a place inside of me, indirectly making decisions playing a role in who I am and in my confidence. Maybe you had a similar moment in school, or you recently had a wakeup moment with your body image or health.

My plea for you is to take it seriously and don't quit. My desire is for you to first, be healthy and live long, second, to walk down the street proud of your vessel. I'm not saying it has to be society's specs, I really just want you to be happy with it.

DO YOU FEEL LIKE I DO?

Just as I discussed in the chapter on business, it's good to have choices. The same applies to our body, as a limited degree of health produces a limited amount of options to work, play and love. I'm going to assume you feel like I do, your primary goals being to live a long, healthy life with plentiful amounts of love and financial security.

It's important to remember, God made Adam from the dust of the earth and created us in His image, giving man dominion over all other animals. He made order out of chaos. And if we attempt to boil down what it means to have a Turned On body it's really the same philosophy or goal, to bring order out of chaos or confusion. As I spoke at the outset of this chapter, the miracle of life is seen in the eyeball and every single organ in our body. This leads us to what? The ability to achieve our greatest dreams and achievements in life depends on these systems of the body granting us the ability to breathe, move, communicate and create. And there you have it, we are all created, but in turn, we also create and, in order to reveal the importance of a Turned On body, it must not be simply viewed as a mobile home or tractor-trailer, taking us to where we need to go. It truly is a temple. It houses our spirit every single day we take a breath, and that will never change. Genesis 2:7 says, *And the LORD God formed man of the dust of the ground and breathed into his nostrils the breath of life; and man became a living soul.* The original text for breath in Hebrew is the word Ruach. It is mentioned in several places throughout the Bible (Job 33.4 - *The spirit of God has made me, the breath (RUACH) of the Almighty gives me life)* and means much more than *to inhale air* as we define breath.

The Ruach is our life force; it gives us all that inspires, encourages, motivates, stimulates and stirs us. It is His breath which he breathed into us and gave us the spirit. God told Moses (Number 11:17) *Then I will come down and talk with you there. I will take the Spirit (RUACH) that is upon you and I will put the same upon them.*

This Ruach then also represents knowledge, wisdom, discernment and truth. When we speak of this breath as the life force, we can draw a correlation to the physical breath that we know in science. The two are very similar. In other words, how do we know if somebody is alive? We check to see if they are breathing.

When you are excited, falling in love, making a big speech, holding your baby for the first time or going down a roller coaster, what happens? Your heart rate increases, you breathe more intensely and you feel what? More alive. When another human being speaks to you in person you can often feel and (for better or worse) smell their breath. It's there and present, although you cannot see it. So when we take care of our body and exercise, the first thing we are told to do is to get our heart rate up. Maybe you've often heard it referred to as a *runner's high* because the endorphins make you feel more present, invigorated, and more alive.

If I had to put in simple terms, turning on your body means that we choose, on a grand level and daily basis, not to separate the flesh from the Ruach. It means that we neither tend to the spirit yet neglect the vessel nor become so enamored with our physical body that we lay waste to any redeemable qualities of our soul. It's balance, peace and an authority over what you control, what you have been placed on this earth to accomplish. Blind trust, therefore, in anybody but yourself should be tempered. Keep the rules pertaining to your body simple, timeless and consistent. Do your research and act with a great deal of common sense. Get in touch with how you feel, not just how you look. Don't allow yourself to go bonkers by succumbing to the constant ebb and flow of the wellness industry.

English philosopher and theologian G.K. Chesterson said, "The trouble with always trying to preserve the health of the body is that it is so difficult to do without destroying the health of the mind." I think that is more interesting and more poignant today than when he said it over 100 years ago. Being almost 300 lbs., and often using self-deprecating humor to deflect his stout shape, I can see how he was troubled. He died young (age 62) of congestive heart failure.

Turning on and keeping the lights on in your body is a big responsibility, but when the lights are on, when you're alert, you have a heightened sense of intuition and wisdom. Angelike and I have seen too many people, including ourselves, become consumed by diets and body image. The human body is complex, and science and technology have given us a quality of life people just a century ago would've never been able to dream up, but never forget, the cruise control button, that automatic pilot, can be one of the most dangerous weapons against our happiness and success. Information is good. Information overload is bad. Convenience and abundance are good, sloth and gluttony are bad. Like everything else you've read in this book, the things that make parts of our life go dark are often cloaked in the terms *progress* or *evolving*. There is a not-so-fine line that says HOLD UP, what makes common sense? That's where we seek to find real solutions.

CHAPTER THIRTEEN

TURN ON
YOUR FAITH

> *"The greatest legacy one can pass on to one's children*
> *and grandchildren is not money or other material*
> *things accumulated in one's life,*
> *but rather the legacy of character and faith."*
> — *Billy Graham*

It was a particularly frigid Sunday in January, and the Pastor stood up to address the congregation. He said, "I knew we'd have a light crowd here today because there was a dusting of snow in Nashville last night." He laughingly emphasized dusting. Everybody chuckled because they knew it was true. He continued, saying, "Some of you are home right now under your blankets sipping a hot cup of coffee watching this on live stream. But I tell you what, if I could, I'd shut it off. If it weren't for the sick people at home or our out-of-state travelers who wanted to watch, I'd choose not to have a live stream."

Everyone in the church awkwardly looked around as the building fell silent. It's because he was right. The Pastor was making an excellent point, a harsh truth, but one that needed to be told. "I don't want to offend anybody, but I do…kinda," he said. "The fact is that a little bit of cold shouldn't keep you home because nothing can replace the community you get by being here in person."

Now, I loved this particular pastor before, but he shot up ten notches in my book that morning. I was the first one to stand up and give him an "Amen." Like that pastor, if we are to be called on to live a TURNED-ON life, we must have the courage to call out others who crave it. Comfort is no excuse to miss community. Being afraid or politically correct means you lack an ability to wake people up to the truth. And here's the truth, you can't always mail it in and watch everything on television or live stream. It's NOT the same. If your wife went into labor, you wouldn't say, "Hun, the docor said he'd set up a camera in the delivery room, so I'm just gonna sit back, pop open some champagne and watch from the couch." You wouldn't say, "Son, I know you're graduating today, but I'm super busy and the college is taping it anyway. I'm gonna watch it next week when I have more time."

And that morning, as I sat in the pews trying to wrap my head around what the Pastor was getting at, I got a very poignant and unique perspective that confirmed his intentions. The eye of that camera live-streaming the service that morning was focused on the stage; the scope of the lens captured the podium where he spoke from and not much else. So, on that chilly morning, if I'd stayed home and mailed it in, I would have missed the father in front of me with his arm around each of his teenage sons on either side of him. I would've missed the look in his eyes, the smiles on their faces, and the lesson that being there in person with your children is a gift that you must be there to receive. I would've missed that community moment, which said, yes, be here together, embracing one another because you only get so many of those in a lifetime, and there's no substitute for that.

In the Old Testament, Uzzah was one of the Israelites tasked with bringing the Ark of the Covenant to Jerusalem for David. However, along the way, Uzzah steadied the ark with his hand in direct violation of God's law and immediately was struck down. Let's be honest, even for the ardent believer, that's a harsh lesson to digest. The Old Testament was about rules, and Uzzah broke them. David then, out of fear, did nothing with the ark, storing it in the house of Obed-Edom for three months. God then blessed the house of Ebed-Edom and David instructed his men to carry the Ark, six steps in fact, then make a sacrifice. This was a success, and the Ark made it to Jerusalem, and all were overjoyed.

However difficult that story might be to digest and reconcile, here is a unique takeaway I've heard from one religious scholar: The Ark, God's word, was never meant to be put on a cart; it was never meant to be carried by mechanics or machine; it was to be borne upon men's shoulders. A-ha, I'd labored over how to take this story, literally or figuratively but this made sense.

The Old Testament was about physical law (The Tabernacle) and then Christ came to renew and make spiritual law (wherever two are gathered in My name). So, my interpretation in a Turned-On world of faith says yes, we can use technology to live stream sermons and bring the good news to people who might otherwise not get it, but the Word of God should still be borne on the shoulders of man, not be left to the internet or social media. That leaves out one of the most important elements—community. Communion is defined as the exchanging of intimate thoughts and feelings on a spiritual level. It's the gathering, just like we spoke of in terms of group exercise in the previous chapter, that is key here. If we take away or remove the fellowship, or friendly association, we lose the depth perception both physically and spiritually. If we can't step out on Sundays, as we have as a nation since its inception, our perspective will certainly be distorted and shaped by those who benefit from a Godless world.

American essayist Henry Louis (H.L.) Mencken wrote, "The urge to save humanity is almost always a false front for the urge to rule it." Reality TV and 24-hour news networks have taken over as our source of both community, entertainment, and dare I say, God. We've become so enveloped by what is going on in other people's homes or lives that we are losing sight of what's happening in our own. We've become so obedient to pop culture that we've lost sight of faith culture. And it's not something that is just affecting our youth. Case in point, one day my parents came to visit and asked me which channel the cable news was on. When I told them I didn't have cable, they actually began to panic. This was an eye-opening moment to me as my mom asked, "What if we miss something?"

Really, I thought. I had to ponder that question mom had asked. I responded by trying to illuminate what I was hearing in a clearer sense. "Mom, do you mean to tell me you're worried that you might miss what they are going to tell you to worry about?" It felt like I was like Will Ferrell's Mugatu character in *Zoolander* who asks, "Doesn't anyone notice this? I feel like I'm taking crazy pills."

Has our culture become addicted to worry? Infatuated with drama? The first 24-hour cable news station was CNN, which began broadcasting in 1980. According to 2018 Comscore TV Essentials data, the number of households tuning into the big three (CNN, Fox News, MSNBC) prime time news slot (8 pm – 11 pm) increased 8% from the year prior to about 125 million people. Their revenue was also up 4% to total $.5.3 billion.

For some perspective, the CBS Evening News held a 15-minute time slot from 1941-1963, but now there are at least a half dozen 24-hour cable news organizations bidding for your eyeballs each day. That's a lot of time to fill and a lot of competition and, thus, the industry has given life to a rather sober yet telling mantra which is "If it bleeds, it leads."

Genesis 6:5 reads, *The LORD saw how great the wickedness of the human race had become on the earth, and that every inclination of the thoughts of the human heart was only evil all the time.* I know from watching the news, the world can feel like that today. According to a 2014 study by Outbrain, negative headlines like Bad, Worst and Never work 30 percent better at getting our attention than positive ones. The average click-through rate on headlines with negative superlatives was a staggering 63 percent higher than that of their positive counterparts.

This leads me to the chicken or the egg question: are we as human beings being fed negative stories, therefore, we have a negative outlook? Or, do we somehow subconsciously crave negative things which the news is more than happy to provide us? Of all people, the comedian Rob Schneider said it best, "If you turn off the news and talk to your neighbors, you'll find that our country is far more harmonious than you're being told."

SEEK AND YOU SHALL FIND

Famed reformer Martin Luther said, "Man must first cry out that he sees no hope; In this disturbance, salvation begins. When man believes himself to be utterly lost, the light breaks."

To put it in layman's terms, when the path is darkest, God illuminates the welcome sign.

It's no secret, the world needs that sign. It needs more light. The broken in spirit are looking for the light switch, and in Matthew Jesus says, "Come to me, all you who are weary and burdened, and I will give you rest.

Would a loving God break us? Would he purposely turn the light outs in our marriage, our business or our health just so we would say, "Ok, you were right, I do need you." No, while some religions or factions of the church have led people to believe that lie, the truth is, God is pure love. He does not test nor inflict strife upon us intentionally. He is a jealous God but not a malevolent one. The fact is God is not micromanaging our lives. We have free will. In fact, most Christians would be surprised at just how much free will plays a part in our lives. People who feel like God has taken a step back or that He isn't good anymore based on what's happening in our world most likely think so for one reason—they haven't opened up their bible in a while, if ever.

I know because I was one of them.

There are three reasons people don't read the bible (1) they are scared (2) they are lazy (3) they just think it's not important. I was a little bit of all three.

There are three ways to view the bible. (1) You could not believe it at all. (2) You can a-la-carte it and try to pick out which parts you like and which you don't (3) you can look upon it as the divine and infallible word of God.

I have no experience when it comes to No. 1, but for most of my life, I hung out comfortably in No. 2. Notice I said comfortably, not happily. Big difference.

Now allow me to lay down the backstory.

I live in Nashville, and Tennessee has about as many churches per capita as any other city in the United States. It's home to 67 megachurches, which are Christian churches where 2,000 or more people attend a weekend service. That's a lot of believers, and, each one believes their theology, services, and Pastors are the best.

Amen.

But there's only one Bible, so where is the disconnect? To the outsider, agnostic, or non-believer, this is awfully confusing, and why shouldn't it be? So many benevolent people with so many different rules or beliefs all stemming from the same book. It a great excuse for non-believers to cast disbelief or doubt on God's word, and I have to admit kind of odd when I think of it that way too.

I've always believed in God. My Aunt is a Catholic nun, and I always say my mother might as well be one too. Like a good Catholic boy, I made my first communion, my confirmation, and began my love for public speaking in the Catholic Church serving as a lector (the people who read scripture to during mass.) In fact, a priest once told my mother after mass one day, "I think David would be a wonderful candidate for the priest-hood." And at the tender age of 17, I graciously thanked him then told him rather bluntly, "Father, you know I really like girls."

In fact, all through college, I continued to attend Catholic Church, but for most of my 20s and 30s, I became a lost sheep.

I was what you'd call a believer but was not a follower. I was far from it. My faith was on cruise control, completely tuned out. That is what we seem to have in the large majority today, what you'd call part-time believers, one foot all in and the other pushing God out because he doesn't fit with the desires of our culture. It's the pick-and-choose menu that I fell victim to for the better part of my twenties and thirties.

But can we really a-la-carte the teachings of a Creator who made the universe? The designer of our lives. I've learned it doesn't work that way and looking back, it's easy to see the root of my problem, I was a habitual-ritual worshiper who experienced a lifetime full of sit/stand, go through the motion, prayer and penance type of church. AKA religion. It provided me with neither the substance nor guidance which I needed, even craved. I had a religion, but no relationship.

A GOD SMACK

Relationships in our twenties are different than those in our thirties. We like to think that an entire decade gives us the experience and insight to know right from wrong. But for me, and many others, it does not. My religion was there for Sundays and holy holidays, but it was conveniently absent when I wanted to experience the pleasures of the flesh, let's just say. But I still had the audacity to pray to and ask God why He was not working in my favor.

Here's is where it changed.

Angelike was the most beautiful girl I had ever laid eyes on. As they say, I totally outkicked my coverage. This woman, who could've had any man she wanted practically, loved me with all my faults, and they were numerous. But because I didn't have a stronger faith, I almost lost her.

One evening, she and I were discussing our upcoming wedding, and I said something like, "Hey, I just want you to know, I'm still going to hang out with my boys every weekend. We're gonna do our thing and stay out late, and if I happen to get a cab ride home at 3 am and stumble in, don't judge me. I just want to make sure you're cool with that."

Guess what? She was not cool with that. "Kinda late in the game to drop that one on me," she said. "I'm going to be your wife, and you can certainly have friends, but if going out with the guys until 3 am every Saturday and them stumbling into our bed is going to be your M.O., then you know where the door is." And get this—I took it. I walked out. Stubborn as the day is long and apparently pretty dumb, I dug in and was ready to call it quits. For three days, I sat like Jonah in the belly of the whale. That's when she called me and said, "Come over, we need to talk."

As we got heated over my reluctance to give up part of my old life in lieu of a new one with her, Angelike said, "David, I know you love God, and I know that you know that I love God too. And the last thing the devil wants if for two people who love God to become one, procreate, and create more followers of Jesus. You're crazy if you don't think he's trying to come between us over some silly, insignificant things right now."

You know what I told her? "No, you're crazy, Angelike. I know God, but I don't think the devil is here concerning himself with David Norrie." To which she replied, well before you walk out that door and out of my life forever, would you do me a favor and open the bible with me to see what it says about that.

Reluctantly, I agreed.

She began with 1 Peter 5:8, *Be alert and of sober mind. Your enemy the devil prowls around like a roaring lion looking for someone to devour.* Then, Ephesians 5:25, *Husbands, love your wives, just as Christ loved the church and gave himself up for her to make her holy, cleansing her by the washing with water through the word, and to present her to himself as a radiant church, without stain or wrinkle or any other blemish, but holy and blameless.*

I mention this story because although it wasn't the first time I'd read a bible, it was the first time I listened to what it said and how it applied to my life. It was like God smacking me on the head (in a loving and fatherly manner) saying, "David, don't be stupid, I just gave you a gift, and you're trying to throw it away." That evening, we read the bible for two hours, and Angelike and I have never been apart from that day forward. It changed everything.

We continued to read the word and become more spiritually Turned On and my religion (in church) began to turn into a relationship (with Jesus). It turns out, it's not just a book of random stories and allegories written thousands of years ago with no relevance to today's world. It's neither random nor made up. It's the best self-development book ever written, and it applies just as much to our world today as it did in the past.

INNOCENT, IGNORANT OR INCOMPETENT

It's no secret that we live in a culture brimming with political correctness. You can't say anything without offending someone.

Unless maybe they are a Christian. We've become society's punching bag, haven't we? But if I'm being transparent, I'll have to admit, before I read the bible, terms like *born again*, *evangelist* and *supernatural* were fair game for mockery. They described the weirdos of faith in my neighborhood. Growing up, some friends and family pointed out born-again Christians as *Jesus Freaks* to be avoided. I'd see evangelists like Billy Graham on television and quickly turn the channel. The only supernatural we knew occurred in books or movies about aliens and psychics.

Part of turning on in your faith is to stop judging and start doing the research; it's about experiencing things for yourself, not just because a priest, parent, or politician said so. Angelike showed me that *Born Again simply means you accept Jesus as an adult and profess it* (John 3:3). She showed me that evangelism doesn't mean you're knocking on doors in your neighborhood or exorcising demons out of people on cable channel 39; it simply means you want and desire to share the good news of the gospel and to give hope to people who may be thirsting for it. And supernatural wasn't a sci-fi term but very real heavenly interventions from God which happen quite often.

I would tell you that my biggest gains in terms of faith came when I stopped the labeling, the pre-judging, and disbelief, and just used my eyes to read, my ears to listen and my brain to think with common sense. Let's put it like this; we don't need to go to a dentist to tell us to brush our teeth, we just know something isn't clean in our mouths. The same goes for our soul. You know when it's not right. You can sense when the darkness creeps in and, like Martin Luther said, sometimes we need to get lost, we need to cry out for help in the dark before the light breaks and we see again.

EVERYBODY NEEDS TO BE PASTORED

Ironically for me, it was women who were my weakness and a woman who saved me. God works in funny ways like that. And while Angelike fed my initial hunger for a relationship with Jesus rather than religion, there was still a thirst in me to go deeper and know more that wasn't nearly quenched. Sometime in late 2017, I prayed to God to deliver me a powerful male mentor to take my faith to the next level. I'd been around priests and around good Christian men, but I needed a man's man who knew the word very well and whom I could respect for his actions and knowledge. And when you ask God for something, He always answers and often, He responds in overwhelming fashion.

He led me to a church in Phoenix called The Trinity Church, which was planted by Pastor Mark Driscoll whom I mentioned several times in previous chapters. Pastor Driscoll took my faith from a faucet to a full-on flood. I'll never forget when I heard him tell the congregation, "There comes a time when boys need to become men," referencing first Corinthians (*When I was a child, I talked like a child, I thought like a child, I reasoned like a child. When I became a man, I put the ways of childhood behind me*). Although I was already 40, I sunk down in my seat and felt like he was talking directly to me. Spiritually, I was still a boy, acting like a boy, leading my family and business like a boy. Then, I read his book *Real Marriage* and it took all that prior biblical knowledge about love, which Angelike had given me, to the next level, helping answer so many of the questions I'd always had about how to be a real man of God.

During the next several months at church, I found answers to my questions about the different nuances in beliefs among the Christian factions. Pastor Driscoll made it very simple for me by telling me that when it came to doctrine, to always ask this one question, "Is it in the Book?" If it's not in the Bible, it's of man. He also introduced me to the concept that there is a huge difference between having a *religion* versus having a *relationship with Jesus* which I've referred to often so far. This was a game-changer as I learned one is an institution, while the other is very personal.

In the summer of 2018, we moved to Nashville and spent the next two years splitting time between two spirit-filled churches. That was a new word to me as well. Spirit-Filled simply means a Bible-led church that is alive, teeming with energy and passion where people come excited and exuberant and in pursuit of the Holy Spirit, rather than out of a sense of obligation and duty. For most of my life, I'd spent time in services that lacked charisma, churches based on sacraments, order and ritual. I could almost count the rhythms; sit-stand, sit-stand, read a scripture, sing a hymn, 15-minute homily, sit-stand, shake hands, and say an *Our Father* and we're out. Back to secular life and living large. Even as a boy, I remember sitting in church so bored thinking, this can't be how Jesus spread the word? No way, he must've been more dynamic than this to have made as big of an impact as he did.

These new spirit-filled Christian pastors were married, they had kids, and they knew scripture back and forth and told stories of problems just like mine. Once more, they never sugar-coated anything. The Word was the Word, and it never wavered. At this point, I felt like God was giving me exactly what I had prayed for in abundance. You see, I knew many people who were *church hurt*, but that wasn't me; I was more like *church disappointed*. Where was this all my life? Why hadn't anybody shown me, or interpreted the Bible like this in my youth? I felt like it would've helped me to have a better understanding of how the Word applies to my everyday life and thus, a better relationship with Jesus in my twenties when my life went off track.

Remember, to a Catholic boy, the word pastor was foreign. It was for *those people*, not *us*. It's critical you understand the word and the difference between a pastor and what it means to be pastored. Pastor (noun) is a spiritual overseer. Pastoring (verb) means to be taught, guided and brought up in the word in order to understand it and to live it. Jeremiah 3:15 says "And

I will give you pastors according to mine heart, which shall feed you with knowledge and understanding." Ezekiel follows it up saying, "For lack of a shepherd, the sheep will scatter."

Yes, to be fed. I was hungry, spiritually hungry, and as Jesus says in Matthew 4:4, *Man shall not live on bread alone but on every word that comes from the mouth of God.* All my life I'd always went to mass to check the box off and make sure that I got into Heaven by acts; go to confession, don't eat meat on Fridays, say the Rosary, etc. Now I understood we are saved not by acts but by grace, and I had the knowledge that gave me the understanding.

FILLING YOUR CUP

Does that honesty make me a traditional church rebel? I'm not trying to be. I just want to help you relate. I was simply a man who wanted to know more about his creator and what his purpose was for me. I'd tried my way. I had tried culture's way. It got me nowhere. If you look at Martin Luther's story, then you know he was labeled a church rebel, but really all he was a man with questions. A man who knew there had to be more to a pious life, a man who desired a more intimate, less imperious way of worshiping. Like Martin Luther, I felt there was a gap between the religion and the relationship. In Matthew 28:19, it says, *Therefore, go and make disciples.* It doesn't say *go and make churches.* Nor does it say go and encourage ritual and make up new rules.

I believe the revival of our time is upon us, and it's going to be done the same way Jesus did it, by teaching the gospels with connection and community. So if you hear people say religion is dying, don't mistake it for faith. For lack of a pastor, the sheep will scatter. Without a shepherd, we don't stand a chance.

The problem I see with our society is we've lost the Word. And we can't forget, in the beginning was the Word and the Word was with God and the Word was God. As a result, you see the scattering of humanity, failing of the family, and wayward-ness among young people.

The challenge is getting back to the Word in its purest state. Pastor Keith Rogan said to me, "A spiritual boycott is going on right now. Young people are saying 'I know what I need isn't there (in religion).' People (like you) are frustrated when they find out the truth, when they find out there is a way to live by faith, in an abundant life and in victory."

I understand that, and I realize what difficult times we are living in. So forgive me if I challenge or offend you, but we are called to be bold and some of you may need a wakeup call. I can only compare it to living in a village and dying of thirst for years only to find out there has been a flowing river on the other side of the valley, but none of the elders knew how to take you there.

THE BOOK OF YOUR LIFE

There is a pastor from Texas named Issac Pitre. I listened to him one day as he spoke. The sermon was about the book of our lives, meaning how thee book, the Bible, relates to our book, the one we write, the one we live. He began by saying, "It's time to unlock the God gene in you."

He said, "You can go to church, sing songs, worship God, and serve in his house and still be out of the will of God, not from a moral standpoint of being devoted to Him but from the point where you are still not doing what he called you to do."

That made me sit up in my seat and lean forward because I had felt that my entire life that I had a calling that God simply refused to reveal to me. In other words, I'd prayed just about every night asking God what he wants me to do with my life, yet I felt like I never got a clear answer. Have you wondered that too?

Pastor Pitre explained how each of us has a specific assign-ment in our life that must be completed and that everything we've been waiting on is in God's will. He said, "Once you really get a revelation of what God created you to be, you'll step back and say, 'Oh God, this is marvelous.'" This was my revelation moment. I was all about the secular self-development world at this point. From a business perspective, I'd been to the conferences, read the Tony Robbins and Dale Carnegie books but still felt left without direction. I knew how to think and grow rich in my wallet, but I didn't know how to think and grow rich in my purpose.

God was always left out of the big conferences I attended. When I attempted to include him in my own speeches for my company, He was edited, censored, and red-lined in lieu of using a safer terminology like the *Universe* or *whatever you believe*. In other words, I was encouraged to temper my faith, that it was in my best interest not to mention Jesus. Maybe you should just keep him for Sundays. But sitting there listening to Pastor Pitre talk about how the book God had written on my life was waiting for me, that I just needed to do a better job searching for and opening it. That changed my thinking.

I began to think to myself, David, you are now a grown man, not just in age or stature, but in the Spirit, in Christ. The universe never spoke to me. Not once during the many trials Angelike and I had faced, death, sickness, etc., did we ever look at one another and say, "Whip out that notebook we used at the last conference to see how to handle this." Nope. We always relied on and counted on Jesus for direction, so why should it be any different in business?

Pastor Pitre's word reminded me of who was really looking to be the influence in my career. It was God. He finished by explaining that most of us never find that book which God wrote for our lives, the one he pre-ordained for us, the one which reveals our true calling. We never find it because we aren't really looking for it. We get sidetracked, distracted, lured in by the earthly world, losing sight of the supernatural power of God who wants nothing more than for us to seek him, seek our book, and open it to live the life of abundance he has written for us.

God spoke through the pastor that day. It was God who speaks to us throughout our days. It's God. It's God. It's God. But if we aren't trained properly on how to listen, we will almost definitely miss the message.

BURNING THE SHIPS

Modern culture has led us to believe the supernatural can occur in almost any realm other than through the divinity of God. People will tell you a crystal can heal you or that Mother Earth is talking to them, but to say Jesus or God is healing or talking, well, that's just silly.

I have to laugh. I get it, that's life in the 21st century where religion is losing, and a la carte spirituality is stepping in to take its place. And therein lies the impasse, a large majority of people have closed themselves off to the Word, either because it's never been taught properly or because they can't check the boxes and order it to fit their lifestyle. Nobody has explained the way, the truth, and the life as it is clearly written. Therefore, we have an abundance of people who adopt a culture up, not Kingdom down, philosophy on faith.

As I mentioned in the chapter on marriage, there's a popular phrase which influencers and aspiring entrepreneurs in the secular world like to use, "Burn the Ships." It was inspired by the story of Hernán Cortés, a Spanish Conquistador who told his men, when they became weary and scared, that once ashore, there was no turning back to go home and quite literally had them burn their ships, leaving no option but to move forward and win. In the self-development realm, "Burn the Ships" was an analogy for pursuing your goals with reckless abandon and not looking back. It was quite inspiring.

One day while visiting Sedona, Arizona, I found myself standing in the Chapel of the Holy Cross, looking out over the beautiful scenery when I made the decision to take a leap of faith and burn my spiritual ship in a sense. I said to God, "I know I'm playing small. I know the plans you have laid for me to prosper and not harm me, but I have not sought out the book on my life in the way I should, the way you would like me to." And then I said out loud, "God, I've held back on making you the center of my life in every way because I was scared and was living by the world's earthly rules and not yours. I will no longer make you (Jesus) a footnote in my business, but rather a headline."

Now it's one thing to say that in the moment, and quite another to actually do it. I know many people who have burned their ships yet still cling to a small lifeboat for an insurance policy. In fact, there is a very intense biblical account in Acts Chapter 5 about a man named Ananias and his wife Sapphira who sold their land to give money to the church but secretly withheld a portion of the proceeds. Their fate didn't turn out well. That was a failed insurance policy in spiritual terms.

As for me, I knew the essential step in proving to myself that I meant business was fully committing to my calling and that if I was being led by the spirit, the challenge would never be too great. I believe that holds true for each of you as well. I believe we are in the midst of a marketplace revival, a time when those with strong convictions don't have to leave them at home Monday through Friday.

LEADING YOUR FAMILY INTO THE LIGHT

Just as we as adults need to be pastored, and need guidance, so do our children. Last Easter, my daughter began asking really difficult questions about God. They'd been talking a lot about the Easter Bunny at school and about Jesus at church. She need-ed to reconcile the two. While we'd love to prolong her childhood as long as we can with things like the Easter Bunny and Tooth Fairy, there comes a time when we know what's most important, and that's truth.

Then came Halloween, and our neighborhood goes crazy for it. But we saw it went too far, witches in a circle in a neighbor's front yard, demonic exorcist looking dolls riding swings on the other's front porch. In the past, we'd always dressed up as a family, the Care Bears, the Incredibles, and Toy Story. Things we felt were extremely innocent yet still allowed us to participate without any reservations. But we decided we could no longer continue to observe the holiday knowing what we know about God's Word. It was a tough conversation for us to have with the children, but we came to an understanding that mommy and daddy weren't trying not to be fun, we were trying to tell them the truth as we understand it.

As parents, we must be armed with knowledge of the Word to be able to answer our kid's most difficult questions, and when culture clashes up against our convictions, it's not an easy choice. But being realistic, we knew this was a time when we would have to be true to our faith. To be Turned On in your faith means you don't have a volume button and turn God up when you need him (when your child is sick) and then mute Him when you're fine (time to play witches and get candy).

In our nine years of marriage, Angelike and I have buried both her parents, her uncle who was like a father, had two kids, moved six times, been through two surgeries, a half dozen ER visits, and a host of other "God, please have my back" moments. If you are going to burn the ship, then burn it. Don't put one foot in for God. Don't hold back by clinging to some type of earthly insurance plan or because you allowed those who weren't walking in faith to mislead you. Because you will be tested.

The world will always offer a path of least resistance, simple pleasures that yield an empty harvest. And while pop culture, social media, Hollywood, and politics will always ebb and flow, God will not. You shouldn't say, I'm putting you down for a bit God until I need you. You can't say I like you here, here and here but not here. It's either all true or none of it is. But the secular world will try to convince you that God is an a la carte God. He is there to please and serve you, not the other way around. Not so. If you believe in God, you believe in a divine being, an infallible God. One with much greater knowledge than any man on earth. Whereas the church prior to Martin Luther was creating too many man-made rules, the churches of today are going the other direction and saying do whatever you please. Both are distortions of the word of God.

So, believe in your calling, turn on your faith, and move forward with all that was placed on your heart and don't look back. Your harvest will only come to full yield when the ship has truly been burned.

FOR CRYING OUT LOUD

It would be nice to think that once we step into our faith that we'd never experience another day of Fear and stress. If that were the case, we'd have a world full of peaceful believers. But the truth is, *the adversary is always lurking, like a lion, seeking to devour us* (1 Peter 5:8). Temptations are bountiful in life, and they never completely go away; you just have to know how to beat them. Alcohol, drugs, pornography, junk food, envy, anger and jealousy will try to find you. You may think you have shaken them, but they call you back. They are referred to as strongholds and they are like doors; they can shut, but they are always in danger of being opened again if you let your guard down.

One of the biggest mistakes one can make in life is not allowing anybody to know you're struggling. I know because that was me. I battled strongholds for most of my youth and into my thirties, and I prayed in silence, by myself at night, in my bed, like good boys are taught to do. So, when it was suggested to me that I pray out loud, it was a big heck no. When it was further suggested that I pray out loud over my wife and kids, I could not think of anything more uncomfortable because I had always been taught that prayer was private.

Oh, how wrong I was.

I resisted praying out loud initially, mostly because I simply thought I just wasn't good at it. I thought I sounded ridiculous. I'd heard others pray, and they were amazing. They sounded like professionals. So I didn't. It's not for me, I said.

Until one day, I forced myself to. Well, I shouldn't say forced — it was literally out of desperation that I mustered the courage. My wife was terribly sick, she was shaking in the middle of the night and scared out of her mind and asked me to pray over her. So, I did. I forced myself to do it out of necessity. I cried out to God in frustration and despair, "Please help her!" I added a few phrases which I can't recall, but it wasn't good by any means. But even though it didn't sound good, it felt good. It felt really good. And most important, it helped her. Her spirit settled, and although we went to the ER, she'd be ok.

After breaking the ice the hard way, I told myself to do it more often. I first prayed over my daughter while in the school drop-off line, and it was very weird for both of us. In fact, I'm not sure who felt more awkward, Ella or me. But, to my surprise, she began to ask me to do it every time I'd drop her off. And it felt great.

I know that for many people of strong faith, let alone those of you reading this with little to none, how this must sound, but hear me out. I'm assuming some of you are like I was, you lay down with your spouse or you lay down with your children to pray, and you either do it in silence or you both say the same prayer like the Our Father. Again, that's ritual, and there is a time and place for it, but it's not a relationship with God, and it's not a prayer relationship with your family. It's more along the lines of, "There, we've both said it, that's great, check off the prayer box, we're feeling good, let's go to bed now." Technically you prayed, but did you communicate with God and with one another?

Now think about during those times, do you know what your spouse was praying for? I'm sure you make assumptions and hope that he or she is praying for your marriage, praying for your health, or praying for abundance in your business. What about your son or daughter? What are they praying for in silence or in ritual prayer? It would be safe to assume they are praying for good sleep, good friends at school, or that new toy. After all, they are kids, right?

But what if you're assuming wrong? What if your spouse is praying for more confidence in her life or more compassion from you? What if your daughter is praying to stop being bullied at school, your son is praying for God to explain why he feels alone or praying for more of his father's affection? Don't you think it's important to know what's being asked of God by the people closest to you so you can all be in union? The petitions of one are the petitions of the family. There is power in declaring your intentions and petitions to your heavenly father.

It all comes down to intention. Prayer time is intention time, and isn't it great to be on the same page? Imagine the love your wife feels when she hears you vocally interceding on her behalf to God. Or how your daughter feels when you lay down, and she hears you speaking to God and asking that she can make good friends and is safe and smart. Better yet, just ask yourself how it would make you feel.

ERASING DOUBT IS THE BEST GIFT YOU CAN GIVE

To be honest, there were nights when Angelike and I would be in a bit of a spat, and I'd lay my head down with some anger or resentment and be fine with just sleeping it off. But when she began to pray, and I could hear her thank God for me out loud, even in my not-so-great moments, well, it's hard to stay mad and not invite forgiveness and understanding in. And isn't that what prayer is, inviting and invoking the teachings of Jesus into our everyday life. This is when the Word comes alive. This is when prayer can save a family by saving a marriage.

Even in the best of marriages, a husband or wife will have moments of doubt. Are they still in love with me? Does she want me to succeed in this new business? Is he still attracted to me?

Our children may be asking, is my dad hoping I make the team? Does my mother think I'm smart? Does daddy want me to do well on my exam?

I've heard my wife go right to the source and ask God to bless me. I've heard her thank God for our marriage and ask him to let this book reach more people because she loves me. It changes everything.

Yes, you can tell your kids they are smart, and that you want them to make friends. You can tell your husband you're proud of him and know he will succeed. And you should. But trust me, it's different when you pray. The stakes seem higher, the authority that much greater. The intercession so much more appreciated. You are going to the King and pleading a case on their behalf.

When my wife or children lift me up in prayer, it lights me up internally and gives me the reassurance and confidence that we were both truly on the same page. And it's one thing to lie and say something you don't mean directly to your spouse; it's another to say it in the presence of God. So, this really forces open and honest communication in a safe environment. When you intercede, broker or reconcile on behalf on another and bring in that third party (God) to the relationship, it turns on a part of your life you never knew was available and makes marriages and families so much stronger.

Don't get me wrong, silent prayer is important, and you should pray silently in the right environment. Praying out loud helps you find your voice, builds your spirit, and teaches your kids that faith is something we should never fear or hide.

WHO ARE YOU WALKING WITH?

Early in our entrepreneurial journey, Angelike and I walked on fire. Walking over hot coals was such a big deal at the time. We thought it would be the big game-changer, spending hours upon hours getting pumped up with courage to do it.

In the years since, we've been through more frightening times than I care to mention, life and death struggles. And looking back, I can say without a doubt that there was never a time when we said to ourselves, "BUT WE WALKED ON FIRE SO WE CAN DO THIS." When Angelike was carrying her dying mother back and forth to the restroom, she never thought, but I walked on fire. When I sat alone in a green room with my heart beating out of my chest about to speak in front of thousands of people, the fire walk never occurred to me. When we've woken up in the middle of the night to care for our daughter who had a 103 fever, we never said, "But that time we conquered fire."

I'm just being honest. And as long as we're being honest, I'll honestly tell you what and who has gotten us through the biggest fears and toughest moments of our lives: Faith and Jesus Christ. He walks with you. When your heart rate skyrockets, walk with Him. When you're faced with major life-altering decisions, walk with Him. When you need courage and confidence in yourself and your abilities, walk with Him.

I'm grateful for the fire walking experience in so much as it taught me this; gimmicks don't move the chains or ease your fears when the real *you know what* hits the fan. But THE WORD OF GOD does. It's tried and true and tested. Lean into your faith. Seek the Holy Spirit. That's the real fire walk.

As I write the final words of this book, the world has taken a turn and fallen into a place nobody alive has quite seen or experienced before. We've been shut in, quarantined at home. So much of what I've been writing over the last three years suddenly seems to have even greater meaning. The stakes seem that much higher. I didn't want to go back and edit and speak of the COVID-19 virus, opting to leave what was already written as is. However, I will add this. This is a pivot point for America, a wake-up call for the entire world. If we go back to sleep, put our lives on cruise control as they were before, I fear the dreams of our children will be put in jeopardy. What sense of privacy will they have? What type of true human connection can they expect? What will they be placing in their bodies? What will the next threat be?

Finding the light just took on an entire new level of importance for the world. We've been given a wakeup call and we've seen a crack in the darkness. Parents are outside playing catch with their children, neighbors are looking for one another, waving more often at each other and craving community. Our commitment to busyness and neglecting one another just got tempered. Many feel this is a sign from God. Many feel this is a time for revival. I couldn't agree more.

I feel like we have an opportunity not just to go back to normal, but we can be better than normal.

Is it time for you to TURN ON? To find the light?

I'll leave you with this from the book of Matthew:

You are the light of the world. A town built on a hill cannot be hidden. Neither do people light a lamp and put it under a bowl. Instead they put it on its stand, and it gives light to everyone in the house. In the same way, let your light shine before others, that they may see your good deeds and glorify your Father in heaven. (Matthew 5:14-16)

ABOUT DAVID NORRIE

David Norrie is a devoted husband, father and entrepreneur and the founder of Turned On, a platform he created along with his wife Angelike to help preserve the lost art of face-to-face connection within the home, workspace and faith community.

He has more than 25 years of experience in all facets of communication; radio, video, newspaper, magazine, social media and sales training. His columns on health and relationships were published in one of the seven largest newspapers in the country and he is co-author of the best-selling book *Faith Into Abundance: 30 Stories of Faith From Successful Christian Entrepreneurs*. In 2015, he founded Socially Speaking, an occupational training program designed to help professionals articulate their passions and products with a greater degree of charisma and marketability for increased profitability.

Over the course of his training, David observed how many of his clients, and much of society, appeared to be moving farther away from one another emotionally, rather than closer together, despite advancements in communication technology. This sparked a desire to create a revival of the spirit by emphasizing principles of basic communication which could be easily incorporated into marital relationships, commerce, parenting and social gatherings.

Identifying himself as "a student of human interaction," his mission is to open the eyes of those people who have put their lives on autopilot and to make them more aware of the disconnection that is rapidly happening in board rooms, bedrooms, living rooms, coffee shops, churches and social media platforms. He desires to help people stop watering down their ability to interact with one another and express themselves more authentically by being "TURNED ON" to see with new eyes and listen with new ears to the possibilities happening all around them. He hopes to restore the light to a world going dark.

Made in the USA
Columbia, SC
11 May 2020